COMPLETE
Early Childhood
CURRICULUM
RESOURCE

MARY A. SOBUT/BONNIE NEUMAN BOGEN

W9-AWF-682

**THE CENTER FOR APPLIED
RESEARCH IN EDUCATION**
West Nyack, New York 10995

4/98

Library of Congress Cataloging-in-Publication Data

Sobut, Mary A., [date]
    Complete early childhood curriculum resource : success-oriented learning
experiences for all children / Mary A. Sobut, Bonnie Neuman Bogen.
        p.   cm.
    ISBN 0-13-87628-238-9
    1. Early childhood education—United States—Curricula.   2. Early
childhood education—United States—Activity programs.   I. Bogen,
Bonnie Neuman, [date].   II. Center for Applied Research in
Education.   III. Title.
LB1139.25.S63   1991   90-37327
372.19'0973—dc20   CIP

Printed in the United States of America

20   19   18   17   16   15   14   13   12   11

Acknowledgments

    Recipe for Animal Crackers from *Kinder Krunchies* by Karen S. Jenkins, distributed
exclusively by Discovery Toys.
    Recipe for Peanut Butter Balls copyright Vicki Lanski from her book *Feed Me! I'm Yours!*,
with the permission of its publisher, Meadowbrook Press.
    Unless otherwise noted, the songs, fingerplays and recipes presented herein have come
from our collection of early childhood materials. While we have made every effort to find the
original sources of these materials, we have generally been unsuccessful. If errors have
occurred, they will be corrected in future editions.
    We wish to thank Gladys Neuman and Delanie Mallie for the many hours spent typing
our manuscript.
    Thanks to our families for the support and encouragement they gave us while we were
writing this resource. Their pride in our endeavor urged us on. Thanks Michael, Andrew,
Jeremy, and Elizabeth Bogen, and Wally, Amy, and Frances Sobut.

ISBN 0-87628-238-9

ATTENTION: CORPORATIONS AND SCHOOLS

The Center for Applied Research in Education books are available at quantity discounts with bulk purchase for educational, business, or sales promotional use. For information, please write to: Prentice Hall Special Sales, 240 Frisch Court, Paramus, New Jersey 07652. Please supply: title of book, ISBN number, quantity, how the book will be used, date needed.

**THE CENTER FOR APPLIED RESEARCH
IN EDUCATION**
West Nyack, NY 10994
A Simon & Schuster Company

On the World Wide Web at http://www.phdirect.com

Prentice-Hall International (UK) Limited, *London*
Prentice-Hall of Australia Pty. Limited, *Sydney*
Prentice-Hall Canada Inc., *Toronto*
Prentice-Hall Hispanoamericana, S.A., *Mexico*
Prentice-Hall of India Private Limited, *New Delhi*
Prentice-Hall of Japan, Inc., *Tokyo*
Simon & Schuster Asia Pte. Ltd., *Singapore*
Editora Prentice-Hall do Brasil, Ltda., *Rio de Janeiro*

DEDICATION

We dedicate this book to the children we teach. They continually help us learn.

ABOUT
THE AUTHORS

Mary A. Sobut has eighteen years of teaching experience in early childhood special education, learning disabilities, and behavior disorders. She holds a B.A. in Special Education, an M.A. in Early Childhood Education, and has completed many hours of post-graduate work. Mrs. Sobut was instrumental in developing the early childhood special education program in Elmhurst, Illinois which includes a comprehensive program of involvement, training, and support for parents. She has supervised student teachers and serves as a mentor to new teachers in the field. She provides in-service training to elementary education teachers and staff, and consults with district ancillary personnel, as well as personnel from public and private agencies that work with young children and their families. Mrs. Sobut is the teacher representative on the Early Childhood Advisory Committee for the North Central Regional Educational Laboratory. The committee reviews early childhood issues and advises the laboratory regarding its efforts in a seven state region.

Bonnie Neuman Bogen has been a special educator for ten years. She has taught early childhood special education and students with learning disabilities, behavioral and emotional disorders. She is presently tutoring children with a wide range of special needs. Ms. Bogen holds her undergraduate degree in Child Development and a graduate certificate in Special Education from the University of Wisconsin. She recently received an M.A. in Special Education from National Louis University in Evanston, Illinois. In addition, Ms. Bogen has expertise in student assessment, curriculum development, and facilitation of parental support and training groups.

FOREWORD

When I first reviewed a draft of this manuscript, I immediately offered to write the foreword. As a former early childhood special education teacher and now director of early childhood education for a regional educational laboratory serving seven states, I can honestly say this book is greatly needed—especially in light of the dramatic increase in preschool programs authorized by state and federal legislation. It will be invaluable whether one teaches handicapped youngsters, those considered "at-risk", or young children in a community- or church-sponsored preschool. Further, for both beginning and veteran teachers, it will be a treasured resource that will supply new ideas and activities and stimulate the development of others.

Research today encourages teachers to utilize hands-on approaches in instruction; to assess children's strengths, needs, and progress continuously; to teach to children's strengths; to integrate and align curriculum, instruction, and assessment; to regard parents as a child's first and most important teachers; to actively connect content and processes to learners' background experiences; and to value their teaching roles as mediator, facilitator, model, and coach. Mary and Bonnie have done a masterful job of showing how all of these concepts are integrated into the early childhood curriculum.

In addition to discussing the importance of establishing goals and objectives, individualizing instruction, establishing a child-oriented environment, and working with instructional aides, the authors provide new and experienced teachers with quick and easy ways to involve parents in the early childhood program. From the monthly concept sheets, to the parent-child activity calendars, to the songs, fingerplays, and recipes, parents are informed of what goes on at school on a regular basis. They also are encouraged to participate actively in the development of their children and their early childhood program and are provided with suggestions to reinforce and extend learning at home during the school year and during the summer months.

But the feature that most sets apart the *Complete Early Childhood Curriculum Resource* from other activity books it its presentation of early childhood curriculum in an integrated, monthly unit approach. Never before has a curriculum guide provided as many instructional activities, games, songs, etc., in as coordinated and comprehensive a fashion. Rationale, directions, and explanations for activities are provided for such developmental areas as language and cognition, fine and gross motor skills, perception, and self-help. Recipes, songs, games, and fingerplays are also provided for reinforcement. Through the monthly unit approach, teachers have greater flexibility in providing sufficient experiences to introduce and expand important concepts and yet meet the varying needs and abilities of each child in the classroom.

Another noted feature of this book is that young children with special needs are viewed as children first. While there has been some concern regarding teacher-directed practices for children with special needs, the authors demonstrate that developmentally appropriate practices and diagnostic prescriptive teaching are not mutually exclusive. Rather, both can work together to meet the *individual* needs of young children.

This book will see years of use by early childhood service providers everywhere. What a wonderful resource!

Linda G. Kunesh
NORTH CENTRAL REGIONAL EDUCATIONAL LABORATORY

ABOUT
THIS RESOURCE

The primary purpose of the *Complete Early Childhood Curriculum Resource* is to help early childhood teachers develop and implement an effective educational program for all regular and special children aged 3 through 6.

The *Resource* is based on the method of diagnostic-prescriptive teaching; this involves an assessment of each child's individual needs, and gearing instruction to meet those needs. From the development of specific learning goals and objectives, the book progresses through the implementation of daily activities. The curriculum focuses on teaching and learning basic concepts and skills through a monthly unit approach, and it is accompanied by specific ideas for parent involvement.

For easy use, materials are organized into two sections: 1. Planning for Instruction, and 2. Monthly Curriculum. Section 1 presents practical guidelines and materials in each of the following areas:

- *Establishing goals and objectives.* Included are procedures for assessing children and creating an early childhood education program. In addition, a sample Individual Education Plan (IEP), and lists of commercial tests are provided. It should be noted that while only special needs children require IEP's, all children learn best when instruction is suited to individual developmental levels and interests.

- *Organizing the learning environment.* Here you will find suggestions for arranging the classroom, scheduling activities, providing learning materials, and evaluating the learning environment, including three sample floor plans, sample schedules, and suggested learning materials by subject.

- *Using a classroom aide.* Guidelines are provided for using an aide most effectively and include specific responsibilities in seven different areas that might be assigned to an aide.

- *Getting parents involved.* Suggestions are included for fostering teaching skills in parents, involving parents in planning their child's Individual Education Plan, a reproducible "Parent Needs Assessment" form, and dozens of suggested activities for home visits.

- *Creating a developmentally appropriate curriculum.* Ten major areas of learning are identified and discussed, followed by special guidelines for facilitating language development in young children.

Section 2, Monthly Curriculum, presents a detailed month-by-month curriculum for September through May, including specific concepts to be stressed and activities for teaching them, in each of these areas: language/vocabulary, fine motor/art, perception, gross motor, premath, sensory experiences, songs and fingerplays, recipe and snack ideas, dramatic play, and children's literature. The monthly activities are followed by information for parents about the concepts being taught that month and suggested parent-child activities in a handy, reproducible calendar format. A summer section is also included.

Each monthly curriculum is presented in a uniform format, including activities for developing the concepts of the month in all content areas. The activities capitalize on children's natural interest in the seasons and holidays, and build upon the concepts and skills learned in prior months. Here, for example, are the topics featured over a number of months in the areas of language and premath.

	LANGUAGE AND VOCABULARY	PREMATH
September:	School, Body Parts	One-to-one Correspondence, Calendar
October:	Fall, Fire Prevention and Safety	0, 1, 2, Circle, Big and Little
November:	Grocery Store, Family, Thanksgiving, Brown	3, 4, Tall and Short, Triangle
December:	Toys, Instruments, Holiday Vocabulary	5, Small, Medium, Large, Square

Moreover, you will find that most of the suggested activities require only simple, inexpensive materials already on hand or readily available.

In short, this book provides a unique practical resource for establishing a comprehensive Early Childhood Program for every child. It will help you make effective decisions about each of the following program components:

- goal setting and formulating the Individual Education Plan
- sequencing learning objectives and selecting teaching procedures
- organizing the time available during the school day
- grouping children for instruction
- setting up the classroom environment

- selecting the concepts and skills to teach
- choosing appropriate teaching methods
- selecting learning materials
- including parents and involving them in their child's education

This curriculum resource addresses all of these issues and should prove itself invaluable to new and experienced teachers alike.

Mary A. Sobut
Bonnie N. Bogen

CONTENTS

Contents

1
PLANNING FOR INSTRUCTION

This first section of the *Curriculum Resource* focuses on child assessment and task analysis. Information about organizing the classroom and materials for effective learning are included.

Establishing Goals and Objectives

Children learn best when instruction is developmentally appropriate and designed to meet their cognitive levels. In part, teachers create a program by informal and/or formal assessment of young learners. Goals and objectives can be informal, as those established for most preschool age children. Formalized assessment of special needs students is completed to establish the unique goals and objectives written for an Individual Education Plan (IEP). Assessment, the establishment of goals and objectives, and the development of an educational plan are dependent upon one another and ongoing in all early childhood programs.

As educators, we are familiar with the semantic difficulty in defining the terms *goals* and *objectives*. In our definition, a goal is long term and broad based. An objective is a behavior or skill which can be defined, observed, and measured. The teacher creates a developmental program for early childhood students by establishing goals and objectives.

One purpose of testing is to provide a score or level of functioning for a child. Another purpose is to provide an index of where instruction should begin. In essence, testing can profile a child's strengths and areas for growth. A wide variety of assessment tools are available to the teacher/diagnostician.

NORM-REFERENCED TESTS

Norm-referenced tests compare the score of a child's performance to that of other children. Norms are frequently based on chronological age. The child's performance is measured against the average score of children his/her own age. These standardized tools are available commercially and contain statistical data regard-

1

ing their validity and reliability. They are ready-made and designed to be used by a trained examiner. The results of formal testing provide an individual performance level as represented by a raw score, scaled score, percentile, or grade equivalent. Experts in the field question the value of using norm-referenced tests with very young children because they are weak predictors of a child's later performance or school success.

CRITERION-REFERENCED TESTS

Criterion-referenced tests assess each child's performance in comparison to mastery of specific objectives rather than the norm of a sample population. Criterion-referenced tests are particularly valuable in identifying and sequencing appropriate instructional goals and objectives.

INFORMAL ASSESSMENT

Informal assessment techniques used in the early childhood setting can include teacher observation, rating scales, checklists, anecdotal records, and other teacher-made materials. These informal procedures yield important information valuable to the teacher, such as level of functioning, approach to problem solving, reaction to stimuli of different modalities, motivational factors, and behaviors exhibited by the child during the assessment process. Informal assessment provides useful information regarding a child who may be too young for more formal measures of evaluation.

Any combination of these assessment techniques can be used in planning the instructional program. The appropriateness of the educational assessment tools is as important as the precision of their administration.

NOTE: See the Appendix for a listing of some available norm-referenced and criterion-referenced tests.

TASK ANALYSIS

Criterion-referenced tests are based on a skill sequence and act as a counterpart to task analysis. When determining goals and objectives, it is vital to sequence skills in order from least to most difficult. Short-term objectives established from the sequence should reflect instructional achievements between the child's current level of performance and the ultimate goal. The process of writing objectives from goals reflects a skills sequence task-analytic approach. Task analysis involves identifying a skill, determining an entry behavior, and analyzing the skill. The teacher records the sequence of task events into small, observable components. It is important to sequence according to the skill, not the child.

The following is an example of one way to task analyze the use of scissors:

1. Place scissors on fingers.
2. Hold scissors correctly on fingers.
3. Open scissors.
4. Close scissors.

5. Snip or make small cuts in paper.
6. Hold paper for cutting with appropriate hand.
7. Cut 1/2-inch strips of paper in half.
8. Cut on a heavy line using continuous movements.

This analysis could be extended and expanded to include higher level cutting skills that progress from cutting curved and zigzag lines to cutting out shapes.

Another example of breaking down a task into components can be applied to color identification:

1. Select one color.
2. Match selected color with an identical sample.
3. Discriminate selected color from others by receptively pointing to the color.
4. Expressively name the selected color.

Once the task has been analyzed, it is possible to construct a checklist of its components. This checklist can be used to determine exactly what the child can and cannot perform and thus be used to determine where to begin teaching each skill. One major advantage of task analysis is its use in recordkeeping. At the end of the year the teacher has concrete information in the form of specific skills which supports the list of the child's accomplishments. This information is invaluable in the evaluation process.

MATCHING LEVEL AND ACTIVITY

The teacher must always be aware of the match between the child's present functioning level and what will be taught. If an activity is too easy, the child may not attempt it because of boredom. If the activity has no grounding in past experience, the child may not have any idea how to approach the task and won't make an attempt. The task must be based on past experience yet novel enough to challenge the child and develop new experiences. Thus a child builds on what he/she already knows. This idea personalizes activities and focuses on specific children and their needs.

Providing the child with activities in which success is possible is good motivation. The more precise the match between the child's stage of development and the activities designed for him/her, the more likely he/she is to succeed. A child who succeeds enjoys learning and takes pride in his/her accomplishments.

WRITING AN INDIVIDUAL EDUCATION PROGRAM (IEP) FOR SPECIAL NEEDS CHILDREN

With individual assessment and awareness of the task-analytic approach complete, the teacher can begin writing an Individual Education Plan for each special needs child in his/her classroom. The IEP is a legal document which is mandated for special needs children by Federal Law 94-142. The IEP minimally must include long-term goals, short-term objectives, methods and materials for achieving objectives, and criteria for evaluation.

When establishing goals, the long-term goal should be a broad-based skill such as "Improve receptive language" or "Improve fine motor manipulation skills." The short-term objective must be a measurable and observable behavior such as "Point to red" or "Make snips in paper." These examples should clarify how task analysis can assist when writing an Individual Education Program.

Setting objectives for each child should be an ongoing process throughout the year. When one short-term objective is accomplished, the teacher then moves to the next-higher level task to be achieved. The teacher must update and expand the child's IEP continually as the child succeeds and masters objectives previously set.

Eight examples of long-term goals and short-term objectives for Individual Education Plans are shown on pages 6 through 9. On page 5 you will find a reproducible "IEP Instructional Objectives" form you can photocopy for immediate use.

This IEP provides for instructional direction and can focus on many areas, including language/concept development, fine motor, perception, gross motor, socialization, and self-help, to name a few. Although the goals and objectives are based on the student's areas to be further developed, the teacher utilizes the student's strengths as she/he implements the curriculum.

The concept of teaching presented in this resource is based on a month-by-month unit approach. We feel that transfer of learning is more efficient when material to be learned is presented in relevant units as opposed to isolated bits from content areas. Within this unit framework, the planning involved makes use of the individual goals and objectives set for each child as well as the group. For example, when teaching the color red, the goal for one child might be to match red. For another child the goal might be to name red at the expressive level. And for another child who knows red, the goal might be to expand language and vocabulary by presenting a wide variety of red objects or pictures for the child to name or tell about. These varied objectives can be addressed in a language lesson presented to a small group of children. When the teacher is aware of each child's educational needs, she/he is able to guide presentation and questioning techniques to accomplish this multileveled objective.

Organizing the Learning Environment

PHYSICAL ENVIRONMENT

Planning space is an important aspect of a good learning environment, especially for young children. Arrangement of physical space reduces congestion and chaos and allows children to explore and learn in safety.

An effective learning environment should create a setting where children can learn both formally and informally. The environment should provide opportunities for students to practice newly developing independent behaviors.

IEP Instructional Objectives

Sept. ___ to Dec. ___

Student: _____   IEP Implementer _____

                                     Title _____

Student Rating Scale

A—Accomplished   U1—Lack of motivation
S—Satisfactory Progress   U2—Frequent absence
M—Minimal progress   U3—Inappropriate behavior
U—Unsatisfactory progress due   U4—Goal inappropriate at this time
   to _____

Long-term Goal:

Short-term Objective	Methods and Materials	Criteria of Successful Performance	Evaluation Schedule	Date and Results

IEP Instructional Objectives

Sept. ___ to Dec. ___

Student: _____ IEP Implementer _____

Title _____

Student Rating Scale

A—Accomplished
S—Satisfactory progress
M—Minimal progress
U—Unsatisfactory progress due to . . .

U1—Lack of motivation
U2—Frequent absence
U3—Inappropriate behavior
U4—Goal inappropriate at this time

Long-term Goal: Improve concept development of body parts.

Short-term Objective:	Methods and Materials	Criteria of Successful Performance	Evaluation Schedule	Date and Results
1. Will *point to* body parts on request: hands, head, legs, arms, etc.	teacher-prepared and commercial games, records, and activities listed in curriculum guide	80% accuracy	ongoing	
2. Will *name* body parts on self on request: hands, head, legs, arms, etc.				
3. Will *point to* body parts in pictures on request: hands, head, legs, arms, etc.				
4. Will *name* body parts in pictures on request: hands, head, legs, arms, etc.				

Long-term Goal: Improve fine motor manipulation skills.

Short-term Objective:	Methods and Materials	Criteria of Successful Performance	Evaluation Schedule	Date and Results
1. Builds a tower (up to ten blocks) with 2-inch cubes	modeling by teacher 1-and 2-inch cubes	80% accuracy	ongoing	

2. Builds a tower (up to ten blocks) with 1-inch cubes

3. Imitates a three-cube bridge after watching an adult

4. Will copy a three-cube bridge, given a model

Long-term Goal: Improve fine motor prewriting skills.

Short-term Objective:	Methods and Materials	Criteria of Successful Performance	Evaluation Schedule	Date and Results
1. Will *imitate* a circle, after watching an adult	chalk and chalkboards, crayons and paper, pencils, markers, play dough, shaving cream, sand table, paintbrush and easel	80% accuracy	ongoing	
2. Will *copy* a cricle, given a predrawn cricle	(See resource for method ideas.)			
3. Will *imitate* a vertical line after watching an adult				
4. Will *copy* a vertical line given a predrawn line				
5. Will *imitate* a horizontal line, after watching an adult				
6. Will *copy* a horizontal line, given a predrawn line				

Long-term Goal: Improve visual perception of shapes.

Short-term Objective:	Methods and Materials	Criteria of Successful Performance	Evaluation Schedule	Date and Results

(continued)

1. Complete a form board puzzle consisting of: circle, triangle, and square	teacher-prepared and commercial puzzles and shapes	80% accuracy	ongoing	
2. Match 3D shapes to models: circles, triangles, and squares				
3. Match pictures of shapes: circles, triangles, and squares				

Long-term Goal: Improve premath skills.

Short-term Objective:	Methods and Materials	Criteria of Successful Performance	Evaluation Schedule	Date and Results
1. Match one-to-one correspondence with objects	reinforce one-to-one correspondence throughout the day, e.g., snack time—one cup for every child; passing out supplies—one pair of scissors for every child; calendar—one symbol for each new day	80% accuracy	ongoing	

Long-term Goal: Improve gross motor skills.

Short-term Objective:	Methods and Materials	Criteria of Successful Performance	Evaluation Schedule	Date and Results
1. Walk on a straight line (masking tape or chalk)	straight line made with masking tape or chalk, balance beam with mat underneath (teacher assistance as needed)	80% accuracy	ongoing	
2. Walk on a balance beam with assistance				
3. Independently walk on a balance beam				

Long-term Goal: Improve social skills.

Short-term Objective:	Methods and Materials	Criteria of Successful Performance	Evaluation Schedule	Date and Results
1. Greets teacher/ peers when entering classroom, i.e., "Hi," "Hello," etc.	reinforce skills at appropriate time, teacher and peer modeling, daily reinforcement	80% of the time	ongoing	
2. Says "please" and "thank you" appropriately at snack time				

Long-term Goal: Improve self-help skills.

Short-term Objective:	Methods and Materials	Criteria of Successful Performance	Evaluation Schedule	Date and Results
1. Removes coat independently	reinforce dressing skills daily, coat, clothing with zippers, dolls with clothing	80% of the time	ongoing	
2. Zips clothing with assistance				
3. Puts on coat with assistance				

Characteristics of physical arrangement to be considered are: (a) attractiveness, (b) cleanliness, (c) stimulative features, (d) child orientation.

A careful inspection of the room will yield important constraints that affect the layout of the room, i.e., outlets, windows, doors, storage space, availability of water, etc. After initial inspection of the classroom, consider the following:

1. Is water near the activities that require it?
2. Are areas requiring physical activities removed from the areas involving little movement?
3. Can students perform noisy tasks without unreasonable disturbance to students in other areas?
4. Are similar activities grouped together to provide for optimal efficiency?
5. Is adequate space provided for large group activities?

6. Is there adequate protection against hazards (e.g., electrical cords, heating vents, etc.) in movement and in the use of materials and equipment?

7. Is there easy access from one area to another?

8. Can the room be modified and adjusted as needs arise?

9. Do students have access to storage areas containing materials designed for their independent use?

10. Are areas clearly defined (e.g., housekeeping, clocks, dramatic play)?

11. Are artwork and bulletin boards displayed at a level where children can easily see and enjoy them?

12. Can the teacher easily view all areas of the classroom at a glance?

Sample Floor Plans. The following pages present three sample plans.

SCHEDULING

A well-planned daily schedule assists the teacher in effectively carrying out the instructional plans. Structure to the day imparts confidence and security. It tells children what to do and what not to do, and what comes next without being told. Order and structure provide teachers and children with greater flexibility and freedom because certain time segments can be counted on.

When planning a schedule, the following should be considered:

1. the needs of the individual child as well as the needs of the total group;

2. physical needs of children;

3. alternating quiet versus active times;

4. flexibility within the schedule;

5. consideration of total school utilization of facility, e.g., gym or playground time;

6. availability of parents assisting in the classroom.

For the schedule to be manageable, it must be based on the needs of each individual or group of children. What works one year may thus not be as effective another year with another group of children. If group composition changes throughout the year as children enter or leave the program, the schedule may need to be altered. When assessing the needs of the individual and/or group, consider the number of children in the group, their ages and attention span, and the degree of their physical capabilities and limitations.

The physical needs to keep in mind primarily involve bathrooming and snack time. In an early childhood program, bathrooming can be very time-consuming. Depending on the location of the bathroom, assistance from an aide or parent volunteer becomes an invaluable timesaver for the teacher. She/he will need to decide if bathrooming should be scheduled as a whole group or dependent on individual needs. Snack time is an important part of the curriculum. In mid-morning or midafternoon, children need a nutritious snack to help them maintain

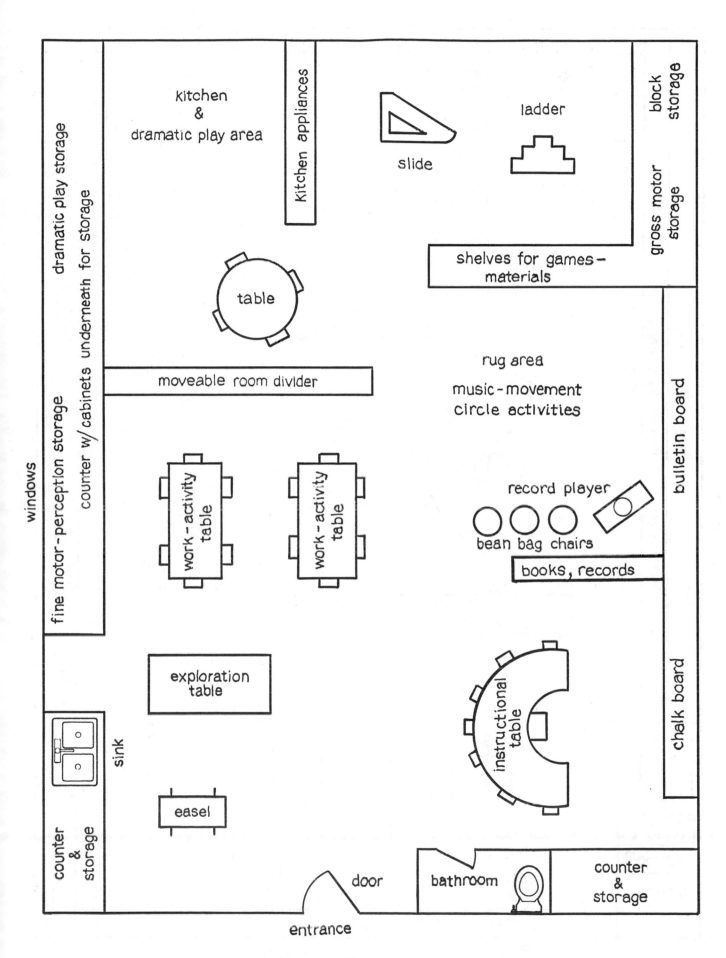

windows

dramatic play storage

counter w/ cabinets underneath for storage

fine motor - perception storage

kitchen & dramatic play area

kitchen appliances

slide

ladder

block storage

gross motor storage

shelves for games - materials

table

moveable room divider

rug area

music - movement circle activities

bulletin board

work - activity table

work - activity table

record player

bean bag chairs

books, records

exploration table

chalk board

sink

instructional table

counter & storage

easel

door

bathroom

counter & storage

entrance

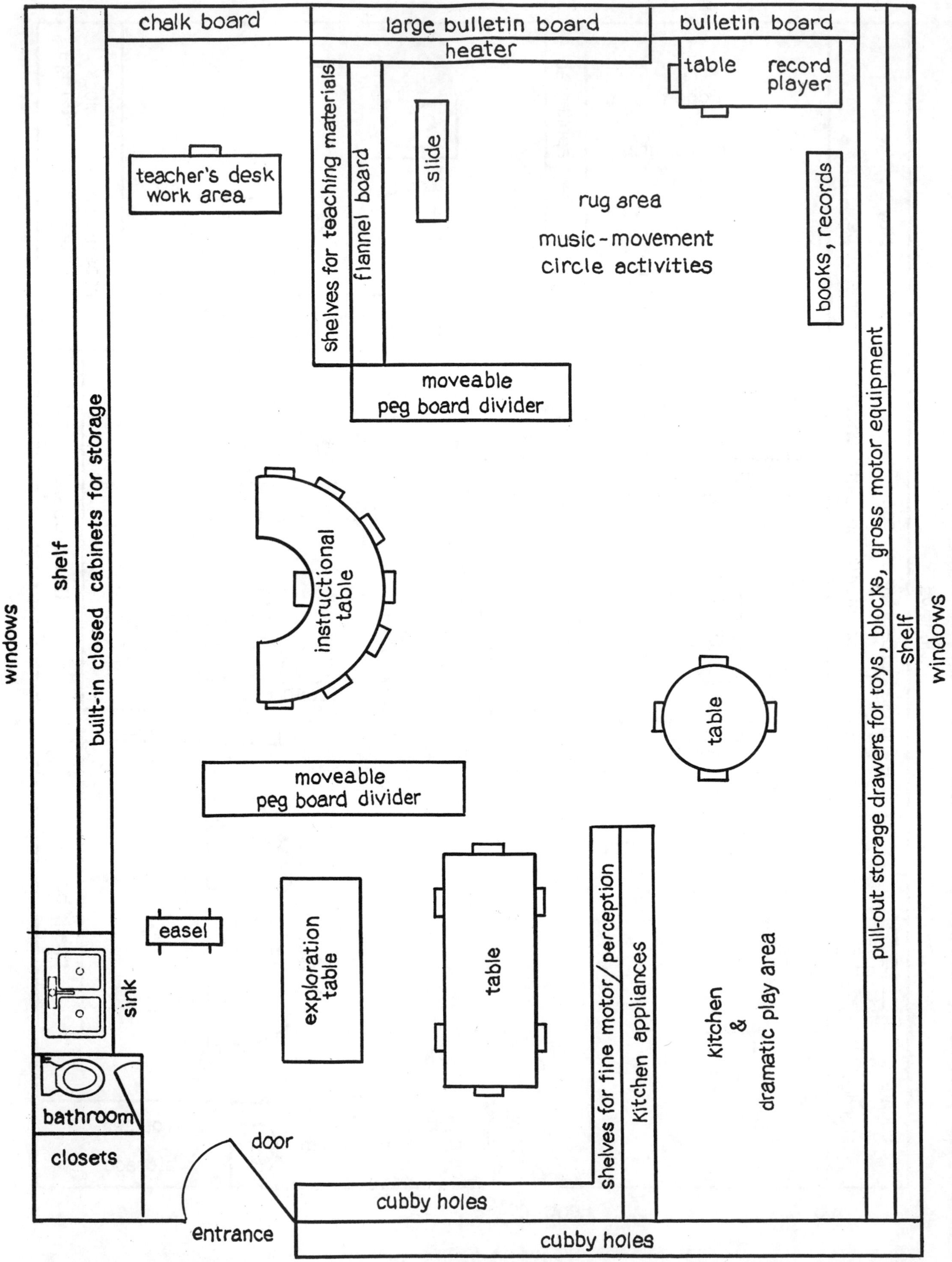
chalk board
large bulletin board
bulletin board
heater
table
record player
teacher's desk work area
shelves for teaching materials
flannel board
slide
rug area
music-movement circle activities
books, records
moveable peg board divider
windows
shelf
built-in closed cabinets for storage
instructional table
table
pull-out storage drawers for toys, blocks, gross motor equipment
shelf
windows
moveable peg board divider
easel
exploration table
table
shelves for fine motor/perception
kitchen appliances
kitchen & dramatic play area
sink
bathroom
closets
door
entrance
cubby holes
cubby holes

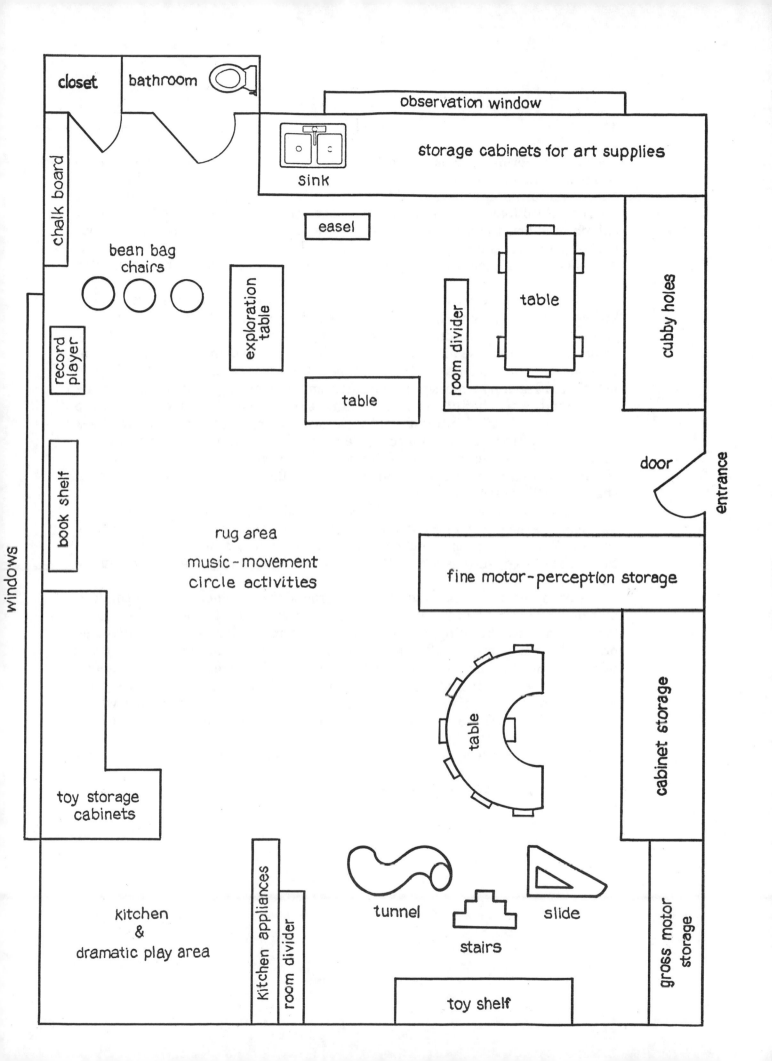

optimum performance. Snack also serves as an integral part of the curriculum in terms of reinforcing language, fine motor, premath, and socialization skills.

Children's ability to attend varies greatly depending on age, ability, and interest. Good teacher planning must focus on these considerations to provide a balance and flow to the child's day. Therefore, alternating vigorous, noisy activities with quieter, more sedentary ones is vital. A structured activity such as a language lesson should be followed by a more active period such as music or movement.

No matter how perfect a devised schedule may appear, a sensitive teacher knows that flexibility within that schedule is imperative. There are several important variables in timing a lesson. Ending a learning experience or activity before the children lose interest can leave them motivated and eager to engage in that activity another day. At other times, the teacher must decide when to lengthen a learning experience if enthusiasm and learning is occurring. On the other hand, a teacher-planned ten-minute activity should be shortened if the children show limited interest or if the concept being presented is above their ability level. This balance in a schedule allows for effective use of instructional time for both the teacher and the student. Experience with a certain group of children increases the teacher's ability to utilize effectively the cues and feedback she/he gets from students.

Flexibility must also be used when accommodating speech, occupational, and physical therapy schedules. If the program is located within a larger school setting, the early childhood schedule must be flexible within the context of the total school need, such as use of the gym, playground facility, lunchroom, and so on.

Depending on his/her style and background, the teacher may feel comfortable using learning centers in the classroom. Certain activities such as fine motor, perception, block building, dramatic play, sand and water play, and language-oriented games easily lend themselves to this approach. Children should be given opportunities to make choices within the teacher-designed learning environment. These choices could include who to work with, which activity to do first or second, and when to ask for guidance. Group projects and learning centers are one way to encourage interaction and conversation, which will help children to develop competence in language.

The schedules which follow are given only as a guide. One is for a teacher working alone in a classroom, while others include the availability of an aide or other classroom assistant or volunteer.

SCHEDULE I—TEACHER, NO ASSISTANT

8:30	Meet bus, assist children with coats
8:40	Bathrooming
8:50	Free-choice centers
9:10	Clean-up
9:15	Sharing circle
9:30	Music and movement
9:40	Language
10:00	Bathroom
10:10	Snack
10:25	Fine motor, perception, or premath
10:45	Gross motor
11:00	Story
11:10	Free-choice centers, clean-up
11:20	Prepare to leave (coats, schoolbags, etc.)
11:30	Dismissal

SCHEDULE II—TEACHER WITH AIDE

Time	Teacher	Aide
8:30	Planning	Meets bus
8:40	Bathrooming children	Assist
8:50	Sharing circle	Assist
9:05	Gross motor	Assist
9:20	Language (Group I)	Perception centers
	alternate groups	
9:40	Language (Group II)	Perception centers
10:00	Bathrooming children	Assist
10:10	Snack	Assist
10:25	Music/movement	Assist
10:45	Individual work with students	Fine motor or other centers
11:00	Story	Prepare materials
11:10	Outside play	Assist
11:30	Classroom clean-up	Dismissal to bus

SCHEDULE III—TEACHER WITH AIDE AND VOLUNTEER

Time	Teacher	Aide	Volunteer
8:30	Planning	Meets bus, assist children with coats	Assist aide
8:40	Planning	Bathrooming	Assist aide
8:50	Sharing circle	Assist teacher	Material preparation
9:10	Music/ movement	Assist	Assist
9:30	Language	Perceptual activity (puzzles, block designs, continue peg board patterns)	Fine motor, art project
10:00	Get snack ready	Bathrooming	Assist aide
10:10	Snack	Assist teacher	Material preparation
10:30	Gross motor	Set up station, get equipment	Assist aide
11:00	Story	Material preparation	Material preparation
11:10	Free-choice centers	Assist with centers	Assist with centers
11:25	Assist students with coats and school bags	Assist	Classroom clean-up
11:30	Dismissal	Take students to bus	Classroom clean-up

MATERIALS

A wide range of materials are typically found in an early childhood classroom. Some materials are likely to be those children use in an independent manner; others are designed to be used most profitably with adult supervision in a structured setting. Some materials can be used flexibly by students alone or in a more formal manner with the teacher. Before selecting and purchasing classroom materials, the teacher must take into consideration what is presently available, the needs of the students, budget limitations, and the durability of each item. After prioritizing needs, the teacher can then decide if a particular item could be found in a regular catalog or in a more specialized catalog offering special developmental materials and equipment. Teacher-made materials and items purchased at garage sales should not be discounted when equipping the early childhood classroom.

Suggestions for selecting materials include the following:

1. Refrain from labeling materials as being for boys or girls only. Children need a wide range of experiences with pretending and manipulating.
2. Rotate materials frequently.
3. Plan the storage of materials carefully. Arrange those to be used independently by the children on low shelves, and keep teacher-directed materials out of students' reach.
4. Materials should be appropriate for the child's interests, needs, and abilities, not so easy as to be boring, or so hard as to be frustrating.
5. Consider the value and purpose of each material.

NOTE: See Appendix (pages 275–278) for a listing of materials.

EVALUATING THE LEARNING ENVIRONMENT

Designing a classroom learning environment does not always guarantee that things will flow smoothly within the room. Again, the teacher must be a good observer of the students. She/he must assess how the children are operating within the space, handling time limits, and using the materials in their environment.

It may be useful to address the following questions when focusing on each area.

PHYSICAL ENVIRONMENT:
1. Is one area of the classroom used more frequently than others?
2. Are children using all the allotted space?
3. Are children trying to find more space?
4. Do the children appear to feel comfortable and safe in the classroom?

SCHEDULE:

1. Does the schedule allow for change as student attention span and concentration levels increase and develop?
2. Does the schedule allow for real flexibility or a sense of fragmentation in various activities?
3. Is time used profitably by students?
4. Does the schedule allow for a blend of teacher-directed and student-selected activities?

MATERIALS:

1. Which materials are most popular?
2. Which materials are never used?
3. Which materials are always used in the same way?
4. Which materials lend themselves best to adaptation and improvisation?
5. Which materials do children combine?
6. Are children using materials in a constructive manner?

Using a Classroom Aide

The school district in which you teach, the number of students in your classroom, and the severity of the students' needs will determine if your classroom is eligible for an aide.

It is the classroom teacher's responsibility to establish the guidelines and framework in which the aide will work most effectively. Initially, the teacher will need to outline and review tasks and responsibilities assigned to the aide. The teacher and aide should set aside a daily or weekly time to review plans and discuss specific needs for that day or week.

Several factors to consider when assigning tasks are:

- Teaching style and philosophy
- Teaching strengths and weaknesses
- Responsibility preferences
- Student needs

Every teacher has his/her own ideas about the best way to foster learning, as well as implement the curriculum. These ideas represent his/her teaching style and form the basis of the teacher's educational philosophy. It is very important for the teacher to share and clarify these ideas with the classroom aide. This will help create a consistent atmosphere within the classroom. In addition, it will help the teacher and aide prioritize tasks to be accomplished within the classroom.

Every teacher and teacher's aide come into the classroom equipped with personal strengths and weaknesses. The aide may be particularly talented in art while it is a struggle for the teacher to mix paint. In this case it makes more sense for the aide to supervise the art project or art center while the teacher sets up the snack. An optimal classroom environment can be achieved if everyone's strengths are utilized.

Within the classroom there are many tasks and activities that either the aide or teacher can accomplish successfully. The division of these tasks can, in part, be made based on preference within certain limitations. The teacher can allow the aide input as to which activities she/he prefers. For example, the aide may feel uncomfortable supervising a music activity. Based on this preference, the teacher could assign another task at that time. It is important to establish a cooperative classroom environment in which everyone feels respected.

Some children may have more significant physical needs, in which case both the teacher and aide may need to devote time to these needs. In a classroom of children with less significant physical needs, the teacher may be able to spend more time directing learning activities while the aide can easily handle the students' physical needs.

It is important for the teacher to be aware of the type of aide assigned to the classroom (i.e., instructional, physical care giver, clerical, etc.) before determining which duties will be appropriate in a particular situation.

The following list encompasses a broad sampling of responsibilities inherent in a classroom. Do not expect the aide to assume any one of these responsibilities unless it is clearly defined. When determining a break time for your aide, be sure to consider the schedule and when you can best function with one less adult.

CLERICAL DUTIES
1. Keep attendance records.
2. File correspondence, reports, etc.
3. Schedule and return audiovisual equipment when appropriate.
4. Requisition and pick up supplies from the office.
5. Record and keep track of permission slips, money, etc.
6. Run Xerox® and dittos when necessary.
7. Prepare material for the week's activities.

HOUSEKEEPING DUTIES
1. Clean snack area daily—wash dishes if necessary.
2. Clean paint and sink areas.
3. Notify custodian when furniture is broken or becomes unsafe.

GUIDING DAILY ROUTINES
1. Supervise children before instructional period begins.
2. Meet children at buses.

3. Assist with toileting.
4. Assist with snack time.
5. Assist children with clothing as necessary.
6. Supervise children as they carry out assigned tasks.
7. Provide transitional activities during gaps (fingerplays, songs, stories, etc.).
8. Supervise children on the playground.

MAINTAINING BEHAVIOR MANAGEMENT PROGRAMS

1. Provide controls for children within guidelines of classroom philosophy.
2. Redirect behavior that is not appropriate.
3. Observe children—inform teacher of changes in behavior or any concerns pertaining to students or the classroom environment.

MAINTAINING PARENT INVOLVEMENT

1. Relate warmly to parents and help make them feel welcome.
2. Model teaching strategy for parents as directed by teacher.
3. Maintain a friendly yet professional attitude with parents.
4. Keep any information you acquire about students and their families *confidential*.

PREPARING THE LEARNING ENVIRONMENT

1. Prepare instructional materials as needed.
2. Mix paint.
3. Arrange materials for accessibility.
4. Organize and collect materials for teaching units as directed by the teacher.
5. Set up motor equipment in the gym or outside.
6. Put away materials and art supplies daily.
7. Make necessary classroom preparations.
8. Put up and take down bulletin boards and decorations.

INSTRUCTIONAL-RELATED DUTIES

1. Reinforce language and concepts throughout the day.
2. Tell stories using books and flannel board.
3. Stimulate play activities and encourage language and conversation between students and between students and adults.
4. Reinforce individual skills.
5. Guide small-group activities.
6. Assist teacher in large-group activities as directed.

7. Arrange field trips as directed by teacher.
8. Supervise learning centers.

Getting Parents Involved

IMPORTANCE OF PARENT INVOLVEMENT

Child development and achievement is enhanced when parents and teachers work together. Research supports the fact that optimal achievement occurs only when parents reinforce learning at home. Federal Law 94-142 not only recommends but actively mandates parental involvement in early childhood special education programs. Research studies have shown that when parents work with their special needs student at home not only is his/her development enhanced, but older and younger siblings also benefit from the parents' involvement. The interest parents exhibit when working with their special needs student demonstrates to the child that his/her progress is important to them. This serves to enhance the child's self-esteem and motivation to learn.

Given this information, one must recognize the importance of including a parent component, particularly when establishing and implementing an early childhood special education program.

Parents are not a homogeneous group, and one type of parent program will not meet the needs of all parents. An effective program must allow for different types of involvement. Educators must analyze the parents' needs just as the children's needs are taken into consideration in the classroom. The parent involvement component in the early childhood program must match and balance its resources with the parents' needs.

The parent involvement component in an early childhood program is multifaceted. Possibly the most critical consideration is that of supporting parents in teaching their children. When parents and teachers share common goals and utilize similar methods in teaching children, progress will be optimal. Given that children spend many more hours at home than in school, it makes sense that for maximum carryover of learning to occur, reinforcement at home is a necessity. The teacher must convey the attitude that the parent-child relationship is of primary importance and that the early childhood program works primarily to encourage and extend that relationship. The teaching staff must exhibit empathy and understanding to the parents and support their efforts to become involved in their child's education program, no matter how minimally. Teachers must convey to parents that they are partners in the education process.

There are many ways to involve and train parents in a teaching capacity. Home visits allow the teacher to observe the parent and child in a familiar setting and learn about special parent skills and parent-child interactions. The teacher can extend the observation by introducing teaching techniques and activities for the parents to utilize at home. The teacher may find it helpful to model a particular activity for the parents to use at a later time. The teacher may assist parents in constructing games and materials to use with the child, or may simply choose to leave pertinent materials with the parents to use until the next home visit.

Another alternative for fostering teaching skills in parents is to have parents come to the classroom and observe the teaching-learning process. The parents may choose to take a passive observational role or may choose to participate actively in the classroom. If the parents choose more active participation, they can assist in classroom activities, prepare instructional materials, collect data, accompany the class on a field trip, or participate in any manner with which they feel comfortable. The teacher serves as a role model in teaching techniques and in fostering learning.

Another option that brings parents and children together at school are school parent-child learning activities. In this situation small groups of parents and children with similar IEP goals come to school together to participate in parent-child activities which are organized by the teacher.

Some parents may choose to become involved in the teaching-learning capacity only through individual or small-group sharing with the teacher, or by simply carrying out teacher-suggested activities at home (see monthly calendars).

Other important facets of the parent component include parent education and support through group meetings with a speaker and/or small-group meetings with other parents. Parent involvement programs should provide opportunities for parents to learn about approaches to child rearing, normal child development, management of the child in the home, and how to find and utilize resources in the community.

Parents should also have direct involvement in policy and decision making and in planning individual education programs. They must understand the rationale, objectives, and activities of the program in which their child is enrolled.

A successful parent program should consider the following:

1. Assessment of parental needs
2. Matching of program resources and parental needs
3. An attempt to include all parents, which may require modification for working parents
4. Provision for change in the program agenda based on parents' interests and needs
5. Maintenance of confidentiality
6. Provision of incentives and reinforcement for parents

Additional considerations may be necessary in encouraging parents to participate in the parent component of the early childhood program. These might include:

1. Providing transportation
2. Providing babysitters

3. Writing or calling parents in advance of meetings
4. Arranging different schedules for working parents
5. Arranging small groups for parents who seem uncomfortable in larger groups

IMPLEMENTATION

When planning the parent component of the early childhood program, the initial step is providing parents with a needs assessment. This gives parents input into the program component that is designed for them in an effort to meet their individual needs. When parents are provided the opportunity to assist in the planning stages of the program, it is more likely that they will be motivated to participate in the various facets of the program.

The needs assessment will vary with each individual early childhood program and the resources and time allotments available. Some needs assessments may include options available for home visits. If the home visit policy is determined by the administration, or the IEP, the parents' choices are limited in this area; therefore, the teacher may choose not to include a section on home visits. The "Parent Needs Assessment" on pages 24–25 provides a sampling of items that can be included.

After compiling the needs assessment, the next step is distributing it to the parents as close to the beginning of the year as possible. If feasible, ask parents to complete the needs assessment at school as part of the early childhood registration. Another option is to mail a needs assessment to each family asking them to complete it within a specified time. Enclose a stamped, school-addressed envelope to encourage more returns. The parent component of the early childhood program for any given school year should be based on the results of the needs assessment. Speakers, meeting times, and topics will all be determined based on the needs of the parents who have children enrolled in the program for that year.

At the end of the school year, the parents can easily assess the parent component. Make a list of the topics included in large and small parent group sessions. The list may include additional questions related to home visits and parents volunteering in the classroom. Ask parents to complete the evaluation form. The information obtained from the evaluation form will help to improve the parent group component in subsequent years. See the following agenda for a sample parent group schedule and the evaluation form on page 26. Both were based on that year's assessment.

EARLY CHILDHOOD PARENT GROUP (SAMPLE AGENDA)

September   Parent Night in Early Childhood 7:00–8:30 P.M.
October   Speech and Language "How to Be a Speech Teacher at Home" 7:00–8:30 P.M.
November   Toy Workshop and Display 1:00–2:30 P.M.
December   Holiday Make-and-Take 1:00–2:30 P.M.—Parents and Early Childhood Children

January	Fine and Gross Motor Workshop—Dads and Children 7:00–8:00 P.M.
February	Behavior Management 1:00–2:30 P.M.
March	Testing and What It Tells Us 1:00–2:30 P.M.
April	Emotional Development 1:00–2:30 P.M.
May	Picnic Field Trip and Early Childhood Olympic Games 12:30–2:30 P.M.
May	Luncheon and Summer Play Activity Suggestions 12:30–2:30 P.M.

THE HOME VISIT

Recent research shows that the years before age five are of singular importance in the developmental process. Learning experiences provided during this time have relatively more impact than at any other time. The parent is the strongest influence on a child's development, and must be considered a very important teacher. One important aspect of home visits is to help parents become effective teachers. The teacher can accomplish this through observation of the parent-child relationship, modeling behavior conducive to fostering parent teaching skills, providing ideas for meaningful daily home experiences, and providing the parents with learning activities that focus on the development of language skills, concepts, motor development, self-help skills, and appropriate socialization skills. Another important aspect of the home visit is the discussion of progress and parental concerns. Parental attitudes are crucial to a child's self-concept. An understanding, sensitive, and informed parent can help the child develop to his/her fullest potential. When a preschool program reinforces the parental strengths, it enhances the development of the child.

Home visits are an intregal part of many early childhood programs. Different programs make various provisions for this component. Some programs may provide a full or half day per week, while others provide one or two days per month, and still others may provide evening time for home visits. For some students, home visits and/or a specific amount of time alloted for home teaching will be written as a goal in the child's Individual Education Plan. However each program provides for home visits, it is extremely important to prioritize the need for the home visit component in the total early childhood program.

A typical home visit might include:

1. Observation of parent-child relationship in the home setting
2. A learning activity that focuses on development: language skills, concept development, or motor development, as specified in the IEP
3. Modeling behaviors conducive to fostering parent teaching skills
4. Discussion of questions/concerns
5. Discussion of progress/IEP
6. Ideas for meaningful everyday home experiences

Parent Needs Assessment

Parent name _____

Directions: Please check the appropriate column for each of the following:

	Very Inter-ested	Inter-ested	Not Inter-ested
I am interested in learning more about or receiving additional information regarding the following:			
1. Stages of child development in various developmental areas including:			
a. Speech and language development			
b. Concept or cognitive development			
c. Social/emotional development			
d. Fine motor development			
e. Gross motor development			
f. Self-help skills			
2. The early childhood curriculum and how it is implemented			
3. Related services, e.g., occupational and physical therapy, speech and language services			
4. How I can help my child at home			
5. How I can be involved in my child's program at school			
6. How I can help plan my child's educational goals (IEP)			
7. Relating with families and friends regarding my child's special needs			
8. Working with and relating to professionals			
9. Family communcation			
10. Community resources for children and parents			
11. Locating medical and related services			
12. Parental rights and responsibilities for parents of special needs students			
13. Family financial planning			
14. Testing and what it tells us			
15. Nutrition and diet			
16. Discipline/Behavior management			
17. Play and home activities			
18. Safety for young children			
19. Toys for young children			
20. Books—using the library			
21. Siblings			

Parent Needs Assessment (*cont.*)

Please include any other areas of interest not included above.

_____

_____

_____

How often would you like the parents' group to meet?

_____ 1 time per month   _____ 2 times per month

I am in need of a babysitting service while attending the parent group.

_____ Yes   _____ No

I would be willing to drive other parents to meetings.

_____ Yes   _____ No

I am mostly interested in: _____ large-group informational meetings

                          _____ small support group meetings with parents

                          _____ both large- and small-group meetings

I prefer _____ daytime meetings _____ evening meetings.

Home/School Learning

I am interested in the teacher making home visits on a regular basis to share ideas and activities I can use with my child at home.

_____ Yes   _____ No

How often? _____ 1 time per month   _____ 2 times per month

I am interested in observing the classroom to learn how best to teach my child at home.

_____ Yes   _____ No

How often? _____ 1 time per month   _____ 2 times per month

I am interested in becoming a classroom volunteer.

_____ Yes   _____ No

I would like to help with the following:

_____ preparing materials

_____ working with groups of children

_____ going on field trips

_____ working with individual children

I am interested in attending school for parent-child learning activities with small groups of parents and children.

_____ Yes   _____ No

Parent Group Evaluation

Meetings	Not Applicable	Poor	Fair	Good	Excellent	Please repeat next yr.
1. Parents Night in Early Childhood (evening)						
2. How to Be a Speech Teacher at Home (evening)						
3. Toy Workshop and Display						
4. Holiday Make-and-Take: Parents and Early Childhood Children						
5. Fine and Gross Motor Workshop—Dad's Night						
6. Behavior Management						
7. Testing and What It Tells Us						
8. Emotional Development						
9. Picnic and Olympic Games						
10. Luncheon and Summer Play Activities						

1. Please list ways in which the parent group helped you and/or your child.

2. Please list ways in which the parent program could have better met your needs.

3. Do you have suggestions for changes in the parent group?

4. What other topics would you have liked us to cover? (nutrition, TV viewing, safety, community resources for you and your child, etc.)

Consider the following strategies when planning for and modeling activities for parents on a home visit:

1. Activities should be kept simple and allow enough flexibility for the parent to modify the learning experience.
2. Activities presented and their suggested follow-up should be kept to five to ten minutes. Parents can decide if they want to work for longer amounts of time with their child.
3. Keep the atmosphere as relaxed and positive as possible. Encourage the parents to do the same when working with their child.
4. Stress to parents that daily activities can be learning experiences for young children. Encourage them to talk to and include children while doing every-day activities such as shopping, cooking, laundry, etc. Many concepts can be reinforced during these times.

The teacher may choose to leave materials with the parents to use until the next home visit or may leave suggestions for activities that include materials which are easily accessible in the home. Some teachers may choose to observe or participate in a home activity such as sorting or folding laundry, or preparing a meal or snack. The teacher can reinforce the parent when she/he uses these simple activities as teaching tools. The teacher may be able to assist parents in understanding how these daily routines can be used to reinforce concepts specified in the child's IEP at home. During a cooking activity, math concepts, language, and fine motor skills can all be enhanced. During laundry sorting, perception, color recognition, fine motor, classification, and other language skills can be reinforced. The teacher may use the home visit to work with parents and children on making materials to play with, such as using egg cartons for counting or sorting materials. The teacher might also use this opportunity to see how parents are utilizing the activity calendars which are sent home monthly. The home visit is a flexible experience that can be used differently for different parents and children, depending on their individual needs.

A reproducible "Home Visit Record" and two samples are presented on pages 28 and 29, along with a reproducible "Home-School Learning Evaluation" on page 30 to be completed by parents.

HOME VISIT IDEAS

Starting on page 31 is a list of ideas to use during home visits. Because the number of possibilities and household materials is limited only by the imagination, only a sampling is included here.

Sample Home Visit

Student name _____ Teacher _____

Address _____

Date	Parent/Adults Present	Objective	Materials	Comments
	Mrs. _____, Parent Mrs. _____, Teacher	To discuss and demonstrate how reading a story can be used to improve and expand vocabulary concepts and answer "wh" who, what, where, when, why questions	Booklet: *Reading a Story* Book: *Is it Larger? Is it Smaller,* by Tana Hoban	Objectives accomplished. Booklet left with parent. Mrs. _____ was able to follow through with story activity after teacher demonstration. She was surprised that _____ responded so well, naming pictures and answering questions. She plans to visit the library and select some books for reading with _____ at home before the next home visit.

Sample Home Visit

Student name _____ Teacher _____

Address _____

Date	Parent/Adults Present	Objective	Materials	Comments
	Mrs. _____, Parent Mrs. _____, Teacher	To involve _____ in a variety of activities that reinforce fine motor development 1. Pincer grip 2. Snipping	Objects to sort into muffin cups (beads, paper clips, safety pins, dried beans) Loop scissors and heavy paper	Objectives were accomplished. _____ worked beautifully today and at one point was eager to try another activity. Once he understood the tasks and focused visually on the materials presented, he was successful on all activities. Mrs. _____ modeled teaching techniques and completed the activities with _____ . Teacher left the loop scissors for _____ to use at home until the next home visit. Mrs. _____ will use a muffin tin and small objects to practice pincer grip and sorting at home.

Home Visit Record

Student Name: _____ Teacher: _____

Address: _____

Date	Parent/Adults Present	Objective	Materials	Comments

Home-School Learning Evaluation

Name _____

1. Were home visits helpful in providing you with ideas/activities to use at home with your child? Were they frequent enough? Too frequent?

2. Were classroom evaluations and parent participation in the classroom helpful in providing you with a better understanding of your child and his/her educational needs?

3. Were conferences useful in helping you to understand better your child's needs and goals?

4. Were you given opportunities for input in your child's Individual Education Program?

5. Were school parent-child learning activities helpful in providing you with ideas to use at home with your child? Were they frequent enough?

6. Other comments:

FINE MOTOR ACTIVITIES

Use paintbrushes and water for sidewalk painting.

Use yarn and fabric swatches for pasting and gluing.

Use plates, cups, etc. for tracing.

Practice cooking/baking, stirring, pouring, rolling, and cutting cookie dough.

Use jars and lids for screwing lids on jars.

Use paper, crayons, markers, and pencils for drawing.

Use clothespins to practice opening and closing. Draw colors or numerals on the pins and match them to the same on paper plates.

Use cereal, macaroni, and strings to make necklaces.

Use nuts and nutcrackers to crack nuts.

Use a knife for spreading peanut butter, cream cheese, etc. on bread, celery, or apples, and cut.

GROSS MOTOR ACTIVITIES

Use large plastic milk jugs with cut-out bottoms to catch balls.

Use soft balls for rolling and throwing into laundry baskets or paper bags.

Use bean bags to toss into a laundry basket, bags, or shapes drawn on paper.

Practice walking, hopping, and jumping to clapped rhythms.

Run, skip, hop, or jump to the mailbox.

Practice jumping from the bottom step.

Make a line from masking tape, and practice walking on it forwards, backwards, sideways, etc.

LANGUAGE ACTIVITIES

Use everyday objects such as combs, brushes, etc., and talk about their functions.

Use old catalogs and magazines for locating pictures, naming objects, and classifying.

Use bath time for naming body parts and teaching concepts of hot and cold.

Use dressing to name clothing terms.

Read books, talk about them, sequence stories, and retell them.

Use grocery shopping to name and classify foods.

Use language prepositions, i.e., *on–off, up–down, in–out, over–under,* when dressing, cooking, cleaning, and bathing.

PREMATH ACTIVITIES

Use butter containers for counting sets and sorting.

Use a deck of cards to match numerals.

While cooking, use measuring and concepts of more and less.

Count with your child through the day—count when cooking, count mail, silverware, etc.

Cut straws in varying lengths, sequence them by size, and use them for counting and sorting by color.

Write a numeral in each section of an egg carton and have children count out cereal or candies to match the numerals.

Count the days on a calendar till Grandma comes, etc., and talk about the day of the week, the month, the seasons and holidays, etc.

PERCEPTION ACTIVITIES

Use egg cartons for sorting.

Use tin cans to repeat rhythms.

Use buttons for sequencing, size relationships, and color sorting.

Use pots, pans, and lids for matching size.

Use laundry to sort by colors and by family members.

Look for colors and shapes while watching television.

Use photographs to mount and cut into pieces, and assemble like a puzzle.

Identify household sounds, e.g., doorbell, refrigerator, and water running.

Help put silverware away, and sort knives, spoons, and forks.

PARENT-CHILD LEARNING AT SCHOOL

If some parents are uncomfortable with having the teacher visit the home, or if the school district does not allow time for home visits, school learning activities for parents and children is another option. In this alternative, small groups of parents and children with similar IEP goals attend school together. The teacher provides activities for children to do together with their parents. The same suggestions for home visits apply to this type of learning situation:

Keep the activities short and simple.

Keep the atmosphere relaxed and positive.

Discuss with parents the ease of doing similar activities at home with their child.

Relate the activities to IEP objectives.

In implementing this type of parent-child learning situation, the teacher might choose to set up learning centers or stations in the classroom. The stations might include the various curriculum areas: fine motor, gross motor, perception, language concepts, etc. Provide a simple activity at each station that parents can do with their children. Provide simple directions at each station and have parents and children rotate stations. A variation on this type of this parent-child learning activity might be to stress different types of activities during different weeks or monthly sessions. One day could be a gross motor session while another could be devoted to fine motor activities.

As with home visits, this type of learning situation is flexible and must be based on the needs of the individual parent-child pair.

BOOKS FOR PARENTS

The following is a selection of books for parents covering a variety of topics and concerns.

Abraham, Willard. *Living with Preschoolers*

Ames, Louise. *Your Four Year Old*

———. *Your Three Year Old*

———. *Your Two Year Old*

Cole, A., C. Haas, F. Bushnell, and B. Weinberger. *I Saw a Purple Cow and 100 Other Recipes for Learning*

Coletta, Anthony. *Working Together: A Guide to Parental Involvement*

Dodson, Fitzhugh. *How to Father*

Dreikurs, Rudolf. *Children the Challenge*

———. *The Challenge of Parenthood*

Faber, Adele. *How to Talk So Kids Will Listen*

Gordon, Thomas. *P.E.T. Parent Effectiveness Training*

Honig, Alice. *Parent Involvement in Early Childhood Education*

Katz, Lilian, G. *Talks with Parents on Living with Preschoolers*

Kohl, Herbert. *Growing with Your Children*

Kuzma, Kay. *Prime Time Parenting*

Lamb, Michael. *The Role of the Father in Child Development*

Lane, Mary. *Education for Parenting*

Lerman, Saf. *Parent Awareness Training; Positive Parenting*

Marzollo, J., and J. Lloyd. *Learning through Play*

Matterson, Elizabeth. *Games for the Very Young: Finger Plays and Nursery Games*

Millman, J., and P. Behrmann. *Parents as Playmates*

Puchaw, D. *Teach Your Child to Talk*

Salk, Lee. *What Every Child Would Like His Parents to Know*

Sutton, Brian. *How to Play with Your Children: (and when not to)*

Early Childhood Curriculum

The content of the early childhood curriculum must be developmentally appropriate for the age and ability of each child. At the minimum, the program components should encompass language concepts and vocabulary, fine and gross motor skills, perception, self-help, and social skills. A curriculum which includes these components recognizes and addresses the many facets of the developing child.

Knowledge of growth and development of children is the essential base on which a particular curriculum must be established. The physical, intellectual, social, and emotional growth of each child in the classroom is the overriding objective. The program must be flexible enough so that sequence and content meet specific needs and situations, and yet structured enough to include all curricular areas appropriate to the ages, interests, and abilities of individuals in the group. Each child must find success in the classroom and find achievement as an individual and as a member of the group.

AREAS OF LEARNING

Language and Cognitive/Thinking Skills and Concepts. Language, thinking skills, and concept development are closely related. Language is the communication system we use to relate ideas and thought through the understanding and usage of words, phrases, and sentences. Thinking skills involve the child's ability to solve problems, share ideas, evaluate and organize experiences, generalize concepts, and recall information.

The content of the cognitive curriculum includes such skills as naming objects, colors, and shapes, and directional-positional concepts. Other examples of cognitive skills are knowing the function and use of objects, answering questions, building vocabulary, and developing verbal reasoning skills.

Perception. Perceptual skills are those related to the senses: sight, hearing, taste, smell, and touch. The word perception doesn't refer to how well one sees, hears, tastes, smells, or touches, but how the brain processes the experiences. Perception applies to just about every experience a child has because the senses are an integral part of learning.

The content of the perceptual curriculum includes such skills as assembling puzzles, copying designs and patterns, and drawing a person. Other examples of perceptual skills include experiences which enable the child to identify and compare sights, sounds, textures, tastes, and odors in the environment.

Motor Skills. Motor skills are generally classified as either of two types: fine motor, which involves small muscles, and gross motor, which involves large muscles. Most fine motor skills relate to the hands. They usually include finger dexterity and the coordination and speed of the finger muscles, wrist flexibility, and the coordination of the hands with eye movement. Activities designed to build these skills include building with blocks, stringing beads, cutting with scissors, doing fingerplays, lacing, buttoning clothes, printing, and coloring. Gross motor skills include such basic abilities as balance and posture, and strength and coordination of the muscles so that the child can walk, run, skip, catch a ball, and climb.

Self-Help Skills. Self-help skills are all the different tasks a child learns in order to care for himself/herself independently. Holding a cup, using a spoon, and holding out arms and legs while being dressed are some of the first self-help skills a young child learns. As the toddler reaches preschool age, the self-help skills become more complex. Feeding, dressing, and toilet training are important achievements in a preschooler's development. As children learn to care for themselves, they develop a sense of pride and confidence that motivates them to try new skills. If children are never given opportunities to care for their needs or if their attempts are criticized, they are deprived of a chance to achieve on their own and feel good about themselves. Children with special needs might take a longer time to learn how to dress, feed, and take care of themselves, but they still feel the same pride and sense of accomplishment that are a vital part of a young child's development.

Social Skills. Social skills include interaction with others and interaction with objects. Interaction with others includes the child's ability to greet others appropriately, deliver simple messages, take turns, share work and play materials, request and offer help, attend and follow directions, and accept praise and suggestions. Interaction with objects includes the child's ability to handle materials with care, put away objects when finished, and play and work independently and appropriately with materials.

Readiness. Readiness skills are the prerequisite building blocks for future success in reading and other academic areas. Abilities, skills, and understanding grow at an individual rate. The content of the readiness curriculum includes following directions, listening comprehension, sequencing, expanding expressive language, and categorizing.

PreMath. Math incorporates the experiences, ideas, and skills to help children organize their world. Exploratory activities and interactions with materials lay the groundwork for the development of mathematical concepts. The content of the math curriculum may include matching, sorting, patterning, comparing, classifying, ordering, measuring, and graphing. Other examples of math skills include understanding of quantitative concepts, shapes, space, numbers, number symbols, one-to-one correspondence, and calendar activities.

Music. Music activities help the child to develop movement skills and spatial awareness by providing opportunities to respond through bodily movements. Children are encouraged to move to the music and express what they think the music says. Children can learn parts of the body more easily when the learning is incorporated with games and songs. In other singing games, children can learn to hop, skip, run, walk, and balance. They use their eyes, hands, fingers, and arms to develop fine motor coordination.

Music in the classroom need not be set apart from other curricular areas. Many songs can be used to enrich the learning experiences in areas such as concept and language development. The children can sing about holidays, safety, weather, animals, birds, and community helpers while they are learning about them in other classroom activities. A learned concept reinforced by a song is remembered more easily and longer. Associating songs and factual content reinforces new learning and can be the stimulus for the child to understand. Carefully planned music activities are particularly helpful for the exceptional child.

Dramatic Play. Dramatic play is an individual or group experience in which every child has the opportunity to express himself/herself as he/she works and plays. It is an ideal way to provide socialization and language expansion for the preschool child. Books, props, guest speakers, field trips, stories, and experiences related by others create themes for dramatic play. Acting out familiar or new experiences provides the child an opportunity to assimilate and accommodate these events. Children's ability to express themselves in both word and action, the creation of a social awareness, and the encouragement of cooperative play can be the outcome of dramatic play in the early childhood classroom.

Art. Art activities for young children should be process rather than product oriented. To foster creativity in children, it is important to avoid using patterns and models for them to copy. The art experience should provide opportunities for learning and discovery through many mediums. The teacher must respect each child's ideas and attempts. Children should be allowed to make choices, and work at their own pace and developmental level. This will encourage them to become spontaneous, imaginative, and creative. In addition, art experiences enhance learning and skill development in other curricular areas including fine motor, visual perception, concept development, and socialization.

Snack. In planning snack and cooking activities, the teacher must focus on learning by experience, exploration, and manipulation. Sensory experiences, including touching, smelling, tasting, and comparing, are basic at this age. These kinds of opportunities provide exposure to, and new knowledge about, food. When the teacher relates curriculum experiences with food selection and preparation, it compliments a unit approach. Fine motor manipulation skills, premath, language, and concept development as well as socialization skills are all encouraged through cooking and snack experiences.

FACILITATING LANGUAGE DEVELOPMENT IN YOUNG CHILDREN

The early childhood teacher is responsible for establishing an environment where children can develop optimal skills. The young child creates language in part due to experience, exploration, and interaction with teachers and peers within that uniquely prepared environment. Meaningful experiences during structured lessons and at center-based activities combined with more exploratory learning which occurs at the exploration table and in sociodramatic play, provide the necessary cognitive base for developing children's language. The teacher's role is to facilitate language in these areas.

Language development follows an orderly sequence. In the young child's language there are many commonalities and consistencies, but a wide range of abilities are likely to exist within any one classroom. Facilitation strategies must be based on an awareness of a developmental sequence. The natural emergence of language provides the direction for language facilitation in the young child and is directly related to the child's cognitive level and subsequent Individual Education Program.

Children open up and become more spontaneous in an environment that has familiar materials as well as some that are new and exciting. A teacher can encourage more ideas to be expressed by introducing a wide range of toys and learning materials at centers, at the exploration table, and during structured lessons. The teacher must provide children ample time to examine and explore materials as well as take the time to talk with each child using increasingly complex and elaborated language.

The classroom environment must be arranged so that groups of children may interact with each other, and with adults, allowing language input, practice, and feedback to occur. Extending children's concrete experiences with materials adds depth to known vocabulary words and brings children in contact with new words through verbal descriptions by their peers and teachers.

Several techniques can be used to enhance the child's language development in every setting of the early childhood environment.

1. *Expansion:* To increase the length of the child's utterance, the child's statement is echoed so that a pattern is provided. (Child: "I see bear." Adult: "Yes, I see a big, brown bear.")

2. *Correction:* To improve the quality of the child's utterance, the child's statement is echoed, but correctly. (Child: "Me want cookie." Adult: "Yes, I want a cookie.")

3. *Extension:* The adult verbalizes to offer new information. (Child: "My car goes." Adult: "Yes, and some cars go fast and some go slow.")

4. *Modeling:* This is the use of adult language structures in response to the child, keeping in mind limits of vocabulary and memory. The adult acts as a language model for the child. Modeling demonstrates that communication is a two-way process characterized by verbal turn taking.

5. *Open-ended Questions:* Provide the child with a question that will move the child beyond the original sentence. (Child: "Truck broke." Adult: "How did the truck break?")

These techniques demonstrate that in language facilitation, the child is not a passive receiver of language and concept instruction, but rather an active participant in developing language through experiences that are meaningful to the child. This implies that the teacher must be an active observer, often allowing the child to direct the interaction.

This approach to facilitating language development should occur in any early childhood program. It capitalizes on a process approach, reflects and respects each child's developmental stage, and encourages teacher, aide, and parent volunteers to learn to interact with children with a heightened awareness.

Understanding children's language, its structures and functions, is an enormous task. The teacher must extract and constantly assess what is familiar and known by the child, relate it to new experiences, and extend the child's knowledge through experiences so that new language can be accommodated. Ideas presented in this resource provide a base of activities and experiences that the teacher may use to accomplish this goal.

2
MONTHLY CURRICULUM

This section presents a month-by-month selection of teaching ideas plus a special collection of summer activities. The monthly ideas cover the following categories:

I. Teacher Information
   A. Monthly Concepts
   B. Activities for Teaching Concepts
      a. Language
      b. Fine Motor/Art
      c. Perception
      d. Gross Motor
      e. Sensory Experiences
      f. PreMath
      g. Songs and Fingerplays
      h. Recipe and Snack Ideas
      i. Dramatic Play
      j. Children's Literature
   C. Evaluation of Monthly Concepts
II. Information for Parents/Home Activities
   A. Monthly Concepts
   B. Suggested Home Activities—Monthly Calendar

The information provided will serve only as a guide. The teacher must take into account her/his own teaching style as well as the needs of the group, time constraints, availability of materials, and socioeconomic factors involved.

In our experience we have found a monthly planning approach to be more effective than a daily or weekly approach. The monthly approach assures that the teacher builds in an adequate number of experiences related to the introduction and expansion of the concepts to be taught. This approach does not have to be rigid. On the contrary, it provides the teacher with the opportunity to adjust expectations and lessons throughout the month within the framework of the concepts to be taught.

One must differentiate between monthly concept planning and writing lesson plans. The monthly plan includes only the general concepts to be taught for the month, whereas a daily plan should include objectives, materials, procedures, and evaluation for each subject taught. Within this approach the teacher can use curriculum ideas presented in this book or from her/his own sources to prepare the lesson plans on a daily or weekly basis, depending on her/his own teaching style and the individual makeup of the class.

When a topic is presented within any month, the teacher must be aware that the concept should be reinforced throughout the year. For example, when self-awareness is introduced in September, the teacher should plan to provide for a variety of activities throughout the year that will reinforce and enhance a child's awareness of self.

SEPTEMBER

CONCEPTS FOR SEPTEMBER

LANGUAGE AND VOCABULARY

1. School—school and bus rules, manners, class routine, naming objects, classmate and school personnel names
2. Body Parts—naming parts, what they can do and how they can move, self-concept ("I'm me, I'm special")

FINE MOTOR

Cutting and gluing, bead stringing, coloring, play dough manipulation

PERCEPTION

Copying peg and block designs, puzzle skills

GROSS MOTOR

Body awareness and movement activities

PREMATH

- Calendar activities
- One-to-one correspondence

SENSORY EXPERIENCES

At the exploration table

SONGS AND FINGERPLAYS

Following simple directions and movements in songs, games, and fingerplays

COOKING EXPERIENCES

- Focus on safety rules
- Cooking vocabulary

SNACK

- Focus on recognizing and naming fruit
- Focus on taste, texture, and appearance

CREATIVE DRAMATICS

- Bus
- School
- Self-awareness

CHILDREN'S LITERATURE

NOTE: During September, an important part of the teacher's role is to observe and assess children as they enter the program. Time will be spent observing children during structured and unstructured periods. Therefore, fewer activities are presented for September than for subsequent months.

ACTIVITIES FOR SEPTEMBER

LANGUAGE AND VOCABULARY

1. SCHOOL

Songs to Teach Names. (Tune: Paw, Paw Patch—FFFF ACAF GGGG EGEG FFFF ACAF)

Teacher: Where oh where is my friend _____ ?
Where oh where is my friend _____ ?
Where oh where is my friend _____ ?

  Child: (raises hand and responds)
"Here I am."

(Tune: Low keys are underlined—CFEDC ABC GAB# AB#C C FEE DC AB# C GC AF)

Hello Everybody yes indeed, yes indeed, yes indeed
Hello Everybody yes indeed, this is (name of school)

    (Teacher says *name* and points to child.)

Here's John

    (and the child responds)

"I'm John Brown."

    (Continue around circle until every child has a chance to say his/her name.)

With a 1 and a 2 (Child holds up one finger and then two fingers.)
And a Me and a You (points to self and then another person)
And a big hello (wave)
And how are you? (Everybody shakes hands.)
And we're all back together again!

Tour of School. Tour your school and meet the helpers.

Learning About School Helpers. Take daily field trips to meet school helpers (custodian, nurse, librarian, school secretary, and principal). Have each school helper introduce himself/herself and show the children some of the activities they perform and the special materials they use.

Learning About School Helpers/Classification. The teacher has prepared photographs of all the school helpers and pictures of objects each helper might use in her/his job. Children name each object and name the person who would use the object.

Language Experience Story. Write a story and draw a picture about each school helper. This can be done as a group, or each child can create his/her own depending on level of functioning.

Listening Game. Make a tape of familiar school sounds, e.g., water running, door opening, singing, etc. Have children listen carefully to identify the sound.

School Bus. Ask your bus driver to give a tour of the school bus. Have her/him name all the parts (door, steering wheel, seat belts, etc.).

Bus Safety. Set up a dramatic play situation using props to simulate a school bus. Role-play safety rules that are appropriate.

Make a School Booklet. Depending on the level of the group, children can either draw their own picture or decorate teacher-prepared pictures of school activities such as snack time, painting at the easel, children listening to a story, playing on the playground, or building with blocks together. Be sure to discuss each activity. Extend this lesson over a period of time.

Labeling. Have the children name classroom materials and supplies they will be using.

Matching. Match real objects with pictures of classroom objects.

Following Directions. Have the children follow one- , two- , or three-step directions. For example, "Bring me the scissors, then pick up the book."

Memory Game. Set out three to five supplies using pictures or actual objects and label them. Children close their eyes while the teacher removes one object. Children guess what school supply is missing.

Sorting and Classifying. Sort school from nonschool items (scissors, paste, dog). Tell why the object doesn't belong.

Riddles. Put school objects on a tray and have children name them. The teacher gives a clue or riddle about one of the objects, and a child guesses the object.

2. BODY PARTS

Responding to Questions Using Full Sentences. Ask "What is your name?" The child must respond in a full sentence, "My name is _____ ." The teacher might ask each child some "wh" questions such as "What color is your shirt?

Where are your shoes? Who is sitting next to you?" For extra fun use a tape recorder and record children's responses. Have the children listen to the tapes and guess who is talking.

Star of the Day or Week. Choose a special day for each student to be star. On that day the child wears a star and brings to school special items such as a baby book, a photo album, favorite toys, pets, and so on. The child can share items with classmates and leave them on the display table.

What I Can Do. Have action pictures prepared ahead of time, showing children doing a variety of activities, such as combing hair, riding a bike, buttoning, painting, and throwing. The child says in a full sentence, "He is combing his hair." The teacher asks "Who can comb his hair?" Children respond, "I can comb my hair." Be sure to use pictures of males and females to stress pronoun usage.

Make a "Me" Book. Include pages for family members, pets, favorite foods, TV shows, and activities for leisure time. This can be extended over a period of days. Children can draw or select from precut magazine pictures.

Mirror, Mirror. Have children stand in front of a mirror and tell one or two things about themselves.

Same and Different. Have two children stand side by side looking into a mirror, and talk about what's the same or different about each other.

Describing Each Other. Have two children stand facing each other. Each child tells about the other.

Person Collage. Give children precut heads. Each day add a feature cut from magazines such as eyes, nose, and mouth. Use yarn for hair. Talk about each part you add and what its function is.

Assemble a Body. Have precut body parts available—head, trunk, arms, hands, legs, and feet. Assemble using brad fasteners. (Name each part and talk about how it moves.)

Body Part Put Together. Have flannel body part pieces precut. Assemble a person using the parts. Start at the head and work to the feet.

Flannel Board.

1. Using a completed model on the flannel board, children tell ways they are the same as the model. For example: I have hair. I have two eyes.
2. With assistance, have children assemble a flannel board person. Children close their eyes while the teacher removes a piece. The children must guess what's missing.

Body Part Riddles. Using an assembled flannel board person, give riddles about a specific body part. For example, "I'm thinking of something that opens and closes. You use me to see. What am I?" Children guess the answer.

Body Parts—Clothing. Have a bag of clothes. Talk about what body parts each piece of clothing covers, then use the clothing for dramatic play.

FINE MOTOR

Hand Tracings. Trace each child's hand and have him/her cut it out, if possible. Use for a helping hands bulletin board.

Body Tracings. Trace each child's body and have him/her cut it out, if possible. Sponge paint clothing on body tracing.

Thumbprint Pictures. Dip thumb into paint and make a picture. Discuss how each fingerprint is unique.

Make a Collage. Let children cut various colors and textures of paper and glue the pieces to another paper to make a collage. Use construction paper, newspaper, brown bags, wallpaper, foil, waxed paper, etc.

Finger Painting. Use a variety of media to paint with. Include shaving cream, whipped soap flakes, paint, etc.

School Bus. Provide cutouts of a school bus shape. Allow children to practice paper tearing to fill in their bus.

School. Draw a simple outline of a school on easel paper and have children paint it. Provide brushes of different sizes.

Cotton Ball Painting. Provide outlines of objects found in the classroom. Use cotton balls dipped into paint to fill in each picture. Vary the activity by having children use clothespins attached to cotton balls.

Paper Tearing. Tear paper to make hair and put on a face collage.

Lacing. Have heavy tagboard apple shapes prepared. Have children lace around the apple.

Fruit Pictures. Provide precut shapes of fruit. Have children snip various colors of paper to fill in each piece.

Cutting Practice. Provide precut shapes of fruit. Have the children snip around the shape.

Fruit Prints. Dip cut pieces of fruit into paint. Print on paper.

Paint to Music. Use different kinds of paper, newspaper, newsprint, etc. Have children paint at the easel while listening to various tempos of music.

Foot Painting. Have children dip their feet into paint and walk across long strips of paper. Provide soapy water for rinsing. Try this activity on a warm fall day.

PERCEPTION

How I Look in September. Have children make a self-portrait after reviewing body parts. Save and make a booklet at the end of the year.

Matching. Prepare about fifteen face pairs. Pairs should differ in obvious ways. Children find and match the faces. The same can be done with school buses and apples.

Easel Painting. Have children paint self-portraits at the easel.

Face Puzzles. Prepare faces with drawn-on features of various shapes, e.g., triangle eyes, circle nose, oval mouth. Prepare cutout shapes which correspond to the predrawn shapes. Children match and paste.

Finish the Face. Draw partially completed figures and faces on the chalkboard. Let the children finish the drawings, then have them draw complete faces and figures.

Body Awareness. Have the children roll their bodies on various surfaces, e.g., grass, floor, rug, blanket.

Mirror Activity. Have two children face each other. One child acts as a leader and moves various ways. The other child copies the leader's movements.

Matching. Prepare a model of a school on paper. Draw doors and windows of different shapes and sizes. Provide cutouts to match doors and windows. Children match and paste.

Picture Put Together. Select pictures of children in a magazine, mount them on paper, cut them out, and have the children assemble them as people puzzles.

Lotto. Prepare a lotto game, using either body parts or school objects. This is done by making a grid with six sections and pasting a picture in each section. A corresponding picture must also be prepared and pasted on a note card, cut to the same size as the grid section. The children then match the picture to the grid.

GROSS MOTOR

Simon Says. Simon can say to touch various body parts or to perform actions such as jumping, hopping, running, etc.

Body Awareness. Children touch various parts of their bodies as the teacher names them. They can raise or move the part named. The same exercises can be repeated with children in different postures: sitting, kneeling, and standing.

Bilateral Movements. Teacher and children sit on the floor, children facing the teacher. Teacher moves an arm or leg and has children imitate the same movement. Gradually increase difficulty until children are able to perform bilateral activities using both arms and legs.

Tightrope. Teacher makes chalk lines outside, and children try to walk the lines like a tightrope walker would do. Encourage children to alternate feet, walk heel to toe, or backwards.

Balls. Sit in a circle, teacher in the middle, or have children sit with a partner. Spread legs apart and roll the ball back and forth. Watch for eye tracking and catching ability.

Jump the Puddle. Draw a line on the ground, and have children take turns jumping over it. To make the activity more difficult, make two lines a few inches apart and have children jump over both lines.

Stop and Go. Children run on command of *go,* and stop on command of *stop.*

Let's Have a Parade. Use records with a good rhythm. Have children move in a line, try kicking legs, bending arms, twisting bodies, clapping hands, etc.

Pop Goes the Weasel. Sing the song "Pop Goes the Weasel." Encourage children to sing along and when they hear the word *pop,* jump up from the floor.

PREMATH

Introduce the Calendar. Point out how every day has a box. Each day put up an object such as an apple, bus, etc., that has a numeral on it. Point to the numeral and count.

Snack Time. Practice setting the table daily. Stress one-to-one correspondence: Each child gets one chair, one napkin, one cup, one plate, etc.

SENSORY EXPERIENCES

The Exploration Table. An exploration sensory table (water table) offers experiences in many areas of development. It is a place where children can work alone, or with other children. Language, premath skills, fine motor, problem-solving, and social skills are all naturally encouraged. It is a success-oriented activity which has no right or wrong way to play. The contents of a sensory table are limited only by the teacher's imagination. It can contain water, sand, rice, feathers, smooth pebbles, shaving cream, soap mixtures, corn meal, styrofoam, etc. Children can be encouraged to use all of their senses—see and feel the substances, hear the noises, smell the soaps, and possibly taste the rice and corn meal.

The contents of the exploration table should be changed regularly. Vary the activities by supplying different objects to use in the medium. Provide utensils for pouring and measuring, plastic boats, cars and trucks, dishes, dolls for bathing, bubbles, materials that float and sink, food coloring, small toys (e.g., dinosaurs, animals, people figures), objects that drip and squirt, containers of different sizes and shapes, plastic tubing and plumbing pipe, wash cloths and towels.

SONGS AND FINGERPLAYS

A copy of some of the favorite songs and fingerplays used at school might be sent home with children each month. The children will enjoy having family members sing along with them.

Wheels on the Bus.

The wheels on the bus go around and around, around and around, around and around.

The wheels on the bus go around and around, all through the town.

The people on the bus go up and down, up and down, up and down.

The people on the bus go up and down, all through the town.

(Continue with these verses or make up your own: Use appropriate hand motions with each verse.)

Wipers—swish, swish, swish
Lights—blink, blink, blink,
Horn—beep, beep, beep
Windows—up and down

Where Is Thumbkin?.

Where is thumbkin? Where is thumbkin? (hands behind back)

Here I am, here I am (left thumb speaks, then right)

How are you today sir? (right thumb)

Very well I thank you. (left thumb)

Run away, run away (left hand behind back, then right)

(Repeat with pointer, tall man, ring man, pinky.

Happy Feeling. (Low notes are underlined—CDEFEDC AAB#C GGAB# AAB#C CCCFEDC AAB#C GG AB# EF.)

I've got that happy feeling
here in my *face,* here in my *face,* here in my *face*
I've got that happy feeling
here in my *face,* here in my *face* today.

(Substitute other body parts, and point to each.)

If You're Happy.

If you're happy and you know it clap your hands, if your're happy and you know it clap your hands.

If you're happy and you know it then your face will surely show it, if you're happy and you know it clap your hands.

Make up your own verses like these:

If you're happy, touch your head, stamp your foot, turn around, etc.

Head and Shoulders.

Head and shoulders, knees and toes, knees and toes. Head and shoulders, knees and toes, knees and toes.

Eyes and ears and mouth and nose, head and shoulders, knees and toes, knees and toes.

(Point to body parts as you say them.)

The More We Get Together. (Tune: "Did You Ever See a Lassie?")

The more we get together,
Together, together,
The more we get together
The happier we'll be.
For your friends are my friends,
And my friends are your friends
The more we get together
The happier we'll be!

Open Shut Them.

Open, shut them (Open hands wide, then shut them.)
Open, shut them
Give your hands a clap! (Clap hands.)
Open, shut them, open, shut them,
Put them in your lap
Creep them, creep them right up to your chin
Open wide your little mouth
But do not let them in.

Ten Little Fingers.

Ten little fingers
Ten little toes
Two little eyes
And a great big nose!

(Point to body parts.)

In the Apple Tree.

Away up high in an apple tree, (Point up.)
Two red apples smiled at me. (Form circles with fingers.)
I shook that tree as hard as I could. (Shake tree.)
Down came the apples and mmmm were they good! (Rub stomach.)

COOKING EXPERIENCES

Before cooking activities begin in September, you must establish safety and health guidelines with the children. The following rules should be a priority; stress and reinforce them throughout the year in the classroom.

1. Always wash your hands with soap and warm water before working in the kitchen.
2. Never turn on any appliances without an adult's help or permission.
3. Always use potholders to lift hot things—even if you are not sure that they are hot.

4. Keep plastic utensils, dish towels, and potholders away from heat.

5. Always turn the pot handles sideways so you don't bump them when passing by. Be careful not to leave them near or over the flames of another burner on the stove.

6. Always carry knives with the point downwards. Never run.

7. Watch your fingers when closing cabinet doors and drawers.

8. Never put knives or cooking utensils in your mouth.

RECIPES

Applesauce.

—2 apples for each child
—a little water
—cinnamon

Wash apples. Cut into small pieces. Boil until soft. Let cool for 10 minutes. Put into foley mill. Let children grind into sauce. Flavor with cinnamon.

Yogurt Pops.

1 carton plain or vanilla yogurt
1 6-oz. concentrated unsweeted orange juice
Optional: dash of vanilla and/or honey

Mix well and freeze in molds. 3-oz. paper cups work well as molds. For handles, insert wooden sticks or spoons when mixture is partially frozen.

Play Dough (stove top recipe)

Mix:

1 cup flour
1/4 cup salt
2 tablespoons cream of tartar

Combine and add:

1 cup water
2 teaspoons vegetable food coloring
1 tablespoon oil

Cook over medium heat and stir (about 3–5 minutes). It will look sticky. When it forms a ball in the center of the pot, remove and knead. Store in an airtight container. Keeps well.

SEPTEMBER SNACKS

Apple Slices. Have children put faces on with raisins.

Apple Chunks. Spread with peanut butter or cream cheese.

Various Fruits in Season. Let children feel, taste, smell, compare shapes and textures.

Breads and Spreads. Cut bread with circle cutter, spread with cheese, peanut butter, or cream cheese, then add facial features.

Fruit Kabobs. Use fruits in season and put on skewers or toothpicks.

Friendship Salad. Each child brings a different fruit to be cut and shared in a fruit salad.

Cooking and snack time provide an excellent opportunity to stress and reinforce premath concepts including more and less, empty and full, one-to-one correspondence, and measuring.

DRAMATIC PLAY

Self-Awareness. Set up a dress-up center. Provide various clothing items which cover different parts of the body. Try to include the following: hats, wigs, jewelry, scarves, shirts, pants, blouses, sweaters, dresses, socks, shoes, gloves, mittens, boots, coats, jackets, robes, slippers, pajamas, nightgowns, bathing suits, etc. Try to have a mirror available in the area. Encourage language and social interaction. Have children dress to look like Mommy or Daddy, etc. Dress for a cold day or a hot day.

Bus. Set up a play situation using props to simulate a school bus. Set up chairs for the bus driver and passengers. Have pretend seat belts, school bags, etc. Encourage language and social interaction. This is a good way for "driver" and "passengers" to review bus safety rules.

School. Have a variety of extra school supplies, such as a small chalkboard, chalk, markers, paper, old books, magazines, etc., available for children to use as they begin to act out school experiences of being teacher or student. Children can also use dishes and silverware from the housekeeping center during their school snack time.

CHILDREN'S LITERATURE

Anderson, Hans Christian. *The Ugly Duckling*

Anglund, Joan Walsh. *A Friend Is Someone Who Likes You*

Behrens, June. *What I Hear*

Bein. *Andy and the School Bus*

Brenner, Barbara. *Bodies*

———. *Faces*

Bright, Robert. *I Like Red*

Carle, Eric. *Mixed up Chameleon*

Child's World. *How Do You Feel?*

Cohen, Miriam. *Will I Have a Friend?*

Conkling. *The Bingity, Bangity School Bus*

Ets, Marie Hall, *Just Me*

Fitzhugh, Louise. *I Am Four*

Gunilla, Wolde. *Betsy's First Day in Nursey School*

Hutchins, Pat. *Fitch*

Iverson, Genie. *I Want To Be Big*

Jackson, Kim. *First Day of School*

Keats, Ezra Jack. *Peter's Chair*

Kraus, R. *Leo the Late Bloomer*

———. *Spiders First Day at School*

Kuskin, Karla. *What Did You Bring Me?*

Manley, Deborah. *All About Me*
_____ . *Me and My Friends*
Poulet, V. *Blue Bug Goes to School*
Relf, Patricia. *The First Day of School*
Rudolf, Marguerita. *Look at Me*
Scott, Ann Herbert. *Sam*
Shapp. *Let's Find Out about School*
Sharmat, Marjorie Weinman. *I Was So Mad*

_____ . *The Day I Was Born*
Symeon, Shimin. *I Wish There Were Two Of Me*
Welber, Robert. *Goodbye, Hello*
Ziefert, Harriet, and Smith, Mavis. *What Do I Hear?*
_____ . *What Do I See?*
_____ . *What Do I Smell?*
_____ . *What Do I Taste?*
_____ . *What Do I Touch?*

Evaluating September Concepts

RECORDKEEPING

Recordkeeping is vital for teacher accountability in any classroom. Informal records should be maintained and updated regularly. A good time to do this might be after the monthly concepts have been taught. Informal records may be in the form of anecdotal records or student checklists.

Anecdotal Records. Keep a written log for each child that can be added to throughout the year. A three-ring notebook is ideal for adding pages. This log is kept for the teacher's benefit and should include dates and notes regarding the child's performance.

Checklists. The checklist may be in the form of a task analysis or may simply list skills and concepts focused on that month. The checklists included in the Appendix of this resource require you to observe the child while performing the task. Simply indicate the child's level of performance by writing the date next to the numeral in the appropriate column. Additional observations may be kept on the checklist form or in the anecdotal record. These checklists can be used throughout the school year.

EVALUATION

The following information can best be kept in an anecdotal record.

Language. Informally assess each child's ability to say his/her own name and that of classmates, teachers, and others introduced during the month.

Evaluate the child's ability to follow classroom routines, such as "find the bathroom," "find your locker," "form a line when requested," etc.

Gluing. Informally assess gluing skills and keep notes in each child's log. Look for these abilities: holding paper to be glued, use of opposite index finger to spread glue, ability to press paper firmly with fingers. Observe use of child's right or left hand and any tactile oversensitivity the child may display while using glue.

Coloring. Observe the child while coloring. Record observations such as grip, ability to use other hand to hold paper, pressure of crayon, type of stroke, ability to color within lines, eye contact, task perseveration, ability to distinguish figure from ground.

Premath. Observe children as they set the snack table, put numbers on the calendar, play at the exploration table, and during cooking activities. In each child's anecdotal log, record understanding of one-to-one correspondence, math-related language, and participation during calendar activities and at the exploration table.

Gross Motor. During September, use the gross motor checklist provided in the Appendix to assess concepts presented. Observe children's performance in the following areas: copying unilateral and bilateral movements, ball handling, moving to music, jumping and running. Gross motor observation can also be included in each child's anecdotal record.

Parent Involvement

REINFORCING CONCEPTS AT HOME

What children learn at school is only the beginning. Learning and growth take place all day. Reinforcing school concepts at home not only contributes to learning and growth, but also helps each child feel good about school and may help him/her to share school experiences. Every month a section on reinforcing school concepts at home is included. A brief concept sheet of what will be taught during the month and a calendar serve as models of what can be sent to parents each month.

The calendar format is easy to follow and suggests a single activity each day. The calendar provides ideas and reminds busy parents of simple activities they may try with their child once a week or every day. The calendar format can also be used to remind parents of school events, parent meetings, show-and-tell day, field trips, community events, etc.

The teacher may opt either to send home a weekly calendar or suggest an activity in a daily note. (An empty calendar is found in the Appendix.)

CONCEPTS FOR SEPTEMBER (parent copy)

LANGUAGE AND VOCABULARY

1. School and bus object naming, and understanding routines
2. Body part naming, how parts move
3. Cooking experiences, safety rules, and cooking vocabulary
4. Snack, recognizing and naming fruit

FINE MOTOR

Cutting, gluing, bead stringing, coloring, play dough manipulation

GROSS MOTOR

Moving body in space, ball handling, simple games

PERCEPTION

Copying peg and block designs, puzzles

PREMATH

1. One-to-one correspondence
2. Calendar activities

CREATIVE DRAMATICS

Experiences related to the bus, school, and self-awareness

ATTENDING SKILLS

1. Following directions and movements in songs, games, and fingerplays
2. Listening to stories and records

SENSORY EXPERIENCES

Touching and manipulating at the exploration table

SEPTEMBER

Parent-child activities

SUN	MON	TUE	WED	THU	FRI	SAT
SHOP TOGETHER FOR SCHOOL SUPPLIES. NAME EACH ITEM IN SCHOOL BAG.	REVIEW NAMES OF PEOPLE YOUR CHILD CAME IN CONTACT WITH TODAY. I.E., TEACHER, AIDE, BUS DRIVER, PEERS.	LOOK FOR AND COUNT SCHOOL BUSES SEEN IN YOUR NEIGHBORHOOD.	TALK ABOUT THE IMPORTANCE OF SEAT BELTS AND BUS/CAR SAFETY.	VISIT THE LIBRARY. GET A LIBRARY CARD FOR YOUR CHILD.	WALK ON THE LINES OF THE SIDEWALK.	MOUNT A PHOTO OF YOUR CHILD ON CARDBOARD. CUT IT INTO PIECES TO MAKE A PUZZLE.
NAME BODY PARTS WHILE BATHING OR DRESSING.	MAKE POPCORN. USE NOSE TO SMELL IT AND YOUR BODY TO MOVE LIKE THE KERNELS.	READ A PICTURE BOOK TOGETHER.	DRESS AND UNDRESS A FAVORITE DOLL.	TALK ABOUT WHAT YOUR CHILD DID AT SCHOOL TODAY.	LOOK IN A MIRROR AND HELP YOUR CHILD TELL SOMETHING ABOUT HIMSELF/HERSELF.	PLAY CATCH WITH FAMILY MEMBERS.
GO FOR A WALK. TALK ABOUT WHAT YOU SEE AND HEAR.	LOOK THROUGH A MAGAZINE. CUT OUT PICTURES OF HAPPY FACES.	STRING CEREAL OR MACARONI TO MAKE A NECKLACE.	HELP SET THE TABLE. GIVE EVERYONE ONE NAPKIN.	TEAR, CRUMPLE, SNIP, OR CUT PAPER.	WHEN OUTSIDE, CLOSE EYES AND TRY TO IDENTIFY SOUNDS YOU HEAR.	LOOK THROUGH A FAMILY ALBUM TOGETHER.
MAKE A BODY PART COLLAGE OF ARMS, LEGS, AND EYES CUT FROM MAGAZINES.	PRACTICE SONGS AND FINGERPLAYS LEARNED AT SCHOOL.	PEEL AN ORANGE OR A BANANA. ENJOY THE SNACK.	PLAY SIMON SAYS TO REVIEW THE BODY PARTS.	PRACTICE COLORING ON NEWSPAPER OR BROWN PAPER BAGS.	MAKE TAFFY APPLES TOGETHER.	VISIT THE GROCERY STORE. LOOK AT AND TRY TO NAME THE FRUIT.
DRAW A PICTURE OF YOURSELF ON THE SIDEWALK.	PLAY A MEMORY GAME. NAME 3 BODY PARTS. HAVE YOUR CHILD REPEAT AND TOUCH THEM.					

OCTOBER

CONCEPTS FOR OCTOBER

LANGUAGE AND VOCABULARY

1. Fall—changes in weather and nature, fall clothing and activities
2. Fire Prevention and Fire Safety—firefighters, what they do and wear, equipment they use, function of fire, hot and cold
3. Halloween—concept of real and pretend, safety and vocabulary
4. Colors—orange and black
5. Directional and Positional Concepts—in and out

Suggested field trips/classroom visitors: visit a fire station, farm stand, nature preserve. Ask a firefighter to visit class.

FINE MOTOR—1. MANIPULATION, AND 2. PREWRITING

Lacing, painting, cutting, coloring, play dough manipulation, making circles, path tracing

PERCEPTION

Same and different, draw a person, sorting, puzzles, copying block and peg patterns

GROSS MOTOR

Organized games, moving to music, eye tracking

SENSORY EXPERIENCES

Sense of touch at the exploration table—hot and cold

PREMATH

One-to-one correspondence, calendar activities, sorting, sets, patterning, numbers and numerals 0, 1, and 2, circle, big and little

RECIPES

- Following directions
- Cooking with fall fruits and vegetables

SNACK

Focus on foods that are orange, black, and circular shaped

CREATIVE DRAMATICS

- Firefighter
- Trick or treating

SELF-HELP

Removing outerwear

REVIEW

Body parts

ACTIVITIES FOR OCTOBER

LANGUAGE AND VOCABULARY

1. FALL

Fall Walk 1. Go on a fall walk. Look for animals such as squirrels and birds. Look at and discuss nature's changes, including colors, cooler weather, falling leaves, acorns, pine cones, and bare branches. Have each child bring a bag and collect items of interest (leaves, acorns, pine cones). Items collected can be used for collages and sorting (see *fine motor* and *perception*).

Fall Walk 2. Take a fall walk outdoors and talk with the children about the signs of fall you observe (need for warmer clothing, leaves changing colors and falling from trees, fall foods ripen and are picked, some birds can be seen flying to warmer climate). When you return to the classroom, write a language experience story.

Walk Talk. Discuss your fall walk upon returning. Label items that were collected. Have children use as many adjectives as they can when discussing the walk.

Language Experience Story. Write a language experience story about your walk. Have each child contribute as much as she/he can remember. Make a copy for each child as well as a large chart story. Give each child an opportunity to use colors or markers to illustrate his/her own copy. Make a class book.

Animals in Autumn. Using pictures of animals, discuss how animals grow thicker fur to keep warm, just as people wear extra clothes to keep warm. If possible, bring a pet into the classroom. Touch its fur, feel the softness and thickness.

Fall Riddles. Have an assortment of fall objects and/or pictures on a tray (squirrel, sweater, acorn, leaves, nuts, football, etc.). Let the children guess what fall object you are describing. For example, "I grow on trees and change colors. I fall from the trees. You can rake me."

Gourds. Prepare a basket of gourds of different shapes, sizes, colors, and textures. Talk about each gourd relating to these concepts. You can then sort gourds by attributes—color, size, shape, smooth, bumpy, etc. This activity offers a perceptual, language, premath, and sensory opportunity.

Autumn Clothing 1. Bring in a bag of summer and fall clothing. Label each item of clothing and decide if it is for fall or summer. Sort into two piles. Use for dress-up play. Review body parts while "dressing."

Autumn Clothing 2. Collect a wide variety of clothing pictures from catalogs and magazines. Mount them on paper and laminate. Children name the clothing and then sort into categories: fall clothing/not fall clothing. They tell why each article of clothing is or is not appropriate for fall.

Leaf Hunt. Walk through the neighborhood and have children find a variety of different types of leaves: a leaf that is green, a leaf that has two colors, a smooth leaf, a leaf that is big. The list can be endless.

Fall Harvest. Talk about foods that are ripened and picked in fall. Have pictures or the actual foods available for the children to touch, describe, and taste (apples, cranberries, acorn squash, pumpkins, nuts, etc.). Introduce the word *harvest.* Practice some discrimination and ask, "Show me the orange one, show me the green, bumpy one," etc.

Sequencing. Have pictures available that show the sequence of changes seen in fall trees: green leaves on trees, colored leaves on trees, leaves falling, leaves on the ground, leaf raking. Have the children tell what is happening in each picture. As their awareness develops, mix up the pictures and have them sequence fall events.

Fall Activities. Have available pictures or actual objects used for activities the children would be familiar with (football, soccer ball, bike, swimming suit, picnic basket, tent, ice skates, fishing pole, pail and shovel, etc.). Name each item. Have the children decide what activities would be appropriate during fall.

2. FIRE PREVENTION AND FIRE SAFETY

Fire Prevention Mystery Box. Introduce fire prevention using the mystery box. Try to use real objects, though in some cases pictures will be necessary. You may want to include a picture of a firefighter, a smoke detector, a hose, firefighter boots, hat, and jacket, ladder, fire extinguisher, tools. Most fire departments are willing to lend extra items for one or two days. Discuss, describe, and label items.

Firefighter. Through pictures, books, or a visit from a firefighter, children can begin to learn the names of the special clothing and basic equipment used by a firefighter. Many children will be interested to learn about why and how these articles are unique to help and protect the firefighter.

Community Helpers. Have pictures of community helpers and some of the basic clothing and equipment they use. Help children name each picture and sort firefighter/not firefighter.

Fire Station Story. After visiting your local fire station or having a firefighter visit the classroom, write a group story. Each child should contribute one or more sentences. The story can be copied for each child to take home, or you can make a class book utilizing the children's illustrations.

Story Sequencing. There are many excellent books written for preschool-age children about fire safety (see list of children's literature on pages 76–77). Read one to the children and have them tell it back in sequence. Provide pictures for visual reminders.

Fire Engine. Using a toy fire engine or a large photograph of a fire engine, label the various parts, i.e., wheels, steering wheel, horn, siren, and ladder.

Go Togethers. Using picture cards (teacher prepared or commercial), have children select cards depicting firefighters and equipment from other community helper cards. Discuss each picture, what it shows, and why it is/is not a firefighter card. This activity can be repeated with seasonal cards, sorting autumn cards from nonautumn cards, or holiday cards, sorting Halloween from non-Halloween cards. Focus on the language elicited during the activity.

Safety Walk. Take a walk inside and outside the school building stressing children's safety. Walk through a practice fire drill with the students. Point out fire extinguishers and fire hydrants and pantomime how these kinds of equipment are used.

Safety Rules. Help children understand the basic safety rules: stop, drop, and roll if your clothes are on fire, and crawl under smoke. Role-play these activities and help children understand why they help us.

Matches. Introduce the positive, helpful use of matches and fire: for cooking and to provide heat. Through pictures and sharing of children's experiences, discuss cooking on a campfire and on an outdoor grill. Discuss how a campfire and a fireplace keep us warm.

Match Safety. When children have a basic understanding of hot versus cold and the functions of fire, it is important for them to learn not to play with matches. Role-play a variety of situations where children learn to give matches to adults.

Function of Fire. After completing a cooking activity, discuss the function of fire—to cook with, to keep warm. Provide a variety of pictures depicting the use of fire.

Hot/Cold Sorting. Use a variety of hot (warm) and cold substances for children to feel, compare, and contrast. You might use water, or hot/cold foods, ice, and a blown-out match. You can follow this introduction by using pictures, discussing them, and sorting them into piles of hot and cold items.

Wax Paper Leaves. Use a hot iron to press leaves between two pieces of wax paper. Hang leaves in windows to display. Have children feel the hot paper after you, the teacher, have closely supervised the ironing portion of the activity. Contrast the hot paper and the cold window. Discuss hot and cold.

Making Popcorn. Make popcorn to use for snack and talk about hot and cold. You can use the popcorn to make ghosts by gluing it on the outline of ghosts, or write names with popcorn by gluing it to the outline of the name. You can reinforce the circle concept by making a circle out of popcorn.

Hot and Cold. Have available a variety of hot and cold objects—ice cube, ice pack, toaster, curling iron, etc. With supervision, allow children to touch/get near these items stressing the concepts hot and cold.

How Do I Feel?. Have a variety of pictures available for the children to name and sort into the categories hot and cold. Pictures might include an ice cream cone, soda soup, coffee, refrigerator, stove, iron, etc.

3. HALLOWEEN

Pumpkin Carving. Carve a pumpkin, review body parts, and use vocabulary words that pertain to monthly concepts (orange, pumpkin, jack-o'-lantern, squishy, slippery). Bake the seeds for a snack (see *recipes*).

Real or Make-Believe. Use magazine pictures mounted and laminated for a categorizing real-or-make-believe activity. Include pictures of dinosaurs, ghosts, fairy tale characters, superheros, dragons, pictures of real animals, and familiar people. Name each picture. Sort into categories.

Costumes. Discuss what a costume is, who can wear them, and why. Talk about costumes that can look real, funny, or frightening. Have children develop a list of costumes that could fit into each category and describe what the costume might look like.

Masks. Discuss the masks worn by people in your community: football helmet, goggles worn by welders or swimmers, hospital mask, sleep mask, ski mask, dark sunglasses, etc. Have some of these masks available for the children to see and try on. Conclude with a discussion of Halloween masks.

Halloween Safety. Discuss Halloween safety rules. Do role-playing incorporating the rules discussed. Some examples are: (1) Make sure you can see out of your mask. (2) Wear a costume that isn't too big so you don't trip and fall. (3) Only cross the street at the corner. (4) Always trick or treat with a grown-up. (5) Only go to homes you know. (6) Never go in a house. (7) Let your mom or dad check your candy before you eat it. Never eat anything that isn't sealed.

You may want to prepare a booklet for each child emphasizing these safety rules or others pertaining to your group.

4. COLORS—ORANGE AND BLACK

Color Mystery Box. Introduce colors for the month on separate days. Bring in orange or black objects and put them in a special mystery box. Children take turns retrieving objects, describing, and labeling them. Make sure children use color words in their descriptions.

Pumpkin. Have a small orange pumpkin available. Let the children talk about its shape, size, smell, and finally stress its orange color. With teacher assistance, the children can scoop out and carve the pumpkin. Talk about the inside and outside orange color. This is a great sensory and language experience.

Orange Box (repeat for black). Cover a large box with orange kraft paper. Gather a wide variety of orange objects and pictures to place inside the box. These objects can be used to reinforce the color orange in a variety of ways:

1. Name each object using a full sentence. (e.g., "I have an orange balloon." Model sentences if necessary.)
2. Describe each object and answer "wh" questions. (who, what, where, when, why)
3. Tell five things about each object.
4. Play a memory game with two to five objects. Tell what orange thing is missing from an assortment.
5. Sort orange from not orange objects.

Orange Hunt (repeat for black). Have children hunt around the classroom for anything orange they can find. Name each item.

Orange Day (repeat for black). Have a day designated as orange day. The children should bring something orange for show and tell and wear something orange. The snack should be orange, and the fine motor activity might be painting at the easel with orange paint or manipulating orange play dough. The extension possibilities are limitless.

Orange Making. Let the children experiment mixing red and yellow paint, finger paint, and food coloring together. Let them create fire, an autumn sky, or just plain orange.

Invented Stories. Have the children invent stories related to the monthly concepts. You, the teacher, start the story with a sentence. The children then take turns adding their own sentences to make a story.

Go-Together Words. Have children listen and choose the word that doesn't go with the others, such as *fire, hat, ladder, truck, apple*. They can clap their hands when they hear the word that doesn't belong. This can be used for visual perception if pictures are added.

5. DIRECTIONAL AND POSITIONAL CONCEPTS—IN AND OUT

Body Movement. Have the children practice following directions using the words *in* and *out*. They can be asked to move in and out of wagons, boxes, a crawling tunnel, etc. Ask the children to respond expressively to the question "Where are you?"

Object Movement. Give the children an opportunity to manipulate objects in and out. Examples of objects to assemble might include chalk and a box, letter and envelope, wallet and purse, bead and cup, etc. Ask each child to follow specific directions, e.g., "Put the letter in the envelope." Then ask the children to use the concept expressively in response to the "wh" question "Where is the letter?"

Directional Pictures. Cut out a variety of pictures from magazines showing objects in and out. Show the pictures to the children and ask the question "Where is the _____ ?" The children can demonstrate their expressive knowledge of the concepts in and out.

FINE MOTOR

1. MANIPULATION

Fall Tree. Make a class fall tree. Provide the outline of a tree on large paper. Using paints in fall colors, have children dip their hands in the paint and then print on the tree for leaves.

Nut Cracking. Crack nuts with a nutcracker.

Leaf Rubbings. Make leaf rubbings. Using leaves you collected on your fall walk, place a leaf bottom-side-up on a piece of paper and cover it with a thin piece of paper (e.g., typing paper). Using a crayon with the paper stripped off, rub the crayon over the leaf. The texture of the leaf will appear.

Fall Tree 2. Let children cut or tear paper to make a tree trunk. Glue onto construction paper. The children can cut/tear construction paper, crumple and glue tissue paper, or sponge paint colored leaves on their tree trunk.

Tree Rubbings. Children can make tree rubbings by rubbing the side of a piece of chalk or crayon on white drawing paper or thinner paper that is held around the tree bark. Encourage children to talk about what the lines and marks look like.

Fall Leaf Prints. Have children spread paint on the raised, vein side of a variety of leaves. Press leaves onto paper to make a print.

Play Dough Prints. Use small rolling pins or cylindrical blocks to flatten play dough to pie crust thickness. Place the raised vein side of a leaf onto the clay. Use the roller to press a leaf image onto the play dough.

Treasure Collage. After a discussion of nature's changes in fall, walk outdoors and collect a variety of seeds, leaves, berries, flowers, etc. Once inside, children can talk about their treasures and glue them on paper, a foam meat tray, or a prepared leaf shape.

Lacing. Cut out simple fall shapes such as leaves, acorns, ghosts, etc., from tagboard. Laminate these pieces and punch holes around the edges with a hole punch. Children can use stiff string or shoelaces to practice lacing.

Fall Planting. After a discussion of planting in spring versus fall, plant some fall bulbs within view of the classroom. Let the children use large spoons or small shovels to dig 6- to 8-inch holes for crocus, tulip, or daffodil bulbs.

Halloween Necklaces. Use tube-shaped macaroni, and paint each piece orange or black. Using yarn with one end taped, string the macaroni. You can alter this activity and make a fire hose using black-colored macaroni.

Costume Collage. In advance, prepare aprons or vests from brown paper bags for each child. Supply a variety of materials the children can use to glue on their costume (e.g., cotton balls, feathers, leaves, fabric and wallpaper scraps, yarn, ribbon, etc.).

Bag Pumpkins. Let children crumple newspaper and stuff in a small, brown paper bag. Close the top with a rubber band and wrap with green yarn. Children can paint their "pumpkin" orange. Supply construction paper, bits of yarn and ribbon, etc., to turn their pumpkin into a jack-o'-lantern.

Pumpkin People. Cut out an orange circle for a pumpkin. Accordian fold (back and forth) black strips for arms and legs. Draw in face.

Masks. Make masks out of brown paper bags. Cut out eyes, nose, and mouth. Use this activity in reviewing body parts.

Witch's Broom. Make witches' brooms by snipping paper.

Fire Hoses. Using play dough, let children manipulate and form long rolls of "firefighter hoses."

Campfire. Using red and yellow finger paint, let children create an orange campfire picture. To stress the helpful function of fire, you may want the children to add a construction paper "hot dog on a stick" to their picture.

Firefighter's Ladders. Provide strips of paper or let children cut strips for making a ladder. Preglue two vertical strips. Have children glue on horizontal strips.

Finger Painting. Finger paint with orange and/or black finger paint. Experiment using hands or feet.

Splash Painting. Place a large sheet of kraft paper on the floor. Using a variety of slightly thinned tempera colors, let the children use large brushes and wrist action to create a "class splash collage" of colors.

Roll-on Painting. Remove the round roller from deodorant bottles and wash in soapy water. Pour thinned tempera paint in the bottle and pop the roller top in place. Let the children enjoy painting at the easel or on a flat surface.

Color Collages. Collect a variety of black and orange materials, e.g., yarn, paper, ribbon, buttons, pompoms, crayons, markers, etc. Allow the children to use these materials to make an orange collage and a black collage. The orange collage can be made on an orange pumpkin shape. The black collage can be glued on a black bat shape.

Easel Painting. Provide orange and/or black paint at the easel. Children can paint freely, or provide predrawn circle or pumpkin shapes. Try negative space paintings (cut circle or pumpkin shapes out of the middle of the paper). Children utilize problem-solving skills in painting around the cutouts.

Group Circle. For a cooperative group fine motor experience, draw a large circle on large paper on the floor. Have the children fill in the circle with crayons, markers, or paint.

Circle Collage. Provide a variety of circle objects (pompoms, plastic milk lids, washers, etc.) and circles cut out of newspaper, foil, sandpaper, construction paper, etc. Let the children create their collage and glue pieces on a large circle shape. Small circles can be created by having children punch paper using a hole punch.

Circle Prints. Cut an orange, lemon, and onion in half. Dip in paint and make circle prints. Talk about the pattern made in each circle.

Fine Motor Center. At your fine motor table, vary the following centers throughout the month.

1. Paper and scissors for cutting, glue to make a collage out of cut paper.
2. Orange and black play dough—provide rolling pins, cookie cutters, dull knives, etc.
3. Yarn and cutouts for lacing pumpkins, fire boots, leaves, etc.
4. Orange and black paints, crayons, markers, chalk for free coloring.

Cutting Center. A cutting center can easily be incorporated into the early childhood setting. You can provide left- and right-handed scissors, loop and safety blade scissors, and four-hole-teacher-assist scissors. A wide variety of materials should be made available for cutting ranging from onion skin and newspaper to fabric and styrofoam. Children can practice snipping, continuous stroke cutting, and cutting out predrawn, teacher-prepared shapes depending on their skill level.

2. PREWRITING

Circles. Provide a variety of experiences for children to copy a circle shape. Children can make circles in the air, trace their finger around a template, or use crayons, markers, and pencils to trace around a template or circular objects. Encourage them to form circles starting at the top and moving counterclockwise.

Path Tracing. Visual tracking activity: On the chalkboard, draw a firefighter and a fire truck about 12 inches apart. With fingers, then chalk, have children trace the path between the objects. Repeat the activity with pictures of various fire safety objects, autumn objects, Halloween objects, etc. This activity can be done with paper and pencil and crayon.

Stencil Tracing. Using Halloween and fall stencils or circle shapes, have the children trace shapes.

Prewriting Center. Set up a prewriting center where children will have opportunities to experiment with various writing materials. You may want to display a chart of designs (circle, plus sign, square, triangle etc.) that children would be interested in copying. Materials to have available might include lead and colored pencils, wide- and fine-tipped markers, colored chalk, magic slates with wooden pencils, all types of paper, old stationery, envelopes, chalkboards, acetate sheets with wipe-off cloths, erasers, shape stencils, etc.

PERCEPTION

Fall Leaf Collection. Collect a variety of leaves (oak, maple, honey locust, beech). Mount them on construction paper and laminate them immediately. Use the leaf cards for a variety of activities: classifying, sorting, comparing. Stress the words *same* and *different*.

Fall Lotto. Make a simple fall lotto game (see p. 47) using signs of fall (acorns leaves, squirrels, apples, pumpkins, sweaters, trees, etc.).

Seed Sorting. Collect a variety of different seeds: apple, orange, sunflower, pumpkin, etc. After seeds have dried, let the children sort them.

Nut Sorting. Buy several kinds of nuts at the grocery store (or cut out shapes of nuts in various shades of brown). Name each nut. Lead the children into an awareness of differences in size, color, texture, and taste. Allow the children to sort the nuts. Talk about the words *same* and *different*.

Clothing Go Togethers. Provide cutouts of fall clothing of various colors and patterns. Talk about what body parts the clothing covers. Match the different pieces of clothing that go together.

Leaf People. Using a leaf collected on your walk, make a leaf person. Use the leaf as the body. Have children draw a head, arms, legs, depending on their ability level.

What's Missing. Using real objects or pictures, place three to five fall items on a tray. Have children look at and label items. While children close their eyes, remove an item. Children guess what is missing.

Autumn Sorting. Upon returning from a fall walk, have children empty contents of bags. Sort like items into piles—similar leaves, acorns, pine cones, etc. Be sure to label items and use descriptive adjectives when talking about objects.

Feel Fall. Have a variety of fall objects that can represent the fall season available (gourds, nuts, a pumpkin, tree bark, leaves, a football, a sweater, etc.). Ask children to touch the objects with their eyes closed and try to identify each object presented. To vary the activity, children can touch and find an item that is identical to the one presented.

Flannel Board Witch. Assemble a witch at the flannel board. Review body parts.

Matching Jack-O'-Lanterns. Prepare eight to ten matching jack-o'-lantern faces. Have children match those that are the same. Talk about how some are different.

Make a Face. Make jack-o'-lantern faces. Provide children with paper pumpkins with outlines for eyes, nose, and mouth. Depending on children's level, have them cut out or give them precut shapes that match the outlines. Glue shapes onto outlines to make jack-o'-lanterns.

Firefighter Lotto. Make a lotto game using pictures of clothing and equipment a firefighter would use. Items might include boots, helmets, jackets, hoses, ladders, fire engines, fire hydrants, etc. Let the children name and match.

Matching—Same and Different. Prepare about fifteen pairs of leaves with different vein patterns, pumpkin faces, ghost shapes, etc. Children find and match pairs. You can vary the activity by placing three pictures on the table. Children can identify the two that are the same or one that is different.

Color Sorting. Use blocks, pegs, beads, unifix blocks, etc., and make necklaces, tall buildings, etc., with only orange or black objects.

Silhouette. Show the outline or silhouette of a variety of familiar objects. Have the children identify the object and decide if it should/could be orange or black.

Circle Puzzles. Cut out large circles in a variety of colors. Laminate each circle. Cut the circle into a number of pieces. Let the children assemble the circle puzzles.

What's in the Bag?. Place circle, square, and triangle plastic attribute blocks in a bag or pillowcase. Let the children reach in to bring out only the circles.

Sorting Cans. Cover four large coffee cans with contact paper. Use a knife to cut a circle, square, triangle, and rectangle shape in the plastic lids. Children can then sort laminated construction paper shapes into the cans, or find only the circles.

Circle Silhouettes. Trace large, medium, and small circles on tagboard game cards. Laminate. Make an overabundance of circle shapes in the three sizes, and laminate. Children can find a laminated circle piece that fits each circle silhouette on the card.

How I Look in October. Make self-portraits. Keep in booklets and watch progress throughout the year.

Perception Center. Create a learning center for perception at a designated table. Alternate activities each week. Activities to alternate are (1) puzzles, varying the difficulty level depending on students' ability, (2) blocks with pattern cards, either teacher made or pictoral, and (3) pegs and designs for copying.

GROSS MOTOR

Who's Missing?. Sit in a circle. Have children close their eyes while one child leaves the room. Other children guess who's missing.

Football. Play catch with a football. Play kick-the-football and practice throwing.

Pumpkin Toss. Play a pumpkin toss game. Toss bean bags or small balls into plastic pumpkins. For older children, you can number the pumpkins one through four and have children toss the bean bags into pumpkins in number sequence.

Ring around the Witch. Instead of playing ring around the rosie, play ring around the witch. "Ring around the witch, she fell into a ditch, ashes, ashes, we all fall down." Or make up rhymes for ring around the ghost or pumpkin.

Balloon Games. Give each child his/her own orange or black balloon. Each child should try and keep it in the air as long as possible by hitting it up.

Balloon Volleyball. Have children divide into pairs. The pairs can play volleyball with the balloons, trying to keep the balloon from touching the ground.

Moving to Music. Play music with fast or slow tempos. Have the children move to the tempo—fast to fast music, slow to slow music. Have them move like witches, ghosts, firefighters going up a ladder, scarecrows in the breeze, etc.

Rake the Leaves. Provide the children with wooden rakes. Let them rake the leaves into large piles for jumping into. The children can jump from the ground or a safe height.

Duck, Duck, Goose and Variations. Teach children how to play duck, duck, goose. When they are sure of themselves and the rules of the game, try variations, e.g., witch, witch, ghost, pumpkin, pumpkin, jack-o'-lantern, etc.

Circle Moves. Teach "Did You Ever See a Lassie?". Children will learn the rhythm of moving to music and copying each other's movements.

Circle Games. Draw a large circle on the rug with chalk. Play circle games such as ring around the rosie and duck, duck, goose.

Firefighter, Firefighter. Teach children to play a version of duck, duck, goose. After a lesson about the firefighter's jobs, the children can play firefighter, firefighter, squirt! Children should be encouraged to come up with other appropriate words that can be substituted for *squirt.*

Movement Experiences. Play instrumental music that has varying tempos. Children can be encouraged to be "ghost dancers" and "falling leaves" as they move to the music.

Falling Leaves. Cut large leaf shapes from construction paper. Tape the leaves on the gym floor. Children can move around their leaf—walk, jump, run, hop, etc.

Obstacle Course In and Out. Set up an obstacle course. Crawl in a box, crawl out. Holding a horizontal ladder, crawl in and out of the rungs. Zig zag in and out of several chairs placed together.

Ladder Games. Try a variety of movements using a horizontal ladder.

1. Walk forward, step between rungs.
2. Walk forward, step on rungs.
3. Creep forward between rungs.
4. Walk backward between rungs.
5. Jump through—between rungs, on rungs using both feet.
6. Step through.
7. Set ladder on side—crawl through (in and out), crawl through (backwards).
8. Walk with one foot on each side rail of the ladder.
9. Walk with one foot between rung and one foot outside rail.

Wind Streamers. Provide children with orange and black strips of crepe paper. Take them outside and let the streamers blow in the wind.

SENSORY EXPERIENCES

Feely Bag. Make a feely bag with items collected on your fall walk. Have each child put their hand in the bag and guess what they are feeling.

Sensory Table. Put crushed or whole leaves, kernels, or ears of Indian corn on the sensory table. Provide containers for pouring and measuring. Use warm and cold water and pour from one container to another.

PREMATH

One-to-One Correspondence. Continue practicing one-to-one correspondence with a variety of fall theme felt or construction paper cutouts. Children can practice giving a hat to every witch, an acorn to every squirrel, a bone to every skeleton, etc.

Sets. Place an assortment of familiar objects on the table, such as books, cars, and crayons. Introduce the word *set* as children group the set of books, cars, and crayons in separate piles.

Set Hunt. Provide a wide variety of experiences for children to find and label sets.

In the classroom, the children can make sets of boys, girls, children with tie gym shoes, children with Velcro™ gym shoes, etc. When children demonstrate understanding of one-attribute sets, try to work on sets with two attributes. Examples might include girls with Velcro gym shoes, boys with blue socks. etc.

Junk Sets and Sorting. Make collections of shells, beads, buttons, keys, washers, bottle caps, etc. Allow a group of children to work with one collection of junk and sort the objects into a variety of sets. The children will need much experience handling and labeling their sets. If the children are having difficulty, you can assist by naming sets the children should look for, e.g., a set of buttons that are circles, a set of buttons with two holes.

Patterns. Encourage children to see patterns in their environment, clothing, in animals, etc. Help them become aware of patterns in their shirts, mittens, in pictures of animals like tigers and zebras, and in carpeting, fabrics, etc.

Calendar Patterning. The daily calendar could have a pattern children can follow. For example, the odd days may be represented by orange pumpkins, while the even days could be represented by black cats. When children begin to see the pattern, encourage them to anticipate what symbol will be next.

Counting Sets. Encourage children to count objects in sets. Form circles with lengths of yarn. Place zero, one, or two objects inside the circles. Assist children in touching and counting items. They can be led to understand that zero means nothing. Let many experiences throughout the day be counting experiences.

Fall Math. Take advantage of fallen leaves to use in the math curriculum. Leaves can be counted, sorted, and patterned (red leaf, yellow leaf, red leaf, yellow leaf, etc.). It's a perfect opportunity to talk about sets (a set of yellow leaves, a set of large, brown leaves, etc.). Children can also order leaves from smallest to largest.

Circle Time. Introduce the circle shape by showing children a circle template or a sandpaper circle shape mounted on construction paper. Name the new shape. Have a variety of objects that are circular shaped in a box (hula hoop, ball, record, necklace, bracelet, penny, button, clock, plate). As each item is removed from the box, children can name the object and then model a sentence—for example, "This is a circle" or "A record is a circle shape."

Circle Search. Provide children with an opportunity to find circular objects in school and in the neighborhood. Children should find and label items like clocks, dishes, bowls, pots, tires, steering wheel, headlights, basketball hoops, etc.

Circle Hunt. Laminate construction paper shapes of different sizes. Include circles, triangles, squares, and rectangles. Put a piece of double-faced tape on the back of each shape and place the pieces all over the classroom. Let the children see how many circles they can find.

Seed Math. Have children dry pumpkin seeds and use them for making sets, counting, and comparing.

Squirrel Hunt. While on your fall walk, look for squirrels. Count how many you see.

Counting Sets. Count objects collected from your fall walk, such as acorns, nuts, and leaves. Use written numerals to label sets.

Gourds. Count gourds from a harvest basket.

Sort and Count. Using egg cartons, label sections 0, 1, or 2. Have children count out the correct number of nuts and place in each section.

Big and Little. Collect a variety of big and little objects found in the classroom. Let children name each object and sort into the categories big and little. The same activity can be done with pictures, comparing the sizes of toys, household objects, animals, etc. Fall leaves and nuts can be compared and sorted. Long sentences can be modeled—for example, "The leaf is brown and big."

SONGS AND FINGERPLAYS

Pretty Leaves (fingerplay).

Pretty leaves are falling down. (Move hands above head, fingers wiggling
slowly coming down to sides).
See them lying on the ground. (Stoop down patting here and there.)
Trees are bending in the breeze. (Sway body back and forth.)
Don't you love the falling leaves? (Move hands above head, slowly coming
down.)

Red Apple (fingerplay).

A little red apple
Hung high up in a tree, (Point up.)
I looked up at it (Look up.)
And it looked down at me. (Look down.)
"Come down please," I called. (Beckon.)
And what do you suppose
That little red apple
Dropped right on my nose. (Touch nose.)

Fall (go through the movements).

I like to rake the leaves in fall
And pile them in a clump.
Then step back a little way . . .
Bend my knees and JUMP!

Little Leaf (fingerplay).

Little leaf, little leaf,
Fly, fly, fly, (Move hands.)
The cold wind will take you
Up to the sky! (Raise arms over head.)

The cold wind will take you around
and around (Turn body around.)
Then slowly—so slowly—
You'll fall to the ground. (Sink to floor.)

This Little Squirrel.

This little squirrel said, "Let's run and play." (Point to each finger in turn.)
This little squirrel said, "Let's hunt nuts today."
This little squirrel said, "Yes, nuts are good."
This little squirrel said, "Yes, they're our best food."
This little squirrel said, "Come climb this tree."
(Hold forearm up, hand open; run fingers of other hand to top
fast, ending with thumb and forefinger making circle.)
"And crack these nuts, one, two, three." (Clap hands.)

Leaves.

Down, down, yellow and brown (Fingers, hands, move down.)
The leaves are falling (Move hands and body to the floor.)
All over the town.

Falling Leaves.

Many leaves are falling down,
(Flutter fingers from above head down to floor several times.)
Yellow, red and even brown.
Falling on the frosty ground.
Falling on the frosty ground.

The Pumpkin in the Dark (tune: "Farmer in the Dell"). Make a large, laminated shape for each Halloween object. Pass out objects before beginning the song.

1. The pumpkin in the dark; (repeat)
   Hi ho on Halloween, the pumpkin in the dark.
2. The pumpkin calls a witch; (repeat)
3. The witch calls a bat; (repeat)
4. The bat calls a ghost; (repeat)
5. The ghost says "Boo!" (repeat)

Five Little Pumpkins (fingerplay).

Five little pumpkins sitting on a gate,
(Hold up hand and move each finger as it talks.)
The first one said, "Oh my, it's getting late."
The second one said, "There are witches in the air."
The third one said, "But we don't care."
The fourth one said, "Let's run and run and run!"
The fifth one said, "I'm ready for some fun."
Whoo-oo-oo went the wind and out went the lights (Close hand.)
And the five little pumpkins rolled out of sight.

A Ghost (movement poem).

A ghost lives in our house, in our house, in our house.
A ghost lives in our house at Halloween time.
He bumps
and he jumps
and he thumps.
He knocks
and he rocks
and he rattles at the locks.
A ghost lives in our house, in our house, in our house
A ghost lives in our house at Halloween time.

Jack-O'-Lantern (tune: "Are You Sleeping?").

Jack-o'-lantern; Jack-o'-lantern
See the light; Oh so bright
Shining in the night time,
Shining in the night time,
What a fright! What a fright!

The Wheels on the Fire Truck (tune: "Wheels on the Bus").

1. The wheels on the fire truck go bumpty bump,
   Bumpty bump, bumpty bump!
   The wheels on the fire truck go bumpty bump,
   All through the town.
2. The horn on the fire truck goes beep, beep, beep.
3. The bell on the fire truck goes cling, clang, cling.
4. The hose on the fire truck goes shhh, shhh, shhh.
5. The siren on the fire truck goes rrr, rrr, rrr.

RECIPES

Pumpkin Muffins.

1. Preheat oven to 400 degrees.
2. Greese muffin cups.
3. Beat 1 egg slightly with fork.
4. Add:

     1/2 cup milk
     1/2 cup canned pumpkin
     1/4 cup melted butter

5. In another bowl, stir:

     1 1/2 cups flour
     1/2 cup sugar
     2 teaspoons baking powder
     1/2 teaspoon salt

    1/2 teaspoon cinnamon
    1/2 teaspoon nutmeg

6. Combine all ingredients and stir. Batter should be lumpy.
7. Add 1/2 cup raisins.
8. Fill muffin cups 2/3 full.
9. Bake 18–20 minutes.

Roasted Pumpkin Seeds.

    1 cup pumpkin seeds
    1 tablespoon vegetable oil
    Salt to taste

Preheat oven to 275 degrees. Remove as much pulp from seeds as you can, but do not wash. Mix with vegetable oil and sprinkle with salt. Spread on cookie sheet and bake for one hour or until seeds are dry.

Pumpkin Pudding.

2 cups cooked pumpkin	1 1/2 teaspoons cinnamon
1 egg	3/4 cup sugar
1 cup milk	1/2 teaspoon nutmeg
1 teaspoon cloves	Dash salt

Place mixture in a saucepan and cook for 15–20 minutes.

Orange Blops.

Blend 3 oz. softened cream cheese and 1/2 cup shredded cheddar cheese together. Then add 1 cup grated carrots. Shape into balls, then roll in wheat germ or ground nuts. Makes about 26 balls.

Peanut Butter Balls.

    1/2 cup peanut butter
    3 1/2 tablespoons powdered dry milk
    A bit of honey

Combine ingredients, roll into balls, and store in refrigerator. Optional additions: raisins, nuts, coconut, wheat germ, sunflower seeds, brown sugar for rolling

OCTOBER SNACKS

Popcorn. Serve on the day you use popcorn for language and fine motor activities.

Fall Nuts. Provide various types of nuts in shells. Let the children try and crack them.

Orange Jello. Make orange jello on "orange day."

Black Licorice. Serve black licorice on "black day."

Breads and Spreads. Put spreads (cream cheese, peanut butter) on bread. Cut bread into circles.

Circle Snacks. Make circular slices of apples, oranges, and bananas to eat.

Orange Pudding. Make vanilla pudding and add orange food coloring.

CREATIVE DRAMATICS

Firefighter. Provide hats, rain coats, boots, lengths of garden hose, wagon, bell, dolls, and a blanket (for a net). Read a story about firefighters. Then let children set up scenarios revolving around the firefighter theme.

Trick or Treating. Role-play trick or treating. Children can dress up in clothes from the housekeeping corner and carry a purse, brown bag, etc. The "parent" can carry a flashlight. Encourage children to knock at the door, say "trick or treat" and "thank you." Continue role-playing the Halloween experience with children. Stress several safety rules: Eat candy after adults check it, go trick or treating with older friends or family members, walk in your costume, carry a flashlight at night. Talk with children in a positive, nonthreatening manner.

CHILDREN'S LITERATURE

Anderson, Lonzo. *The Halloween Party*

Atwood, Ann. *The Little Circle*

Aylerill. *The Fire Cat*

Balian, Lorna. *Humbug Witch*

Barth, Edna. *Jack O' Lantern*

Bond. *Poinsettia and the Firefighter*

Bracken, Carolyn. *Here Come the Fire Engines*

Bridwell, Norman. *Clifford's Halloween*

Bright, Robert. *Georgie*

_____ . *Georgie and the Noisy Cat*

Bundt, Nancy. *The Fire Station*

Chlad, Dorothy. *Matches, Lighters and Firecrackers Are Not Toys*

Curren. *The Fire Fighters' Counting Book*

Dr. Seuss. *The Shape of Me and Other Stuff*

Elliot. *A Visit to a Sesame Street Firehouse*

Gibbons, Gail. *Halloween*

Glovach, Linda. *Little Witch's Black Magic Cookbook*

Greene. *I Want To Be a Fireman*

Hall, Adelaide. *The Wonderful Tree*

Hankin, Rebecca. *I Can Be a Firefighter*

Hannum, Dotti. *A Visit to the Fire Station*

Haywood, Carolyn. *You Can Drive a Fire Engine*

Hoban, Tana. *Circles, Triangles and Squares*

Johnson. *Firefighters: A to Z*

Keats, Ezra Jack. *Hi Cat*

Kroll, Steven. *Amanda and the Giggling Ghost*

_____ . *The Biggest Pumpkin Ever*

Lionni, Leo. *Frederick*

Low, Alice. *Witch's Holiday*

Marston. *Fire Trucks*

Mayer, Mercer. *There's a Nightmare in My Closet*

Miller, Edna. *Mousekin's Golden House*

Peters, Sharon. *Trick or Treat Halloween*

Peterson, Glen. *Let's Visit the Fire Department*

Prelutsky, Jack. *It's Halloween*

Rey, Margaret, and H. A. Rey. *Curious George and the Costume Party*

Rose, David. *It Hardly Seems Like Halloween*

Sendak, Maurice. *Where the Wild Things Are*

Seuling, Barbara. *Stay Safe, Play Safe*

Slobodkin, Louis. *Trick or Treat*

Stevenson, James. *That Terrible Halloween Night*

Unurn, Nora. *Proud Pumpkin*

Von Hippel, Ursula. *The Craziest Halloween*

Whitehead, Pat. *Best Halloween*

Yesback, Steven. *Pumpkinseeds*

Zion, Gene. *All Falling Down*

Zolotow, Charlotte. *Tiger Called Thomas*

Evaluating October Concepts

RECORDKEEPING

During October, continue to update progress in each child's anecdotal log. Observations and individual child responses can be recorded in the log for the language concepts presented. The checklists presented in the Appendix will continue to be used throughout the entire school year. This information will be useful in assessing progress on each child's Individual Education Program and when reporting progress to parents.

PREWRITING

In addition to charting progress on the prewriting checklist, observe each child at the prewriting center. It is important to observe the child while copying or imitating designs using a variety of instruments. This process is as important as the child's end product. You should consider keeping samples of the child's designs drawn throughout the year.

LANGUAGE AND VOCABULARY

    1. Autumn's changes, weather, nature, and activities
    2. Fire prevention and fire safety
    3. Halloween safety, real and pretend
    4. Cooking experiences
    5. Colors, black and orange
    6. Directional and positional concepts—in and out

FINE MOTOR

Lacing, painting, cutting, coloring, play dough manipulation, making circles and path tracing

PERCEPTION

Same and different, draw a person, puzzles, sorting, copying block and peg patterns

GROSS MOTOR

Organized games, moving to music, eye tracking objects

PREMATH

One-to-one correspondence, calendar activities, sorting, making sets, patterning, 0, 1, and 2, circle, big and little

CREATIVE DRAMATICS

SENSORY EXPERIENCES

OCTOBER
Parent-child activities

SUN	MON	TUE	WED	THU	FRI	SAT
HELP MAKE ORANGE JUICE FOR BREAKFAST.	FIND CIRCLE-SHAPED OBJECTS IN THE HOUSE—PLATE, BALL, RECORD, ETC.	VISIT THE LIBRARY. SELECT STORIES ABOUT FIREFIGHTERS.	PRACTICE A FAMILY FIRE DRILL AT HOME.	PRACTICE STOP, DROP, AND ROLL.	TALK ABOUT HOT AND COLD THINGS FOUND IN THE KITCHEN.	GIVE YOUR CHILD BOOTS, GARDEN HOSE, WEAR A FIRE HAT. PLAY FIREFIGHTER.
PRACTICE RUNNING, JUMPING, AND BALL HANDLING.	RAKE SOME LEAVES AND THEN JUMP IN.	COLLECT FALL LEAVES. SORT AND COMPARE THEM—BIG AND LITTLE, SAME AND DIFFERENT.	VISIT THE LIBRARY. SELECT BOOKS ABOUT FALL, ANIMALS, ETC.	SING OCTOBER SONGS TOGETHER.	CUT ORANGE CARROTS INTO CIRCLE PIECES. COUNT THE CIRCLES.	TALK ABOUT WHERE THINGS ARE. FOCUS ON THE WORDS IN AND OUT.
PRACTICE OCTOBER FINGERPLAYS.	MAKE AN ORANGE COLLAGE. PRACTICE CUTTING ORANGE MAGAZINE PICTURES.	PRACTICE DESIGN COPYING. MAKE CIRCLES.	PEEL AN ORANGE, SEPARATE INTO PIECES. COUNT THE PIECES.	VISIT THE LIBRARY. SELECT SOME HALLOWEEN AND MAKE-BELIEVE STORIES.	MAKE ORANGE JELLO.	PRACTICE DRESSING SKILLS WITH COATS AND BUTTONS.
GO ON A FALL WALK. LOOK FOR SQUIRRELS AND COUNT THEM.	PLAY DRESS-UP WITH OLD CLOTHES.	PRACTICE USING PENCILS, CRAYONS, CHALK, AND SCISSORS WITH SUPERVISION.	MAKE A CIRCLE SANDWICH. USE A GLASS TO CUT BREAD, CHEESE, ETC.	DECORATE A BROWN BAG FOR HALLOWEEN. USE FABRIC, PAPER, YARN, PAINT, CRAYONS, ETC.	REVIEW BODY PART NAMES. THEN DRAW A PERSON.	CARVE A FAMILY PUMPKIN TOGETHER.
COUNT SOME PUMPKIN SEEDS. MAKE SETS OF 1, 2, AND 3.	ROLE-PLAY AND PRACTICE TRICK OR TREATING. PRACTICE KNOCK-ING, SAYING "TRICK OR TREAT", AND "THANK YOU."	HAPPY HALLOWEEN!				

NOVEMBER

POTATOES
59¢/lb.

89¢
ea

CONCEPTS FOR NOVEMBER

LANGUAGE AND VOCABULARY

1. Grocery Store—naming, classifying, and sorting vegetables
2. Family—family members, their jobs, responsibilities, clothing and activities, sorting to family members, practice pronouns *he, she,* and *I,* practice possessives *his* and *her.*
3. Thanksgiving Theme—sharing, good manners, things to be thankful for, vocabulary
4. Color—brown
5. Directional and Positional Concepts—up and down

Suggested field trips/classroom visitors: Visit a grocery store, vegetable-fruit market. Ask moms, dads, and grandparents to visit class.

FINE MOTOR: 1. MANIPULATION, AND 2. PREWRITING

Lacing, painting, cutting, coloring, gluing, bead stringing, tower building, play dough manipulation, making vertical lines, path tracing

PERCEPTION

Same and different, draw a person, puzzles, copying block, peg and bead designs, patterning

GROSS MOTOR

Organized games, jumping (over objects and consecutively), ball handling and balance

SENSORY EXPERIENCES

Sense of touch at the exploration table—rough and smooth

PREMATH

One-to-one correspondence, calendar activities, sorting, numbers and numerals 3 and 4, tall and short, triangle

RECIPES

- Cooking with vegetables
- Baking

SNACK

Focus on vegetables and other foods that are brown and triangular shaped

CREATIVE DRAMATICS

- Grocery Store
- *Goldilocks and the Three Bears*
- McDonald's (fast food restaurant)

SELF-HELP

Work on fasteners, snaps and buttons, put on outerwear

REVIEW

Body parts, orange, black, directional and math concepts

ACTIVITIES FOR NOVEMBER

LANGUAGE AND VOCABULARY

1. GROCERY STORE

Grocery Store in the Classroom. The setting for your grocery store theme can be a classroom store. Ask parents to send empty containers, boxes, cans, and bottles. Provide grocery bags, receipts, cash registers, play money, plastic fruits and vegetables, shopping carts, and any other grocery store items you can think of. The grocery store can be the theme for creative play or more structured language activities.

Shopping List Game. Give each child a picture shopping list. Cut out small pictures of five to ten items for each child. Children will look at their list and find items that match pictures in the store. They can check items out and pay for them.

Shopping by Memory. Depending on each child's level, tell them one or more items to shop for. Children must use auditory memory when shopping for items.

Grocery Store Field Trip. Prepare a shopping list based on a November cooking project or projects. Try to include as many sections of the grocery store as possible, e.g., produce, bakery, canned goods, boxed items, refrigerator section. Give each child a shopping list to shop for at the store. Let each child pay for his/her own items and receive the change. Many grocery stores are pleased to give behind-the-scenes tours of their stores including the meat department, bakery, and produce sections. Some stores are also willing to let children scan and check out their own items. Arrangements should be made beforehand.

Food Classification by Picture. Ask parents to send coupons (with pictures) that they don't plan to use. After a simple discussion of the four food groups, classify the picture coupons. Provide four shoeboxes. On the front of each attach a picture to represent the food group. Children can sort their coupons into the appropriate box. If parents don't have coupons with pictures, food pictures cut from magazines and mounted on paper can be substituted.

Food Classification with Real Food. Provide a variety of foods representing each food group and four shopping bags. Label shopping bags with pictures. Sort foods into appropriate bags. This activity is a good follow-up to the grocery store field trip.

Guessing Game. Using your school grocery store, give children the opportunity to shop for an item, put it in a bag, and then have classmates guess the item. If children have difficulty formulating clues, you can give clues or help the children give clues by encouraging them to tell about color, size, when you eat it, and so on.

Vegetable Science. Cut off the top of a potato and let children stick toothpicks into it. Fill a glass or jar with water and place the potato so part of it is in the water. Watch it grow. Encourage children to talk about changes they notice each day.

Introduce Vegetables. Show children a variety of vegetable pictures, plastic pieces, or actual vegetables, if possible. Talk about the color, shape, and size of each. Compare, contrast, and taste, if possible.

Musical Vegetables. Pass a picture of a vegetable around a circle as music plays. When the music stops, the child holding the vegetable card must name it. Then change the vegetable card to be passed and continue the game.

Veggie Riddles. Play a riddle game: "I'm thinking of a vegetable that is long and orange and grows under the ground. What am I?" You may have two or three pictures on the table as children point to or name the correct vegetable. The clues should be attributes introduced or previously discussed/observed by the class.

Where Do They Grow?. Cover the bottom of a flannel board with brown kraft paper to represent soil. Place some clouds and the sun at the top. Older pre-schoolers can tape pictures of different vegetables above or below "the ground" to show where they grow.

Pumpkin Science. Children can fill a jar with cotton and place seeds between the cotton and the glass. Wet the cotton and keep it damp. After several days, encourage children to tell what they see: pumpkin shoots growing "up" and roots growing "down."

Name the Vegetable. Have a variety of vegetable dish pictures cut from magazines—vegetable casseroles, pumpkin pie, french fries, mashed potatoes, etc. Have children name the vegetable used to prepare the food shown in the picture.

Name the Food. Have two or three food/vegetable pictures on the table. Children can use pictures as prompts to respond to teacher questions: What food can you eat raw? Cooked? What vegetable is juicy? Crunchy? Which ones have seeds? Which one can you eat with your fingers? The list of questions is endless.

Same and Different. Put two vegetables/pictures on the table. Talk about how they are the same and how they are different.

2. FAMILY

Making a Family Album. This activity can be completed over several days or during the course of the month. Children bring in pictures of various family members including self. One day add pictures of Mom, another day add pictures of Dad, continue with sisters, brothers, grandmothers, grandfathers, aunts, uncles, cousins, pets. Depending on the time allotment, you may choose to limit the album to immediate family. Children can dictate a sentence about each picture for the teacher to write.

Family Visitors. On the day you add each family member to the album, you can invite family members to visit the classroom. Each child may choose one or more family visitors. One child might invite a dad. Another child might invite a grandmother. Each classroom visitor might do a special activity with the class such as read a book, sing a song, share a snack, or whatever the visitor feels comfortable doing.

Mom/Dad Pictures. When talking about moms or females, make a picture. Have children look through magazines and find pictures of females to make individual or group collages. Write a story about moms, everyone adding to it. This activity can be repeated with dads.

Whose Mom or Dad Is It?. Ask parents to write a short paragraph telling what they do at home and/or work. Each day read one or more of the paragraphs to the class and see if children can identify their parents.

Picture Sort. Using pictures of family members that were sent to school, sort into groups of male/female. Using items or pictures that are uniquely male or female (e.g., shoes, wallets, purses, etc.), have children decide if the items go with the group of male or female pictures. Have children tell why when making their decisions. Attempt to elicit male and female pronouns when children are talking.

Finding Families. Using the flannel board, display figures of men, women, boys, girls, and babies. Ask each child to select the appropriate figures that make up his/her family. Have the child tell as many things as possible about each family member (e.g., What they do, what they like or dislike.).

Story Sequence. Read a story about a family such as *The Three Bears*. Have children tell the story back in proper sequence or order pictures in sequence. Use terms such as *first, second, third,* last. Follow up by dramatizing the story.

Families. Using pictures, puppets, dolls, or 3D people figures, introduce family members: mother, father, sister, and brother. Depending on the dynamics of families in your class, you may need to introduce grandmother, grandfather, aunt, and uncle. Help children understand many concepts: Families can be big or small; they can be headed by one adult or more; family members love each other; families can work and play.

Family Albums. Have each child bring in a family album or family pictures. Give children an opportunity to name each person and state their relationship, if possible. Encourage children to tell about each picture brought to school. (Parents can write simple information on the back of pictures, so you can more effectively prompt the child.)

Family Clothes. Have pictures of clothing or actual articles of clothing worn by family members. Include a blouse, shirt, pants, skirt, necktie, sweater, swimsuit, bathing trunks, socks, slippers, robe, pajamas, etc., placed in a laundry basket. Allow children to name and help sort laundry to family members. Encourage children to practice *he* and *she* or *his* and *hers,* e.g., "He has a shirt, she has a sweater" or "The necktie is his, the skirt is hers."

Family Jobs. Encourage children to talk about the jobs and responsibilities held by each family member. They need to be made aware that roles and responsibilities *vary greatly* and can be *shared* by family members. Show a picture and state a job associated with it. Children can then share whose job it is at their house. In this activity there are no right or wrong responses. Some items to include might be.

PICTURE	JOB
doll	I put my dolls away.
garbage can	I take out the garbage.
vacuum cleaner	I vacuum the rug.
lawn mower	I cut the grass.
dishes	I set the table.

Family Activities. Show children pictures of families doing things together. Then name activities/objects used or enjoyed by family members. Children can identify family members associated with each object or activity. Items to include might be a book, bike, skateboard, dolls, puzzles, models, various sport balls, swimsuit, golf clubs, a game, deck of cards, a record player. Encourage children to tell about other activities or hobbies that family members enjoy.

He or She. Show children figures of family members. Children can identify them and state which family members are girls and which are boys.

Family Wish List. Give each child an opportunity to make a wish list for each family member. Write down responses, or children can cut out catalog pictures. Have children tell why the family member would like each item.

A Busy Family. Play a game with the children to strengthen memory skills. Have them remember and tell back sentence sequences. Examples: "Mom was busy today, she cut the grass and washed the car." The child can tell what Mom did first and last. "Dad went to the grocery store, he bought corn, meat, and crackers." Children can tell what Dad bought. "Danny played with his dolls, puzzles, and trucks today." Children can tell what Danny played with.

I Grow up. Have children bring in a baby picture of themselves. Talk about things babies do and like. Then encourage children to tell about and demonstrate things they can do now, e.g., "I can button. I can jump. I can hop."

What Doesn't Belong?. Place three or four objects or pictures on the table, e.g., bib, rattle, crib, and airplane. Have children name each object and then identify the object that doesn't belong. Extend the activity; have children tell who could use the objects and why.

Thanksgiving Sound Blending. Divide Thanksgiving-related words into syllables and slowly say them to the children. Children can be encouraged to listen carefully, put the sounds together and then say it fast. Words to try to include: *tur–key, gra–vy, pump–kin–pie, In–di–an, po–ta–to,* etc.

Turkey. Introduce a turkey by showing a picture. Have children tell about how it looks. Have them find and name the feathers, beak, clawed feet, etc. Talk about the sound it makes. Compare its size and shape to other birds such as chickens and ducks.

Auditory Directions. Provide children with a cutout turkey shape and feathers cut from various colors and sizes. Give children verbal directions to complete the turkey. *Example:* "Put the small red feather next to the green feather," or "Put the large orange feather between the two green feathers."

Thanksgiving Story. Simplify the story of the first Thanksgiving. Highlight only the main events: (1) Pilgrims arrived on a large ship called the Mayflower. (2) Indians helped the Pilgrims. (3) They had a large feast to celebrate. Draw simple pictures to go with the story. Have children sequence the pictures in retelling the story, then have them dramatize the story.

Things to Be Thankful For. Brainstorm about things children are thankful for. Write or draw ideas on separate slips of paper and hang from a hanger to make a mobile.

Dress-up. Do some role-playing with the children in the housekeeping corner. Children can dress up and take turns pretending to be the mom, dad, a child, or a baby. Encourage language and creative displays of roles.

3. THANKSGIVING THEME

Thankfulness Story. Review the idea of being thankful. Write a class story in which children can tell what they are thankful for (family, food, pets, clothes, toys, etc.). Children can draw a picture or cut out a magazine picture to illustrate their sentence story.

Thanksgiving Feast. Review the ideas of fall harvest (see October *language*). Display pictures of food enjoyed at the first Thanksgiving. Have children name the food.

Class Feast. Plan a simple Thanksgiving feast with the children. Let them assist in selecting foods they will shop for on a field trip to the grocery store and help to prepare in school. The children can make a shopping list that will be brought on the field trip. Children can look for magazine pictures of foods chosen, cut them out, and glue them on a large sheet of construction paper.

Manners. As children gain skill in setting the snack table (one-to-one correspondence), take time to talk about and model good manners: saying "please" and "thank you," taking only what you can eat, and sharing the food. Encourage children to display good manners as they play in the housekeeping corner kitchen.

Manners Match. Use old magazines to find pictures of people using good or poor manners, or draw pictures depicting the same. Use a large sheet of paper divided in halves labeled *good manners, bad manners.* Discuss each picture. Decide where to place it. Mount pictures and hang on the wall. Practice using good manners at snack time as well as throughout the day.

Share Fare. One day, have children bring food and toys to share with each other. Each child can bring in a special snack item. Put all items together on a tray and have all the children share all the snacks. This can also be done with favorite toys. Children bring in favorite toys and tell about them. During free play, children share toys with each other.

4. COLOR—BROWN

Mystery Box. Introduce the color brown using your mystery box (see October). Fill it with brown items such as paper, nuts, brown toys, cooking utensils, or any other brown objects you can find in the classroom or at home. Give the children clues about each item. Have them guess each brown item in the box.

Scavenger Hunt. Brainstorm together things that are brown in school. Make a list. Have children go to other classrooms, the principal, secretary, or nurse, trying to collect the brown items. This activity could be added to or varied by including things that are triangles.

What is Brown?. Look through magazines for brown pictures. Cut out the pictures and mount them. Give pictures a caption.

Brown Hike. Take the class for a walk or hike to look for brown items. Give each child a bag for their brown collection. Upon returning from the hike, glue brown objects onto brown construction paper to make a collage.

Brown Riddles. Upon returning from hike, help children write riddles about what they found. Children do this by describing objects without telling what they are. Make a class book of riddles.

Brown. See the suggested activities for introducing colors listed in October. These activities may all be used by substituting brown objects.

Brown Bag. Place a brown object in a brown paper bag, then give descriptive clues about what's inside and let children guess what's in the bag. To vary the activity, some children may be able to tell clues about what they have in their bag as other children guess the contents.

Thinking of. Show children a piece of brown paper. Have them identify/name the color. Encourage children to name anything they can think of that can be brown or reminds them of brown. List their ideas on paper and send the list home with children to extend the "brown activity." Parents and children then can look for the listed brown objects at or around their home and neighborhood and circle those they find.

5. DIRECTIONAL AND POSITIONAL CONCEPTS—UP AND DOWN

Slides and Stairs. Introduce the concepts of up and down on the playground. Climb up and slide down a slide. Children should be encouraged to tell what they are doing, where they are going using the words *up* and *down.* Try the same activity with climbing up and down stairs in the school building.

Up and Down Walk. Go for a walk outside. Children can look for and name things found up in the sky and down on the ground.

Up and Down Sorting. Divide a flannel board in half. Talk about what part is up and what part is down. Children can name and place pictures in the appropriate section using double-faced tape. Provide pictures such as helicopter, cloud, airplane, bird, kite, wagon, dog, car, grass, etc.

Up and Down Object Movement. Bat balloons up in the air, roll balls down on the ground. Encourage children to give directions using the words *up* and *down.*

Chair Game. Have children stand *up* on a chair and *down* on the ground. Repeat using objects.

Birds in a Tree. Draw a picture of a tree or use a flannel board tree. Have children place cutout birds up in the tree or down on the ground.

Paper Airplanes. Depending on the level of the children, either provide them with paper airplanes or give directions for making them. Fly the airplanes using vocabulary words *up* when the airplane is up in the air, and *down* when it flies down.

FINE MOTOR

1. MANIPULATION

Family Puppets. Staple a tongue depressor to a paper plate or small paper bag. Provide children with crayons, markers, construction paper, and yarn to create family puppets.

Paper Dolls. Have children play with paper dolls. They will enjoy putting on and removing clothing that fits.

Doll Dress-Up. Allow children to put clothing on dolls. Some children will be ready to work on fasteners: buttons, snaps, Velcro™ closures, etc.

Draw a Family. Give children crayons, markers, colored pencils, etc. Let children draw a picture of their family. Children can dictate a family story for you to write down.

Indian Drum. Children can make an Indian drum using an empty oatmeal box. Each child can decorate a drum using crayons, markers, construction paper, or scraps of fabric.

Lacing. Cut out Indian teepees, canoes, or vegetable shapes from tagboard. Laminate these pieces and punch holes around the edges with a hole punch. Children can use stiff string or shoelaces to practice lacing.

Chalk Teepees. Cut out triangle-shaped Indian teepees from old sheets. Wet the fabric teepees and smooth on a table. Children can decorate the teepees using colored chalk. When dried, hair spray can be used as a fixative.

Eye-Dropper Corn. Cut two or three pieces of corn-on-the-cob shapes from manila paper for each child. Wet the paper and show children how to use the pincer grip to fill an eye dropper with different colors of paint. To make Indian corn, squeeze paint on the corn cob paper.

Indian Clothes. Make a vest, apron, or loin cloth for each child from kraft paper or a large brown grocery bag. Children can decorate with prints made from vegetables (carrot, potato, celery, etc.) dipped in paint.

Stringing a Necklace. Children can paint styrofoam pieces or rigatoni noodles with brown and orange paint. They can string the dried pieces with heavy thread or yarn. If children pattern the colors (orange, brown, orange, brown, etc.), the activity also strengthens visual perception.

Fall Negative Space Picture. Cut a variety of nut shapes out of the children's painting paper. Have a variety of brown shades available for easel painting on the negative space paper.

Turkey Collage. Give children an outline of a turkey shape. Provide a variety of materials children can use to decorate and glue on their turkey shape. Use pieces of magazine or newspaper, sandpaper, pieces of yarn, string or ribbon, fabric scraps, noodles or beads to make interesting feathers.

Class Totem Pole. Give children a variety of boxes of different sizes. Encourage the class to stack the boxes cooperatively and creatively. Assist them in gluing the boxes together. Children can paint and decorate the totem pole.

Torn Paper Collage. Tearing paper strengthens pincer grip and using fingers in opposition. Provide children with various kinds of paper ranging from thin pieces to full-sized wide pieces. Demonstrate controlled tearing. Children can tear paper and then glue on construction paper.

Crumpled Paper Bear Skins. Give children a large piece of irregularly shaped kraft paper or an opened brown paper bag. Children can repeatedly crumple, then open and smooth the paper using both hands. Children can paint or use markers on the bear skin.

Squeeze Pictures. Allow children to squeeze freely school glue onto heavy paper. They can shake on, sprinkle, or put sand or dried coffee grounds (brown) onto the glue. Let dry. Children shake off the excess.

Fall Necklaces. Provide children with fresh cranberries, apple chunks, and golden and dark raisins to string onto heavy thread. Let the necklace dry for several weeks. (If children pattern the pieces, visual perception is strengthened.)

Indian Corn. Give children two or three pieces of manila paper shaped like ears of corn. Provide scraps of orange, red, yellow, and purple paper. Children can tear or snip paper and then glue onto the ears of corn.

Corn Cob Painting. Roll a dried corn cob on a styrofoam tray that has a thin layer of paint in it. Children roll the cobs in different directions across their paper.

Vegetables. Give children an opportunity to shuck corn, snap beans, scrape carrots, tear lettuce, remove peas from the pod and so on.

Folding. Fold napkins into triangle shapes.

Snipping. Give children outlines of a variety of different vegetables. Children can practice snipping 1- or 2-inch strips of construction paper. They can glue orange pieces on a carrot, green on the lettuce, etc.

Potato Prints. Cut a potato in half and carve a simple design in the potato with a knife. Children dip the potato in tempera paint and make prints on paper.

Glue a Shape. Children can use a template to make a shape with a marker or pencil. They can spread or squeeze glue on the shape and place dried beans, seeds, paper snips, etc., on the glue. After glue dries, these can be a good way to practice tactile discrimination of shapes.

Turkey Hands. Trace each child's hand. Depending on ability level, cut the handprint out or have the child cut it out. Decorate the handprint as a turkey. The thumb is the head, fingers are feathers. Use markers, crayons, paper scraps, or other collage materials to decorate.

Thanksgiving Placemats. Placemats can be made in various ways depending on the ability level of each child.

1. Using large sheets of paper, children snip fringe around edges, and decorate the remainder of the mat with crayons, markers, paint, or collage materials
2. Using precut strips of paper, have children weave a placemat in an over-under pattern. The children can choose their own colors, or you can use brown and orange to reinforce October and November colors.

3. Children can copy designs (0, 1, etc.) and/or Indian symbols on brown construction paper. They can fringe around the edges of the paper.

Papoose Lacing. Provide cutout oval shapes to lace a papoose holder. Punch holes around the oval to use for lacing. Children can put a paper baby into their holders. They can cut their babies out of construction paper or tagboard and decorate with markers and yarn for hair.

Indian Beads. Using colored macaroni, lace onto pieces of yarn for making necklaces. Children can create their own color patterns to follow when lacing.

Vegetable Prints. Use various vegetables cut in half. Dip them in paint and print onto paper. Try using various vegetables—potatoes, carrots, celery, zucchini, beets, onions, squash, etc.

Triangle Pictures. Provide children with paper with a triangle drawn or taped on. Let each child create a picture from the triangle. Some children might simply decorate while others produce a representational picture. This open-ended activity can be varied by using a chalkboard, easel, or chalk on the sidewalk.

Fine Motor Center. The fine motor center (see October) can be utilized throughout the year. You may want to add to or vary the materials to follow your monthly unit approach. For November, you may wish to add additional brown materials, e.g., paper, markers, crayons, and collage materials. You might add feathers to your collage materials. Provide lentils and pasta products for coloring, gluing, and stringing. Children can practice cutting tall and short strips of paper. Ask them to cut *up* the paper and *down* the paper. Provide triangle shapes for tracing, snipping, cutting, and decorating like teepees. Almost all concepts for the month can be incorporated at the fine motor center.

Tall and Short Play dough. Roll play dough into tall and short sticks or lines.

2. PREWRITING

Triangle Teepees. Make teepees by connecting dots to make a triangle teepee. Decorate at the art table.

Easel Painting. Paint brown triangles at the easel. For a variation, cut triangles out of easel painting paper. Paint around the triangles.

Chalkboards. Practice prewriting skills at the large chalkboard or at small individual boards. Connect dots to make triangles. Use the vocabulary words *up* and *down* when practicing vertical lines.

Tall and Short Lines. Using any of the writing materials available (chalkboard, markers, crayons, paints, etc.), children can practice vertical lines by making them tall and short.

Path Tracing. Vertical paths can be created for paper/pencil, chalk/chalkboard, or paint/easel activities. Trace mom to dad, sister to brother, turkey to pilgrim, or vegetables to pot.

Up and Down Lines. Using the chalkboard or paper and paint or various other writing utensils, practice making lines by going up and down.

Dot to Dot. Prepare a variety of simple dot-to-dot pictures for children to connect: vertical lines, vegetables, nuts, etc. Use a color cue, e.g., start on the green dot, finish on the red dot.

PERCEPTION

Patterning. Cut a headband for each child from kraft paper. Supply children with 1- by 1-inch snips of orange and brown construction paper. Children can make a pattern with the colors (orange, brown, etc.) and then glue on the headband.

Turkey Feathers. Give children two colors of Indian feathers. Children can pattern the feathers and glue on a headband.

Teepee Lotto. Make lotto cards picturing different colors and designs of teepees. Laminate pieces. Children match the teepees that are the same.

Feely Box. Prepare a cardboard box with a hole in the side that is large enough for the child to put in his/her hand and bring out an object. Children can be asked to feel and find vegetables, Thanksgiving objects, etc.

Necklaces. See fine motor ideas that incorporate patterning to strengthen visual perception.

Vegetable Sorting. Sort pictures of food into two categories: vegetables and not vegetables or vegetables, fruits, etc.

Matching. Have children match pictures of cut vegetables to the whole. Vary the matching activity and have children match the outline or silhouette of a vegetable to the picture of the whole.

Fishing for Colors. Cut at least six fish shapes from each color of construction paper. Laminate these pieces and put a paper clip on the end of each fish. Attach a magnet to a string that is tied to a dowel rod. This becomes a fishing pole. Make a blue river out of kraft paper, or use yarn to make an outline of the fishing area. Place fish in the "water." Children can fish for only brown, orange, etc. This activity also strengthens fine motor skills.

Fishing for Shapes. Make at least six fish shapes for each geometric shape. Cut enough circles, squares, triangles, rectangles, etc., to be glued on the fish. Laminate these pieces and put a paper clip on the end of each fish. Make a fishing area. Children can fish for only triangles, circles, etc. This activity also strengthens fine motor skills.

Family Lotto. Make lotto cards with pictures of family members. Two children can take turns and match like pictures.

Potato Faces. Each child can use a potato to represent a head. Features can be added on by using toothpicks to attach paper, raisins, yarn, marshmallows, etc., for facial features.

Food Puzzles. Children can find full-page food pictures from magazines. These can be mounted and glued on heavy paper. You or the children can cut the food pictures into puzzle pieces. Children can assemble the puzzles and tell about the foods they see.

People Puzzles. Cut pictures of people out of magazines. Cut each person in half vertically and then match people halves.

Photo Puzzles. Ask parents to send a photograph of each child. Have children mount the photos on construction paper, then cut into pieces. When finished, children can assemble their own or a friend's puzzle.

Grocery Item Memory Game. On a tray, display three to five grocery store items. Ask children to look at the items, and then close their eyes. Remove one or two items from the tray. Children must guess what's missing.

Turkey Feather Patterns. Provide children with paper plates and various colored cutout feathers. Children can paste feathers onto paper plates according to a specific color pattern.

How I Look in November. Make November self-portraits. Add to booklet begun in September.

Perception Center. The materials and activities at the perception center (see October) can be varied to reinforce concepts for November. Thanksgiving lends itself to patterns in the perceptual area. Children can follow color patterns while making Indian headbands and beads. Various food items (e.g., nuts, lentils) can be sorted. The concepts tall and short can be incorporated into block designs. Peg designs can be utilized in learning about triangles.

Sorting Dried Foods. Provide a variety of dried foods such as nuts, cereals, beans, and different types of pasta. Use egg carton sections, margarine containers, or small paper cups for the sorting activity. Children can sort the foods according to various attributes on separate occasions. For example, on day 1 sort by color, day 2 sort by size, day 3 sort by food type.

What's Behind the Window?. Use pictures which relate to the monthly concepts. Mount on paper and play a guessing game. Cover the pictures with construction paper in which window flaps have been cut and can be opened. Open windows one at a time until children can guess what's behind the paper.

GROSS MOTOR

Mother May I?. This game is a variation of Simon Says. One child is chosen to be Mother. Mother gives directions to the others. Children must remember to say "Mother May I?" before doing an action. The game can be varied. Use "Father May I?", "Brother May I?", etc.

Farmer in the Dell. Play Farmer in the Dell using members of a family. For instance, father takes a mother, mother takes a son. Allow children to decide on substitutions.

Jumping Rope. Use a rope about 10 feet long. Two teachers can swing the rope, or tie one end to a stable object such as a tree or post. Swing the rope slowly back and forth while children take turns jumping over it. If it is too difficult for children to jump over a moving rope, hold it still while children jump over it. Start with the rope on the ground and then very slowly move it higher.

Jump over the River. Draw a chalk river with two wiggly lines. Encourage children to jump over the river so they don't fall in. To add a balance component to the activity, build a bridge out of blocks, and children can walk across the bridge.

Hopscotch. Begin this activity with single squares for both feet. Children can simply jump through the sequence of squares. Make the activity more difficult by allowing for hopping on one foot and resting on two feet. This follows the more traditional hopscotch game.

Bean Bag Turkey Toss. Draw a turkey on the floor or make one out of wood or tagboard. Give the turkey a large open mouth in which to toss the bean bag. A variation of this could be played by tossing the bean bag into a pilgrim's hat or into a teepee's door.

Circle Catch. Children stand in a circle with the teacher in the middle. The teacher goes around the circle throwing the ball for each child to catch.

Bowling. Set up a bowling game. Blocks can be substituted for pins. Children try to knock the pins/blocks down.

Basketball. Use a round laundry basket with the bottom cut out. Fasten it to a tree outside or inside. Children throw the ball through the basket. The height of the basket can be raised gradually.

Hot Potato. With music playing, children sit in a circle and pass the "hot potato" (ball, bean bag, or real potato). When the music stops, the child holding the "potato" sits in the middle of the circle. To vary the activity, children can roll or push the "potato" around the circle.

Freeze. Play lively music while children move to the beat in free-form exploration. When the music stops, the children must freeze in their positions.

Body Movement. Review body part names as children experience a variety of body movements: bend—knees, waist, elbow, fingers, neck; twist—wrist, ankle, waist, neck; lift—arms, legs, heel, chin.

Balance. Children can learn how to balance by walking a line of masking tape placed on the floor. Encourage them to walk forward alternating feet, walk heel-toe, walk backward, walk with hands extended laterally for balance, walk with hands held at side, walk sideways, walk on tiptoe, or with a bean bag on top of their heads.

Balance Beam. Children can repeat the foregoing balance activities on a balance beam. You may want to place a mat under the balance beam.

Jumping. Place a strip of masking tape on the floor. Children can line up and take turns jumping over the line. Then place another strip of masking tape parallel to the first piece (about 8 inches apart). Children can pretend that the space between the lines is a river they are to jump over. Widen the space between the strips when children are ready.

Jump Fast. Play lively music and have children jump consecutively. Observe each child to make sure both feet leave the floor. You may want to clap the jumping beat.

Obstacle Course. Set up a simple obstacle course where children can jump over low objects, balance on straight and zig zag lines, and walk across a low balance beam. Some children may feel comfortable jumping off low objects.

Roll the Ball. Children can roll a ball back and forth to a partner while sitting, kneeling, or standing. Children can also roll balls through chair legs, through people's legs, and through croquet wickets. Children will also enjoy simple bowling games where they knock down light objects.

SENSORY EXPERIENCES

Sensory Table. At the sensory table, provide materials that are rough and smooth. Some examples are aquarium gravel, smooth stones, smooth and bumpy gourds, sandpaper, cellophane paper, hopsack cloth, pieces of smooth cloth such as satin or nylon, and furry material. Let children explore the various textures and try to elicit vocabulary which describes the textures. Also provide various textured substances for pouring and measuring such as corn kernals, soapy water, dried and broken-up leaves, corn meal, water mixed with gelatin and colored water.

Feel Your Clothes. Talk about children's clothing, using the words *rough* and *smooth.*

Food Textures. Incorporate the sense of touch and vocabulary terms at snack time when referring to food, e.g., jelly is smooth, crackers are rough.

Silly Putty. Make silly putty using the following recipe:

> 1/2 cup Elmer's Glue™
> 1 cup starch (Sta-Flo™)
> Touch of food coloring

Mix with hands until thoroughly mixed. Keep in an airtight container.

PREMATH

Family Graphs. Children can make a pictorial graph of their family by drawing a picture of each family member. They can count the number of adults, boys, and girls.

A class family member chart can be made the same way. Children can then compare class results in each column. Who has the biggest, smallest family? Who has the most brothers, the least sisters? Who has the same number of brothers?

Counting Songs. Make felt sets of fall-related objects: ten nuts, Indians, turkeys, feathers, canoes, carrots, etc. Place pieces from left to right on a flannel board. Touch and count as children sing to variations of the tune "Ten Little Indians." Give children opportunities to touch as the song is sung.

Calendar Activities. The class November calendar could have a pattern following the vegetable or Thanksgiving theme (turkey, canoe, turkey, canoe or potato, carrot, potato, carrot). Children should learn to anticipate what will be next for tomorrow. Count the numbers on the calendar each day. Chart the names of the days of the week. Talk about activities related to yesterday, today, and tomorrow.

Rote Counting. Rhythmic chanting, songs, and fingerplays help children to learn rote counting, the sequence of number words.

Clip the Can. Cover small cans or milk cartons with self-stick vinyl. Use a permanent marker to write a numeral between zero and four on the container. Children can "read" the numeral and clip the correct number of clothespins on the can. This activity strengthens the fine motor pincer grip. Vary this activity by putting the correct number of small objects in the container.

Indian Canoes. Cut out canoes from construction paper and write a numeral between zero and four on each canoe. Cut out enough oars to correspond to the numerals on the canoes. Laminate these pieces. Children can give each canoe the correct number of oars.

Tall and Short. Introduce the concepts tall and short by comparing the height of objects in the classroom.

Structures. Let children build a variety of tall and short structures using 1-inch cubes, Unifix ™ blocks, and wooden blocks. Encourage them to express the height of their buildings, etc.

Sorting. Cut out a variety of pictures children can use to compare and sort into the tall-short categories: trees, bushes, people, buildings, appliances, etc.

Circles and Triangles. Have a real pizza for snack or make a pizza using tagboard for the crust and yellow, red, and brown construction paper to represent the cheese, sauce, and sausage. Talk about the circle shape of the pizza. Have children suggest different ways you could cut the pizza. Finally, cut the pizza into triangular-shaped wedges. Talk about the number of sides and corners each piece of pizza has now. Eat and enjoy!

Ask children to think of other foods that can be cut into triangular pieces: pie, quiche, apple, cantalope, etc.

Clay and Cut. Children can use rolling pins to make pizza out of play dough. Cut the pizza into triangular pieces using a pizza cutter. Serve on circle-shaped plates.

Feely Bag. Place a variety of attribute blocks in a bag or pillowcase. Children can reach in and pull out only those shaped like a triangle. This is a good activity to strengthen tactile perception.

Shape Lotto. Make a lotto game where children can match triangles with sides of different lengths. Stress that they are all triangles because they each have three sides and three corners.

Triangle Construction. Provide children with straws, toothpicks, pipe cleaners, etc. Encourage them to make triangles. Some children may want to glue their shape on paper.

Vegetable Graphing. Choose three familiar vegetables and place a picture of each at the top of a grid chart. Let children choose their favorite vegetable and record their choice. Compare class results. For example, "How many votes did each vegetable receive? What is the favorite, least favorite?"

Treasure Count. Following your classroom scavenger hunt, count the brown items collected.

Dice Game. This group game reinforces counting and one-to-one correspondence. Use a large, teacher-made or commercial die. Two dice can be used if children are at a higher level. Children line up at the start line and take turns shaking the die. Depending on the number shook, each child takes the number of steps she/he shook. The object is for all children to get to the finish line.

Clothespin Counting. This activity can be varied depending on children's level. Put a numeral on a small paper plate. Children put that number of clothespins on the plate. (Vary by putting on the plate pictures of dots, balls, etc.) Children match the number by putting on that number of clothespins. Write numerals on clothespins and draw sets on the paper plates. Children match the clothespins to the sets.

Match Rhythms. Provide children with numeral cards, 1 through 4. You may also want to illustrate sets 1 through 4 on the card. Show cards to the children one at a time. Ask children to clap as many times as the card says. Vary the activity by stomping feet, beating a drum, tapping heads, etc.

Math Pictures. Make a booklet. Number the pages 1 through 4. Have children cut pictures from magazines and paste them on pages to match the numerals.

Sorting Shapes. Using margarine containers or egg cartons, label sections with a circle or triangle. Provide various colors and sizes of circles and triangles. Have children sort into appropriate containers.

Golf Tee Match-ups. Cut triangular pieces of styrofoam and mount them on pieces of tagboard. On each piece of tagboard, write a numeral 1 through 4 (or above, depending on children's abilities, draw a set of small triangles which correspond to the written numeral). Provide children with golf tees. The tees are to be put in the styrofoam corresponding to the numeral on the card.

Flannel Board Sets. Put numerals 1 through 4 on the flannel board. Provide flannel cutouts of objects. Children can place the corresponding set of objects next to the appropriate numeral.

Turkey Sets. Provide each child with four turkey cutouts. Each turkey should have a numeral from 1 through 4 on it. Make feathers available for each child She/he can glue the corresponding number of feathers to each turkey.

Tall-Short Sort. Using two shoeboxes, one longer than the other, stand them upright so they look tall and short. Label one box tall and the other box short. This can be done with words or pictures, i.e., the short box has a picture of a short tree, the tall box has a picture of a tall tree. Sort tall and short pairs of items into the corresponding boxes. Suggestions include straws, strips of paper, cutout teepees, sticks, or feathers.

SONGS AND FINGERPLAYS

Indians and Pilgrims (tune: "Row, Row, Row Your Boat").

Beat, beat, beat the drum,
Beat it loud and clear.
To tell brave Indians everywhere
That hunting time is near.

Cut, cut, cut the logs,
Make them long and short.
To help the pilgrims build a house,
A warm and friendly fort.

Turkey Dinner (tune: "Are You Sleeping?"). Make a drumstick out of construction paper and laminate. Pass around as first verse is sung

Turkey dinner, turkey dinner, gather round, gather round.
Who will get the drum stick? yummy yummy yum stick.
All sit down, all sit down.

Corn bread muffin, chestnut stuffin', pudding pie one foot high.
I was so much thinner, before I came to dinner.
Me oh my! Me oh my!

One Little Indian.

One little, two little, three little Indians, four little, five little,
six little Indians, seven little, eight little, nine little Indians, ten
little Indian boys.

(Repeat with Pilgrims and turkeys.)

Five Little Turkeys (fingerplay).

Five little turkeys flew up in a tree (Hold up hand with fingers spread.)
The first one said, "There's a man I see." (Point to thumb.)
The second one said, "He's coming this way." (Point to index finger)

The third one said, "It's Thanksgiving day." (Point to middle finger)
The fourth one said, "What's he going to do?" (Point to ring finger)
The fifth one said, "He's coming after you." (Point to little finger)
Chop went the axe before the turkey flew away (Clap hands on *chop*.)
They all were on the table that Thanksgiving day.

Mr. Turkey (fingerplay).

Mr. Turkey's tail is big and wide. (Spread hand/fingers wide.)
He swings it when he walks. (Swing hands.)
His neck is long, his chin is red. (Stroke chin/neck.)
Mr. Turkey is so tall and proud. (Straighten up tall.)
He dances on his feet. (Fingers dance.)
And each Thanksgiving day, (Fold hands in prayer fashion.)
He's something good to eat. (Pat stomach.)

The Family at Home (tune: "Farmer in the Dell").

The family works at home,
The family works at home,
Hi, ho the derry-O
The family works at home.

Verses: Repeat refrain "Hi, ho the deery-O . . ."
1. The dad cleans the house.
2. The mom cuts the grass.
3. The kids wash the car.
Add verses for grandma, grandpa, or other family members.

The family plays at home,
The family plays at home,
Hi, ho the derry-O
The family plays at home.

Verses: Repeat refrain "Hi, ho the deery-O . . ."
1. Dad and kids play catch.
2. Mom and kids dance.
Ask children to help add other verses.

My Family (fingerplay).

Here is my mother, (thumb)
Here is my father, (pointer finger)
Here is my brother tall, (middle finger)
Here is my sister, (ring finger)
Here is the baby, (little finger)
O how I love them all. (Clap left hand over all fingers just indicated.)

Vegetable Harvest (tune: "Are You Sleeping?").

Vegetable garden, vegetable garden, harvest time, harvest time.
Gather corn and snap the beans, dig potatoes, pick the peas.
Veggies taste good, veggies taste good!

Being Thankful (tune: "If You're Happy and You Know It").

If you're thankful and you know it clap your hands.
If you're thankful and you know it clap your hands.
If you're thankful and you show it,
Let you family and friends know it.
If you're thankful and you know it clap your hands.

(Add verses by substituting other actions.)

RECIPES

Oatmeal Raisin Crispies.
Mix:

2 cups oatmeal	1 egg
1 cup brown sugar	1/2 teaspoon salt
1/2 cup oil	1/2 teaspoon vanilla
1/2 cup raisins	

Drop teaspoonfuls of the mixture onto a greased cookie sheet. Bake at 350 degreees for 12–15 minutes. Yields 3 dozen.

Cranberry Sauce.

2 cups water
2 cups sugar
1-pound package of cranberries

Boil water, sugar, and cranberries until cranberries pop. Chill and serve.

Cheesy Corn Muffins.

2 beaten eggs	3/4 cup shredded cheddar cheese (3 oz.)
1 8 3/4-oz. can creamed corn	2 7-oz. packages of corn muffin mix
1/3 cup milk	

Combine eggs, corn, and milk. Add cheese and muffin mix. Fill muffin cups. Bake at 400 degrees for 15–20 minutes.

Apple Pizza.

2 tablespoons flour	2 apples peeled and sliced thin
1/2 cup brown sugar	1 can refrigerator biscuits
1/2 teaspoon cinnamon	Dab of butter or margarine
1 cup grated cheddar cheese	

Mix flour, sugar, and cinnamon in a bowl. Press biscuits into flat circles and put on a lightly greased cookie sheet. Sprinkle grated cheese on each biscuit. Put apple slices on each biscuit. Put brown sugar mixture on top. Dot with butter. Bake for 20–30 minutes in 350-degree oven. Let cool.

Carrot-Raisin Salad.

Grate 2 cups of carrots
Add 1 cup raisins

Stir in 1 cup of chopped nuts
Mix with plain yogurt

Corn Bread Muffins.

1/4 cup vegetable oil	4 teaspoons baking powder
1 cup corn meal	1/2 teaspoon salt (optional)
1 cup flour	1 cup milk
2–4 tablespoons sugar (optional)	1 egg beaten

Heat oven to 400 degrees. Combine dry ingredients, add oil, milk, and egg.
Mix until blended. Pour into muffin tins. Bake 15–20 minutes.

Butter.

Pour a carton of whipping cream into a jar that is suitable for shaking. Take
turns shaking until butter is formed.

NOVEMBER SNACKS

Celery Stuffers. Children stuff celery with yogurt, cottage cheese, cheese spread,
or peanut butter.

Ants on a Log. Spread peanut butter on celery, then add raisins on top.

Crescent Roll Up. Let children roll up triangular pieces of refrigerator rolls to
form a crescent. Children can put 1 teaspoon of preserves or whole cranberry
relish on the roll before rolling the crescent.

Friendship Soup. Children wash, peel, and cut into pieces a vegetable brought
from home. Add vegetables to beef broth or vegetable/tomato broth. Cook until
vegetables are tender.

Things that Are Brown. Serve the following brown items for snack.

graham crackers with cream cheese or peanut butter

peanut butter on toast

chocolate pudding

cinammon on toast

pretzels

raisins

brown breakfast cereals

Things that Are Triangles.

bread cut into triangle shapes and spread with various toppings

cheese cut into triangles

graham crackers broken into triangles

Vegetables. Let children feel, taste, smell, and compare the shape and texture of a wide range of raw and cooked vegetables (e.g., popcorn, corn on the cob, cream style corn, canned and frozen corn). Cut up vegetables such as carrots, celery, or zucchini sticks, flowerettes of broccoli, raw or cooked green beans, pea pods, slices of cucumber or zucchini.

Tall and Short Snacks. Serve tall and short carrot, celery, and zucchini sticks, and tall and short bread sticks.

Peanut Butter and Banana Toast. Using toast or bread, top with peanut butter and slices of banana cut into triangles.

Snack Mix. Mix the following in a bowl: varied brown breakfast cereals (e.g., Cheerios™, Chex™), pretzels, raisins, peanuts, and chocolate chips.

DRAMATIC PLAY

Grocery Store. See November language activities for ideas on setting up a classroom grocery store. Allow children to use the store during free-choice time. You can be present to encourage language and verbal exchanges between children.

Fast Food Stand. Many fast food restaurants such as McDonald's, Wendy's, or Burger King are happy to lend props for a limited time. You will need uniforms— hats and jackets, food containers, cups, boxes, and bags. Draw a picture menu on the chalkboard. Provide a cash register and play money. The children can use the area for free-choice time, with a teacher helping to elicit language, or in more structured teacher-directed activities.

Goldilocks and the Three Bears. Read the story of *Goldilocks and the Three Bears* to the children several times throughout the month. As they begin to become familiar with the story, let them help to tell the story by "reading" the pictures. Tell them they will get to act out the story. Encourage them to find or make simple props they can use to help act out the story (e.g., three different sizes of bowls and spoons, chairs, and blankets). Keep the props simple. You can be the narrator. Allow children to attempt simple lines depending on their levels of language competence. You should be flexible in assigning roles. If interest is high, allow two Goldilocks or four bears, etc. Encourage all children to attempt something, and positively recognize their efforts.

CHILDREN'S LITERATURE

Alda, Arlene. *Matthew and His Daddy*
_____ . *Sonya's Mommy Works*
Berenstain, Stan. *Berenstain Bears and Too Much Junk Food*
Berenstain, Stan and Jan. *He Bear and She Bear*

Brown, Marc. *Arthur's Thanksgiving*
Brownstone, Cecily. *All Kinds of Mothers*
Child, Lydia. *Over the River and through the Woods*
Cohen, Miriam. *Don't Eat Too Much Turkey*

Dalgliesh, Alice. *The Thanksgiving Story*

Edelman, Elane. *I Love My Baby Sister (Most of the Time)*

Francoise. *The Thank-You Book*

Gleiter, Jan. *Color Rhymes*

Gundersheimer, Karen. *Colors to Know*

Hillert, Margaret. *Why We Have Thanksgiving*

Janice. *Little Bear's Thanksgiving*

Kroll, Steven. *One Tough Turkey*

Lakin, Patricia. *Don't Touch My Room*

Lerner, Sharon. *I Like Vegetables*

Manley, Deborah. *What Color Is It?*

Marilue. *Baby Bear's Thanksgiving*

Martin, Bill. *Brown Bear Brown Bear What Do You See?*

McGovern, Ann. *Stone Soup*

Moncure, Jane. *Tasting Party*

———. *Word Bird's Thanksgiving Words*

Overbeck, Cynthia. *The Vegetable Book*

Oxenbury, Helen. *Family and Mother's Helper*

Quackenbush, Robert. *Sheriff Sally Gopher and the Thanksgiving Caper*

Rayner, Mary. *Mrs. Pig's Bulk Buy*

Rogers, Lou. *The First Thanksgiving*

Seuling, Barbara. *What Kind of Family Is This?*

Sharmat, Marjorie. *One Terrific Thanksgiving*

Smith, Peter. *Jenny's Baby Brother*

Spinelli, Ellen. *Thanksgiving at the Tappletons*

Stevenson, James. *Fried Feathers for Thanksgiving*

Wantanabe, Shiego. *Where's My Daddy*

Westcott, Nadine. *The Giant Vegetable Garden*

Williams, Barbara. *Chester Chipmunk's Thanksgiving*

Evaluating November Concepts

Throughout the month, you should continue to update and record significant progress and/or changes made by the children. Use the checklists and individual logs to assess concepts taught in November. Record each child's receptive and/or expressive knowledge of the names of vegetables and foods taught throughout the month. Observe children at play and snack time to see if sharing and good manners have carried over into less structured times of the day. Encourage children to share family experiences.

You may want to keep samples of each child's work to share with parents and see growth over the course of the year. These samples can also be used to demonstrate significant strengths and check progress in weak areas that have been set as goals for the child on his/her IEP.

CONCEPTS FOR NOVEMBER (parent copy)

LANGUAGE AND VOCABULARY

1. Vegetable naming, sorting, learning about the grocery store
2. Family member jobs, clothing, and activities
3. Thanksgiving theme, sharing vocabulary
4. Cooking experiences
5. Color—brown
6. Directional and positional concepts—up and down

FINE MOTOR

Lacing, painting, cutting, coloring, stringing, tower building, play dough manipulation, making verticle lines, and path tracing.

PERCEPTION

Same and different, draw a person, puzzles, copying block, peg and bead designs, patterning

GROSS MOTOR

Games, jumping, ball handling, and balance

PREMATH

One-to-one correspondence, calendar activities, sorting, numbers and numerals 3 and 4, tall and short, triangle

CREATIVE DRAMATICS

SENSORY EXPERIENCES

NOVEMBER
Parent-child activities

SUN	MON	TUE	WED	THU	FRI	SAT
PRACTICE CUTTING, TEARING, AND FRINGING. BROWN BAGS ARE GREAT.	PRACTICE FOLDING NAPKINS INTO TRIANGLES. TALK ABOUT 3 SIDES AND 3 CORNERS. GIVE 1 TO EACH FAMILY MEMBER.	LET YOUR CHILD HELP SELECT AND PREPARE A VEGGIE FOR DINNER. (SCRUB POTATOES, SCRAPE CARROTS, ETC.)	CUT OUT PICTURE OF VEGETABLES FROM MAGAZINES OR GROCERY ADS. GIVE ON A PAPER PLATE.	THINK OF AND TASTE FOODS THAT CAN BE BROWN—BREAD, MUFFINS, COOKIES, POTATO SKINS, ETC.	FIND SOMETHING BROWN TO BRING TO SCHOOL.	FRINGE A BROWN PAPER BAG.
PRACTICE JUMPING ON 1 FOOT AND BOTH FEET. COUNT JUMPS.	DRAW A PICTURE OF EVERYONE IN THE FAMILY.	LISTEN TO A STORY, THEN RETELL IT BY "READING" THE PICTURES.	COMPARE TALL AND SHORT OBJECTS INSIDE AND OUTSIDE—SHORT BUSH, TALL REFRIGERATOR.	TOUCH AND COUNT THE TREES IN YOUR YARD.	SHARE A TOY WITH SOMEONE.	MAKE A SANDWICH, CUT IT INTO TRIANGLES, THEN SHARE AND ENJOY.
GO OUTSIDE. NAME WHAT'S "UP" IN THE SKY AND "DOWN" ON THE GROUND.	TRACE AROUND YOUR CHILD'S HAND TO GET TURKEY SHAPE. COLOR OR DECORATE.	HELP SORT FAMILY LAUNDRY— HIS OR HERS.	PLAY DRESS-UP WITH OLD CLOTHES.	LOOK AT THE FAMILY PICTURE ALBUM TOGETHER.	MAKE A BLANKET TENT TOGETHER. WHO FITS INSIDE?	FAMILY NIGHT— PLAY A GAME, READ A STORY, OR WATCH A TV SHOW WITH THE WHOLE FAMILY.
DINNER TIME ACTIVITY—TALK ABOUT NICE THINGS EACH FAMILY MEMBER DOES.	TALK ABOUT MANNERS AND WHAT CHILDREN CAN EXPECT TO HAPPEN ON TURKEY DAY.	FIND GREEN, YELLOW, AND BROWN VEGGIES AT THE GROCERY STORE.	PRACTICE USING CRAYONS, PENCILS, AND CHALK WITH SUPERVISION.	HAPPY THANKSGIVING! SING SONGS AND DO THANKSGIVING FINGERPLAYS.	STACK PLASTIC CONTAINERS— MAKE TALL AND SHORT BUILDINGS.	PRACTICE SNAPPING AND BUTTONING CLOTHES.
GO FOR A WALK. TOUCH SOMETHING SMOOTH AND ROUGH.	LISTEN TO MUSIC. MOVE TO THE RHYTHM.					

DECEMBER

CONCEPTS FOR DECEMBER

LANGUAGE AND VOCABULARY

1. Toys—naming, describing, classifying, and sorting
2. Instruments—naming, describing, playing, listening to, and comparing
3. Exposure to holiday vocabulary through the curriculum
4. Color—green
5. Directional and Positional concepts—bottom and top

Suggested field trips/classroom visitors: Visit a department store, music, or toy store. Take a walking trip to look at neighborhood decorations. Attend a musical production designed for children. Ask a musician to visit class.

FINE MOTOR: 1. MANIPULATION, AND 2. PREWRITING

Lacing, painting, cutting, gluing, bead stringing, play dough manipulation, block tower building, woodworking center, path tracing, horizontal line

PERCEPTION

Same and different, draw a person, puzzles, copying block, peg and bead designs, patterning

GROSS MOTOR

Organized games, ball handling (throwing and catching), movement experiences, scooter boards

PREMATH

One-to-one correspondence, calendar activities, sorting, number and numeral 5, small, medium, and large, square

SENSORY EXPERIENCES

Sense of touch at the exploration table—hard and soft

CREATIVE DRAMATICS

- *The Little Engine That Could*
- Department store

RECIPES

Holiday treats

SNACK

Foods that are green and square shaped, holiday-shaped snacks

SELF-HELP

Continue to work on putting on outerwear, work on fasteners, including zippers

REVIEW

Body parts, colors, directional concepts, and math concepts

ACTIVITIES FOR DECEMBER

LANGUAGE AND VOCABULARY

1. TOYS

Fun with Toys. Place a variety of toys or pictures of toys in a holiday wrapped box. Pull out one toy at a time. Encourage children to tell about each toy: its color, shape, and function.

Categorizing. Have children categorize toys: toys to build with, toys that move, toys that feel soft, etc. Expand thinking skills by having children identify a toy having two attributes, e.g., "Name a toy that feels soft and moves."

Comparing. Place two toys on the table. Children can be prompted to tell how they are the same and how they are different.

What Doesn't Belong?. Place three toys on the table, for example, a car, a doll, and a truck. Children name the toy that doesn't belong and tell why. Increase the difficulty level of this activity.

Toy Stories. Have children dictate a short story about their favorite toy. Pass out a different toy to each child. Have each child dictate a list of things that tells about their toy.

Riddles. Make up riddles for a variety of toys found in the classroom. Say the riddle and let children guess what toy was described. Children can then find the toy in the classroom.

Sharing. Display a variety of pictures showing children playing with toys. Talk about the importance of sharing. Role-play some situations involving sharing/cooperation and encourage children to tell what they saw, how the situation could have been resolved, etc.

Share a Toy Day. Have each child bring his/her favorite toy to school in a bag or box. Children can give clues about the toy with or without teacher prompting, while the other children attempt to guess the toy. The children can then share toys and enjoy each other's favorite toy.

Memory Game. Set up a toy store in the classroom. Children can be sent to shop for specific toys, for example, Jane went to the toy store, she bought a fire truck, a puzzle, and a game. Children can go to the store and buy the toys.

Inside-Outside. Show a variety of picture cards with toys cut from magazines or catalogs. Have children name each toy and decide if it is an inside or outside toy. Decide what toys can be used in both places.

2. INSTRUMENTS

Rhythm Instruments. Place rhythm instruments (rhythm sticks, triangles, bells, drums, cymbals, tambourines, maracas, and sand blocks) in a large box. Invite children to guess what's inside the box. Carefully remove one instrument at a time. See if the children can name the instrument and demonstrate how to make music the correct way. Stress the importance of handling the instrument gently and carefully.

Rhythm Experiments. After a general introduction of instruments, present one to three instruments during a lesson. Again encourage children to name the instrument, talk about what it is made of (wood, metal, etc.), and what the sound might remind them of, e.g., maracas—popping corn. Each child needs an opportunity to experiment with the different sounds the instruments make. Play the instrument loudly, softly, fast, and slow. Continue presenting new instruments throughout the week.

Play It, Name It. Play lively music. Give each child a rhythm instrument to pass around the circle as the music plays. When the music stops, each child should play his/her instrument and then name it.

Musician. Explain to children that a person who makes music is called a musician. Invite a musician to visit the classroom and play for the children. Children can learn that pianos, guitars, violins, trumpets, etc., are instruments they can learn to use.

Creative Sounds. Encourage children to use rhythm instruments to imitate familiar sounds heard in their environments: rain, thunder, footsteps, clocks ticking, horse's hooves, doors slamming, sirens, etc.

Listen and Play. Let children listen to music that has different tempos, rhythms, and sounds. Encourage them to talk about what they heard. Play the music again as children use their rhythm instruments in a manner that reflects their ideas.

Musical Memory. Play two or three instruments as the children watch. The children then repeat the order in which the instruments were played.

Marching Band. After children have had experience using the instruments, create a marching band. Try to play music of varying speeds. Change the volume of the music. Children can be encouraged to change the way they play their instruments as they follow the leader.

Musical Guessing Game. Set up a screen in your classroom which will conceal one child at a time. Have the child hide behind the screen and choose an instrument from a variety placed behind the screen. The child then plays the instrument and the other children guess what instrument is being played.

3. HOLIDAYS

Holidays. Talk with children about how their families celebrate holidays. Children can bring in family pictures showing Halloween, Thanksgiving, Chanukah, and Christmas themes. Be sure to talk about preparations, feelings of excitement, etc. During this holiday season, parents may be invited to visit the class and share Jewish, Christian, or other traditions, e.g., make potato latkes, play with a dreidel, decorate a small Christmas tree, sing Christmas carols.

Holiday Wish List. After talking with children about various kinds of gifts, discuss with them the fun of giving presents and helping to make others happy. The class can develop a wish list of presents they would like to give. Children can cut and glue gift pictures cut from magazines. Encourage them to share why they picked each gift.

Holiday Safety. Show pictures with holiday themes such as baking cookies, decorating a Christmas tree, plugging in holiday lights, lighting candles on a menorah. Talk about what is happening in each picture. Develop a list of simple safety rules with the children.

1. Never touch or get near the hot oven.
2. Never pull on tree ornaments or lights.
3. Candles are hot and can burn—stay away.
4. Let grown-ups unplug electrical cords.

Send the list home with students so safety can be reinforced at home.

Holiday Classification. This activity can be used after children are familiar with both Christmas and Chanukah. Bring in a variety of holiday objects such as ornaments, menorah, dreidels, candles, gift boxes, candy canes, etc. Have children identify the objects and sort them according to Chanukah, Christmas, or either holiday.

Chanukah or Christmas?. After children have been familiarized with both holidays through a variety of activities throughout the curriculum, have them classify activities as unique to Christmas, Chanukah, or either holiday. Use pictures that were cut from a magazine and mounted on paper or family snapshots that depict familiar holiday scenes such as lighting candles or decorating a tree. Have the children tell about the picture, then decide if it depicts Christmas, Chanukah, or either holiday (e.g., opening a gift).

4. COLOR—GREEN

Mystery Box. Introduce the color green by using the mystery box idea. Children name and tell about objects or answer "wh" questions (what, when, where, why, who) about the objects or pictures found in the box. Occasionally, surprise the children with an object that is not green and let them catch your mistake.

Green Hunt. Look in the classroom, within the school building, and in the neighborhood for green things. Later, see how many objects the children can recall from their observation walk.

Scavenger Hunt. Predistribute familiar green objects to other classrooms, e.g., green sweater, paint, socks, paper, book, tissues. On the day of the scavenger hunt, give children a simple picture cue sheet of objects they are to find. Divide the class in half—one group can go with the aide or parent volunteer and one group can go with the teacher. Each group brings back all the green objects they could find. A special green snack can await the children on their return.

Green Day. Choose a day to be "green day." Request that children wear green. Provide a green snack and do activities which include the color green throughout the day.

Class Collage. Ask children to look for a green object or magazine picture at home with their parents. Have them bring their green item to school. Have them talk about their green item. Then mount all items on one large sheet of paper or on a bulletin board to make a class collage or bulletin board.

Green Book. You can have children make individual books or a class book, depending on the age and developmental level of the students. Have children draw a picture or pictures of things that are green. Ask each child to tell about the picture(s) and write his/her words on the page with the picture. Assemble into books.

5. DIRECTIONAL AND POSITIONAL CONCEPTS—BOTTOM AND TOP

Bottoms and Tops. Introduce the directional and positional concepts of bottom and top. Name objects in the classroom (pictures, puzzles, tables, toys, doll clothes, etc.) and have children tell or show the bottom and top part of each object.

Body Parts. Play a game like Simon Says. Children can touch the bottom or top of parts of their body: arm, leg, head, and foot.

Toy Clean-Up. Empty a bookshelf in the classroom. Have children demonstrate receptive knowledge of the concepts of bottom and top by following auditory directions, e.g., "Put the books on the top shelf." Let children pretend to be the mom or dad as they direct their children in toy clean-up. As children give directions, assess their expressive knowledge of bottom and top.

Flannel Board. Divide a large flannel board in half with a chalk line or strip of masking tape. Have a variety of flannel cutouts on the table. Give each child a chance to be "teacher" and give directions to another—"Put a star at the top," "Put the rabbit at the bottom."

Bottom and Top. Decorate a tree, either real or on a flannel board or bulletin board. Provide children with ornaments and give them directions to place their ornament either at the bottom or top of the tree.

Float or Sink. Use your water table or a large clear bowl for this activity. Provide a variety of items that will either float at the *top* or sink to the *bottom*. After putting an object in the water, ask the children if the object stayed at the top of the water or went to the bottom.

FINE MOTOR

1. MANIPULATION

Playing with Toys. Allow children to move and manipulate the movable parts of toys. Children can dress and undress dolls, stack blocks, catch balls, assemble and disassemble toys, guide wheeled toys and vehicles around obstacles. The fine motor activities are endless.

Tops Off. Give children a variety of boxes, canisters, or jars. Have them match a top to a bottom, then snap on, place on, or twist on the top.

Lacing. Cut the shapes of simple toys, instruments, or holiday objects out of heavy tagboard. Laminate these pieces and then punch holes around the edges. Children can lace around the pieces. Laminate the fronts of old holiday cards and punch holes around the edges. Children can lace around the holiday cards.

Paper Chains. Give children strips of red and green paper to make paper chains. Children glue the loops together.

Garland. Let children string popcorn, Fruit Loops™, or macaroni to make holiday garlands.

Paper Plate Wreath. Cut out the center of a paper plate. Children can snip green paper or crumple green tissue to glue on the plate. They can add red holly berries with crumpled paper.

Lid Ornaments. Have children use colored rigatoni and other collage materials to glue to both sides of the plastic lids of coffee cans or margarine tubs. You then punch a hole in the lid and tie a piece of yarn on the ornament for hanging.

Pine Cones. Have children paint pine cones with a mixture of glue and green food coloring. They can decorate the pine cones with sequins, glitter, etc.

Collages. Children can cut and glue magazine pictures to make various collages. Examples include toys, instruments, or things that can be green.

Holiday Cards. Help children fold a sheet of paper in half to form a card. They can dip sponge pieces in red, white, and green paint to decorate their card.

Children can dictate a message inside and sign their name (scribbles are acceptable) to the card.

Wrapping Paper. Children dip cookie cutters into red and green paint. Make prints on tissue paper.

Roll a Wrap. Cover a large rolling pin with flocked wallpaper. Use rubber bands to keep the paper in place. Brush paint on the wallpaper. Children then roll their wrap on newsprint.

Marble Tree. Place a construction paper green Christmas tree in a shirt box. Have children drop a small dab of red, yellow, and blue paint onto the tree. Put a marble in the box. As children move the box, they will create an instant garland.

Chanukah Candle. Have children paint a paper towel or toilet tissue tube. Children can crumple yellow tissue paper to stuff in the tube to "light" the candle.

Color a Cane. Draw a large candy cane on white paper. Children color the candy alternating with their red and green crayons. This activity strengthens visual perception.

Spin a Dreidel. Prepare a small square of tagboard for each child. Punch a hole in the middle of the square. Children decorate the square dreidel with crayons or markers. Have children put a pencil through the hole and help them spin their dreidel.

Shaker. Have children put rice, dried beans, peas, etc., in a small milk carton. Then staple on a tongue depressor for a handle and staple the milk carton securely across the opening. Children then decorate the shaker with paint, or glue on pieces of holiday wrapping paper.

Cutting Squares. Have children practice cutting little squares from pieces of sandwich-sized bread.

Templates. Let children use commercially prepared or teacher-made templates to make squares and holiday symbols. Some children may want to color and cut out their pictures.

Stacking. Children can stack large cardboard boxes or various sized square wooden blocks.

Guitars. Have children stretch four large rubber bands across a cigar box, shoebox, tissue box, etc. They will enjoy plucking the rubber bands to hear the sounds they produce.

Chanuka Menorah 1. Give children construction paper that has nine candles and flames cut out. Also provide various colors of cellophane for children to glue over the cut out portion. Hang in a window.

Chanukah Menorah 2. Provide long, thin rectangle shapes or have children cut strips. Glue on construction paper. Have children squeeze a drop of glue above the strips, and shake on glitter to make the flames.

Drums. Ask children to bring empty oatmeal boxes or coffee cans. Decorate them and use them for drums. Children can play the drums with their hands or make drumsticks from unsharpened pencils or tongue depressors.

Kazoos. Make kazoos out of toilet tissue tubes and wax paper. Have children decorate their tube. Give them each a square of wax paper. Have them cover one end of the tube with the paper and secure it in place with a rubber band.

Bells. With a large needle and yarn, have children sew three to four bells onto a strip of felt. Use the bells for music and rhythm activities.

Sponge Printing. Cut sponges into various holiday, instrument, or toy shapes. Dip into paint and print onto paper. To extend the activity, shapes can be labeled and classified into things to play with, instruments, or holiday items.

Glitter and Glue. Have children make pictures or designs with a squeezable glue bottle. Have them sprinkle glitter over the glue to complete their designs. Shake off excess glue and dry.

Decorate a Tree. Provide children with cutout green triangles or have them cut their own. Have them squeeze an eye dropper into paint and then drop onto the tree to decorate it.

Easel Painting. This month at the easel, try some of the following ideas. Paint with green paint, draw holiday shapes on easel paper, use negative space holiday shapes (cut holiday shapes out of the easel paper and have children paint around the cutout portion). Try varying the consistency of the paint from thick to thin. Have children practice painting squares at the easel.

Finger Painting. Finger paint with different shades of green paint. Apply paint either directly to finger paint paper, or finger paint on the table and blot it into construction paper.

Stockings. Provide children with stockings cut from construction paper or tagboard. Punch holes in the stockings and have children lace them. Have children decorate the top of the stocking with cotton balls.

Fine Motor Center. You can extend the holiday theme to your fine motor center. The color green and the square shape can also be reinforced daily at this center. Provide shapes for children to glue collage materials on. Shapes might include wreaths, menorahs, gingerbread boys, gifts, dreidels, triangle shapes for trees, and candles. Things to glue onto the shapes include small squares of tissue paper, ribbon, pine cones, pieces of fabric, raisins, small candies, cotton balls, and bells. Provide gift boxes for stacking and tower building. Provide boxes, wrapping paper, tape, scissors, and ribbon for wrapping packages. In one of your December activities, have children make green play dough. Use it at the fine motor center. Provide holiday-shaped cookie cutters for use with the play dough. String popcorn, green noodles, bells, or beads to decorate the classroom.

Woodworking Center. Woodworking involves many developmental areas. Fine motor skills are utilized when the child works with tools: visual motor skills are encouraged when the child pounds a nail with a hammer; perceptual skills are strengthened when the child tries to copy a model or follow a pattern with woodworking materials. Socialization and language skills are enhanced as children work side by side, talk about what they are creating, share materials, and problem solve. Premath skills are used as children measure lengths and widths, count nails, screws, or the number of times it takes to pound their nails. Children see woodworking as a time to feel grown up using adult tools and supplies. Self-concepts are strengthened, and the activity is enjoyed by all. Children are allowed to explore various textures, explore the differences between hard and soft, rough and smooth, and many other sensory concepts. Different sounds can be explored such as sawing, hammering, and drilling. The learning opportunities are virtually endless at the woodworking center. Safety at this center must be planned in advance. Rules must be discussed and enforced. If possible, you, the aide, or classroom volunteer should be present to supervise the children at the woodworking center. Safety rules can be brainstormed by the class, listed by you, or you may choose a combination of both. Be sure to include the number of children allowed at the center at one time, safe use of tools, and the importance of putting tools in the proper storage area when finished.

The following is a list of materials you will want to include at the center.

tree stumps for pounding nails and screwing	hand drill
wood scraps—free of splinters	glue
cardboard	spools
styrofoam	bottle caps
hammer	golf tees
flat-head nails of various sizes	rubber bands
screwdriver	sandpaper
screws	pliers
saw	

To avoid overwhelming children, bring out materials gradually, over time. You may wish to start by hammering nails into a tree stump or pushing golf tees into styrofoam and gradually increase the complexity of the materials.

2. PREWRITING

Dot to Dot. Have children use pencils, crayons, or markers to complete simple dot to dot pictures of toys, instruments, and holiday symbols.

Driving. Draw several thick horizontal lines on a large piece of paper with felt-tip pens. Children can follow the line with their finger moving from left to right. They can then dip the wheels of a small plastic car into a shallow pan of paint and "drive" their car on the road.

Path Tracing. Prepare several horizontal paths for the children to follow. They may use a crayon, pencil, or marker. Draw a line from the drum to the stick, from the doll to the girl, etc.

Stencils. Provide stencils of holiday shapes, instruments, and toys for children to use with markers, crayons, pencils, or chalk.

Chalkboard. Allow children to use the chalkboard to practice making horizontal and vertical lines. Show children how to connect the lines to make a square.

Play Dough. Practice forming horizontal lines and squares using play dough.

PERCEPTION

Name the Instrument. Place three instruments in front of the children. Play and name each instrument. Children close their eyes as you play one instrument. Children name the instrument that was played.

Feel the Music. Place a rhythm instrument in a pillowcase. Let children feel the shape of the instrument and guess what it is. You may place three instruments or pictures of instruments on the table that children can use as visual cues.

Loud-Soft. Let children repeat simple patterns made using rhythm instruments, e.g., loud, soft, loud, soft or loud, loud, soft, loud, loud, soft.

Where Is the Sound?. Children sit in a circle with the same instrument placed in front of them. Children are to close or cover their eyes. Tap the shoulder of one child who is to make a sound with the instrument. Children then open their eyes, guess where the sound came from, and who made it.

Sorting Activities. Use objects or pictures that children can sort into categories, such as instruments and not instruments, toys and not toys, etc.

Paper Chain Patterning. Children can make paper chains following two or three color patterns with strips of construction paper, e.g., red, white, green, red, white, green or red, green, green, red, green, green.

Holiday Matching. Prepare about fifteen pairs of ornaments, decorated trees, presents, etc. Pairs should differ in obvious ways. Children find and match the objects that are the same. Vary the activity by placing three holiday cards on the table. The child must indicate which one is different.

Gingerbread Man. Children can use raisins to add facial features to a paper gingerbread man or one that has been cut out from play dough or cookie dough.

Fishing. Using fish prepared for colors and shapes (see November activities, p. 93), children can fish for only green fish or for only square fish.

Will It Fit?. Place several different sizes of square-shaped boxes and various toys and instruments on the table. Let the children decide what toy or instrument would fit in each box.

Shaker Sounds. Children can compare the sounds made by their shaker instruments (see FINE MOTOR, p. 115). Children can try to guess what is inside each child's shaker, which sounds high, low, loud, or soft.

Feel a Square. Place a circle, triangle, and square-shaped attribute block in the feely box or bag. Children touch the shapes and bring out only the square.

Shape Patterns. Provide plastic attribute blocks, flannel pieces, or construction paper cut into circle, triangle, and square-shaped pieces. Let children copy, continue, or create their own patterns with two or three shapes.

Shape It. Give children various sizes of plastic attribute blocks and flannel pieces cut into three shapes: circle, triangle, and square. Children use the shapes to copy or make pictures of train engines, houses, people, etc.

Geoboards. Help children to reproduce simple shapes, including squares and triangles, by stretching rubber bands on a commercial geoboard. This activity also strengthens fine motor skills.

Santa's Feely Bag. Fill a pillowcase with familiar toys. Have children reach in and feel a toy and then try to guess what it is, using only their sense of touch. To make the activity easier, let the children watch you fill the bag and name the toys as you put them in.

How I Look in December. Have children draw pictures of themselves to add to their books. If children are developmentally able, have them draw themselves in a favorite holiday scene.

Musical Hands. Have the children use their hands as instruments, and clap patterns. Begin with simple patterns such as two to three consecutive claps. Make the patterns more difficult by adding pauses or varying the rhythm of claps. Allow children the opportunity to clap a pattern for classmates to follow.

Loud and Soft Sounds. Provide pictures of animals or objects which produce either loud or soft sounds. Have children tell what the picture is and put it in the appropriate pile for things that sound loud or things that sound soft.

Perception Center. At your perception center, use the holiday theme and colors. Puzzles might include pictures depicting holiday scenes, e.g., gifts, menorahs, Christmas trees, Santa, etc. Peg patterns might include green triangles (trees), menorah shapes, candles, or other simple holiday shapes. Block patterns can also utilize the holiday theme. Provide paper or flannel shapes at the center to make Santa's parts (hat, face, bag, boots, mittens) to a premade Santa form. Add auditory perception to the center by providing a tape of familiar holiday sounds for children to identify. Include bells, familiar songs (Hanukah and Christmas), Santa's voice, *Ho, Ho, Ho,* a sled moving through snow, a crackling fire.

GROSS MOTOR

Creative Movement 1. Have children listen to music that has different tempos, rhythms, and sounds. Pass out scarves or lengths of crepe paper and encourage children to move to the music.

Creative Movement 2. Have children listen to music that has different tempos, rhythms, and sounds. Encourage children to hop, jump, skip, gallop, or move specific body parts as they listen to the music.

Toy Movement. Give children the opportunity to move like a certain toy, such as a stuffed animal, truck, toy soldier, airplane, etc. Play music and have a toy parade.

People Shapes. Children will enjoy experimenting with their bodies to form the shapes square, triangle, and circle.

Red Light, Green Light. Show children a red and green colored card. Help them learn that green means "go" and read means "stop." Hold up one sign at a time as children move or stop by "reading" the color cards.

Bottom to Top. Starting at the bottom, have children walk or climb to the top of a slide, the stairs, or other playground equipment.

Ball Throwing. Children should have experiences participating in a wide range of ball-throwing activities. Balls should range in size from small tennis balls to large, rubber playground balls. Some activities could include:

> Throw a ball as high as they can.
> Throw a ball as far as they can.
> Throw a ball at a target.
> Throw a ball into a box or basket.
> Throw a ball through hoops from varying distances.

Encourage children to track the ball as soon as it leaves their hands. Children can practice throwing underhand and overhand.

Ball Catching. Children can practice catching big, soft balls thrown by you or by a partner. Start at about 3 feet and gradually move farther apart. Vary the type and size of the balls children use. Children can attempt to catch balls bounced to them or thrown to them.

Children will catch a ball with their arms, hands, and chest before being able to catch a ball with their hands.

Dodge Ball. Have one child stand in the center of a circle of children. The child in the middle tries to throw a ball and touch those in the circle. Use a soft Nerf™ ball or beach ball. Children in the circle move around the circle to avoid being hit.

Catch around the Circle. A child or the teacher stands in the center of a circle of children. The middle person rolls, bounces or throws a ball to a child standing in the circle. Encourage children to watch carefully and be ready for their turn.

All by Myself. Give each child a ball. Have him/her gently toss the ball into the air and try to catch it with two hands. Vary the activity. Have the child bounce the ball about waist high and try to catch it.

Scooter Boards. Give children opportunities to use alternating arm and leg movements as they move on scooter boards. Children will also enjoy scooter board relays.

1. Lay chest on board. Hold feet off the floor. Arms pull forward using a left-right alternating swimming motion.
2. Sit on scooter board. Place hands securely at the sides of the board. Pull forward with feet using a left-right alternating motion.
3. Sit on scooter board. Place hands securely at the sides of the board. Move backwards with feet using a left-right alternating motion.
4. Kneel on scooter board. Lean forward and use hands and arms to move forward using a left-right alternating motion.

Bean Bags. Play simple bean bag games. To reinforce the square shape, have children toss a bean bag into a square drawn on the floor. To reinforce the color green, play with green bean bags. Make up bean bag relay games in which children throw bean bags to team mates, or one child throws the bean bag and another child runs for it. Have children move to music while balancing a bean bag on their heads, shoulders, or other body parts.

Whistle Stop. Have the children move in a directed way such as run, jump, skip, or hop. When they hear the whistle blow, they stop moving.

Looby Loo. Sing and play "Here We Go Looby Loo." This game is an excellent way to review body parts, follow directions, and move to music.

SENSORY EXPERIENCES

Hard and Soft. During December, reinforce the sensory concepts of hard and soft.

Soft cotton is a natural material to use for art projects. Use it for snow, Santa's beard, and decorations on your holiday bulletin boards. The concept of hard will naturally be reinforced at the woodworking center. Many substances found there are hard, such as wood, tree stumps, nails, hammers.

Hard and soft can also be stressed during holiday cooking activities. Discuss the ingredients and utensils which feel hard or soft.

Exploration Table. At the exploration table, include hard and soft substances for touching, manipulating, pouring, and utilizing. Some examples might include gravel, coins, woodchips, cotton balls, shaving cream, feathers, small cars and trucks, pasta shells and noodles, soft fabric swatches, foam rubber, sawdust.

Ordering. Give children an opportunity to order at least three different sizes of measuring spoons and cups used at the sensory table.

Cornstarch Mixture "Goop." Have children help mix two parts cornstarch with one part water at the sensory table. They may want to add a few drops of green food coloring. Allow children to add too much water or more cornstarch to see what happens. When children squeeze and manipulate the crumbly/soupy mixture, the consistency changes will amaze them.

Shapes and Faces. Let children make shapes and faces in the sand, woodchips, shaving cream, rice, or other such substances found at the sensory table.

PREMATH

Musical One-to-One Correspondence. Ring bells, clang cymbals, or beat the drum, one to five times as children count the number of sounds. Give each child an opportunity to ring the bells five times, or play other instruments as the other children count.

Dice Game. Make a large die from a small, cube-shaped container. Draw from one to five dots on each side. Children toss the die and clap whatever number they tossed. Vary the activity by using musical instruments to play the specified number of times.

Count the Candles. Prepare several pictures of Chanukah menorahs. Let children touch and count how many candles are lit and how many are not lit.

Ordering Toys. Place an assortment of toys on a table or rug. Children can arrange the toys from largest to smallest. This is also a visual perception task.

Toy Math. Let children touch and count toys. Count the trucks, the blocks, the stuffed animals, dolls, etc.

Sort by Size. Children can sort classroom instruments and toys by size: large, medium, and small. Have available a variety of pictures which might include household objects or animals. Children can sort the pictures to extend the activity. This activity strengthens perception.

One-to-One Correspondence. Cut out several large candle shapes and the same number of flames. Have children give each candle a flame.

Set of Five. Fold a piece of 18- by 24-inch paper into six sections and number the sections 0 through 5. Have children cut and glue one magazine picture into each section. They can find and make a set of five toys, five instruments, etc. They should touch and count each set made.

December Calendar. Use cutouts of toys, instruments, or holiday symbols for the December calendar. Number the cutouts so a pattern is formed by the shape and/or the color. Children can anticipate what symbol will be next. You may want to place a menorah and a Christmas tree on the correct dates. Children will love to count how many days until Chanukah and Christmas.

Decorate a Tree. Cut out a large Christmas tree from paper or flannel. Children can decorate the tree with stickers or small flannel ornaments. Give each child a specific number of ornaments to place on the tree.

Square. Introduce the square shape made from felt or sandpaper. Have children touch the shape and compare it to the circle and triangle shapes already introduced. Have children touch and count the sides and corners.

Square Sorting. Cut out three sizes of squares and laminate. Children can sort by size: large, medium, and small.

Making Squares. Give children clothespins, straws, toothpicks, or Popsicle™ sticks to form the square shape. They may want to glue their square on paper.

Square Hunt. Look in the classroom or walk outdoors to find and label objects that are square shaped. Extend the activity by giving children riddles about square-shaped objects, e.g., "I'm thinking of something square. It plays records. What is it?"

Bean Bag Toss. Cut out several large circles, triangles, and squares. Children can stand in a circle or behind a line and take turns throwing their bean bag on a shape and then naming it.

Three Bears. Tell the story of *Goldilocks and the Three Bears* using flannel pieces. When the story is over, help children give the large bed, chair, and bowl of porridge to Papa Bear, the middle-sized pieces to Mama Bear, etc. Stress the words *large, medium,* and *small.*

Holiday Walk. Take a walk around the school neighborhood. Count the houses that have lights, wreaths, those with Christmas trees, and those with 3D holiday decorations.

Dice Match. Use the die you prepared for the dice game activity (p. 122). Have children shake the die and match the number on the die by finding the same number of objects. For example, if a child shakes three, she/he might collect three toys from around the room. If she/he shakes five, she/he might collect five musical instruments. Allow the child to choose what category of items to collect.

Dominoes. There are many commercially prepared domino sets which match numbers, animals, etc. Use one of these sets or make your own. Prepare cards with one to five dots on them. Children find a matching card and place it next to the number they are trying to match. Use a minimum of twenty to twenty-five cards.

What Comes Next?. In a wrapped box with a removable lid, provide three to five smaller boxes which children can order by size. They can build a tower with the largest box on the bottom, building from bottom to top, or simply order the boxes in a row. Try putting other objects that can be ordered by size in the gift-wrapped box—e.g., small, medium, and large cars, dolls of varying sizes, or different sized spoons.

Bingo. Prepare a Bingo game using numerals and/or numbers from one to five. Separate your Bingo cards into four sections, each containing a numeral or set from 1 to 5. You or a child calls out numerals 1 to 5 while the players cover the appropriate sections of their cards.

SONGS AND FINGERPLAYS

Christmas Season—(tune: "Are You Sleeping?").

Christmas Season, Christmas Season, will it come? So much fun.
Wrapping all the presents, eating tasty cookies.
Yum, yum, yum. Yum, yum, yum.

Sleigh bells ringing, children singing
In the night, oh so bright.
I can't wait for Santa, Jolly, jolly fat man
Ho, ho, ho! Ho, ho, ho!

We Wish You a Merry Christmas.

(Chorus)
We wish you a merry Christmas,
We wish you a merry Christmas,
We wish you a merry Christmas,
And a happy New Year.
(Verse 1)
Let's all do a little clapping,
Let's all do a little clapping,
Let's all do a little clapping,
and spread Christmas cheer.

(Other verses could include snapping, tapping, jumping, twirling, etc.
Substitute words *happy Chanukah* for Merry Christmas.)

Ring the Bells (tune: "Row Your Boat").

Ring, ring, ring the bells
Ring them loud and clear.
To tell the children everywhere
That Christmas time is here.

Ring, ring, ring the bells
Around Santa's sleigh,
He's bring children everywhere
Games and toys for play.

I Have a Little Dreidel.

I have a little dreidel
I made it out of clay,

and when it's good and ready
Oh dreidel, I shall play.
I made it out clay
Dreidel, dreidel, dreidel
Now it's time to play.

Big Red Truck (tune: "Mulberry Bush").

I give my friend a big red truck,
A big red truck, a big red truck.
I give my friend a big red truck,
Because I want to share.

(Substitute the name of other toys or instruments.)

When Santa Comes.

When Santa comes down the chimney (Move hands down.)
I would like to peek. (Peek through fingers.)
But he'll never come, no never (Shake head and finger.)
Until I'm fast asleep. (palms together beside head)

Santa's Shop.

Here is Santa's workshop (Form peak with both hands.)
Here is Santa Claus (Hold up thumbs.)
Here are Santa's little elves (Wiggle fingers.)
Putting toys upon the shelves.

Christmas Bells.

Five little bells, hanging in a row.
The first one said, "Ring me slow."
The second one said, "Ring me fast."
The third one said, "Ring me loud."
The fourth one said, "Ring me soft."
The fifth one said, "I'm like a chime."
Which you can ring at Christmastime.

Include traditional holiday songs: *Jingle Bells, Rudolph, the Red-Nosed Reindeer, Up on the House Top.*

RECIPES

Oats and Honey Candy.

1 cup honey	1 1/2 cup nuts
1 1/2 teaspoon peanut butter	1 1/2 cup raisins
1 1/2 cup powdered milk	1 cup oat flakes

Combine and mix the above ingredients. Shape into walnut-sized balls or shape into logs. Refrigerate and slice before serving.

Potato Latkes.

4 medium potatoes	1/2 teaspoon pepper
1 small onion	1/2 cup oil
1/2 cup Bisquick™ or pancake mix	2 tablespoons sour cream
1 teaspoon salt	2 eggs

Peel potatoes and onion, grate them into a bowl. Pour off any extra liquid. Add eggs, pancake mix, sour cream, salt, and pepper and mix well. Heat oil until it sizzles. Drop the batter into the oil by tablespoonfuls. Flatten each pancake with a spatula. When pancakes are golden brown, turn carefully. Serve with sour cream, applesauce, or plain.

Honey Nut Granola.

2 1/2 cups uncooked oats	1/3 cup margarine
1/2 cup firm brown sugar	1 teaspoon cinnamon
1/2 cup sunflower seeds or chopped nuts	1/2 cup raisins, apricots, or
1/2 cup honey	dates

Preheat oven to 325 degrees. Combine all ingredients in a large bowl, except raisins. Mix well. Bake in a lightly greased 9″ × 13″ pan for 20–25 minutes, stirring occasionally. Stir in raisins. Spread mixture onto an ungreased cookie sheet to cool. Store in a cool, dry place or refrigerate.

Hershey Kiss ™ Peanut Butter Cookies.

1 3/4 cup flour	1 egg
2 tablespoons milk	1/2 cup sugar
1/2 cup brown sugar	1 teaspoon vanilla
1/2 cup margarine	1 teaspoon soda
1/2 cup peanut butter	

Combine all ingredients except kisses. Shape into balls and roll in sugar. Bake at 375 degrees for 10 to 12 minutes. Immediately after cookies come out of oven, push kiss into middle of each cookie. Makes about 4 dozen cookies.

Sugar Cookies (nonroll dough).

1 cup margarine	1 teaspoon vanilla
5 tablespoons sugar	2 cups flour
Pinch of salt	

Cream margarine, sugar, salt, and vanilla. Gradually mix in flour. Refrigerate dough about 20 minutes. Roll dough into small balls and flatten with a sugar-dipped fork in a criss-cross fashion. Bake in a 350-degree oven for approximately 15 minutes.

Cranraspberry Holiday Punch.

1 6-ounce can frozen lemonade	1 10-ounce package frozen raspberries
3 cans water	1 32-ounce bottle ginger ale
1 quart cranraspberry juice	

In a punch bowl, mix lemonade, water, and juice together. Add raspberries and pour in ginger ale.

Rice Krispie ™ Squares.

> 1/4 cup margarine
> 1 package (10 ounces) or 4 cups miniature marshmallows
> 6 cups Rice Krispies™ cereal

Melt margarine over low heat. Add marshmallows and stir until melted. Remove from heat. Add cereal stir until well coated. Press mixture into a buttered 13″ × 9″ pan. Cut into squares when cool. Works well in an electric skillet used right in the classroom.

DECEMBER SNACKS

Green Snacks.

Pistachio pudding

Celery and green pepper strips
    served with dip

Kiwi fruit

Honeydew melon

Granny Smith apples

Lime Jello℗

Grapes

Pickles, olives

Lettuce

Square-shaped Snacks.

> Wheat thins
>
> Saltines
>
> Graham crackers, etc.
>
> Sandwich bread can be cut into four small squares and topped with jelly, cream cheese, flavored cream cheese, and other toppings to make mini sandwiches.
>
> Children create hors d'oeuvres with the breads and spreads by adding toppings of olives or fresh fruit.

Holiday-shaped Snacks. Use holiday cookie cutters on different varieties of breads, waffles, or cheeses. Enjoy eating all the delicious foods prepared from the December list of holiday foods and treats!

DRAMATIC PLAY

The Little Engine That Could. Children will enjoy dramatizing the story by W. Piper. Any number of children can easily participate. Simplify the story so children can focus on the sounds and movements of the toys and engines, and the repitition of the little engine "I think I can, I think I can." Allow children to name a toy or engine they would like to be. Children can hold a toy as a prop or move and make the sound of a toy, e.g., dolls cry ma-ma, drum beats da-dum, da-dum. Train engins might wear an engineer's hat, hold a whistle, or make the *choo choo* sounds as they rumble along a chalk-drawn track. Children would enjoy getting "over the mountain" by climbing up and sliding down a classroom slide.

Department Store. In your creative dramatics/play area, set up a department store for creative dramatics. Children can role-play many different roles including shoppers, clerks, cash register operators, Santa Claus and his helpers, gift wrappers, etc. Within the department store setting, children can play independently, you or volunteers can play and facilitate language and vocabulary, or you can use the center for structured lessons in the various areas of the curriculum.

Include as many departments as your space allows, or change departments periodically. Include departments for clothes, shoes, toys, housewares, foods, jewelry, accessories, sporting goods, and furniture. If space allows, you might set up a small restaurant area. Props include cash registers, money, bags, boxes, and the items belonging in each department.

CHILDREN'S LITERATURE

Adler, David A. *A Picture Book of Hanukkah*

Baylor, Byron. *Plink, Plink, Plink*

Bemelmans, Ludwig. *Madeline's Christmas*

Berenstain, Janice and Stan. *The Berenstain Bears' Christmas Tree*

Brett, Jan. *Twelve Days of Christmas*

Burstein, Chaya. *Hanukkah Cat*

Charette, Beverly Rae. *The Story of Chanukah for Children*

Daly, Eileen. *Rudolph the Rednosed Reindeer*

Daly, Niki. *Vim the Rag Mouse*

Donaldson, Lois. *Karl's Wooden Horse*

Duke, Kate. *What Bounces*

Fisher, Arleen L. *My First Hanukkah Book*

Freeman, Don. *Beady Bear*

_____ . *Corduroy*

_____ . *A Pocket for Corduroy*

Geliman, Ellie. *It's Chanukah*

Glovach, Linda. *The Little Witch's Christmas Book*

Gorsline, Douglas. *The Night before Christmas*

Greene, Jacqueline D. *The Hanukkah Tooth*

Grifalconi, Ann. *The Toy Trumpet*

Grimm. *The Elves and the Shoemaker*

Hastings, Evelyn Belmont. *The Department Store*

Hayward, Linda. *The Curious Little Kitten's First Christmas*

Hill. *Where's Spot?*

Hill. *Spot's First Christmas*

Hoban, Lillian. *Arthur's Christmas Cookies*

Hoff, Sydney. *Santa's Moose*

_____ . *Where's Prancer?*

Hutchins, Pat. *The Best Train Set Ever*

Isadora, Rachel. *Ben's Trumpet*

Keats, Ezra Jack. *Apt. 3*

Kellogg, Stephen. *Mystery of the Magic Green Ball*

Kredenser, Gail. *One Dancing Drum*

Lionni, Leo. *Alexander and the Windup Mouse*

_____ . *Geraldine, the Music Mouse*

Mayer, Mercer. *Merry Christmas Mom and Dad*

McClosky, Robert. *Lentil*

McGovern, Ann. *Too Much Sound*

McGuire, Leslie. *Bialosky's Christmas*

McPhail, David. *Mistletoe*

_____ . *The Train*

Moncure, Jane B. *Christmas Is a Happy Time*

Nakatani, Chiyoko. *My Teddy Bear*

North, Carol. *The Christmas Sled*

_____ . *The Christmas Tree Book*

O'Brien, Anne Sibley. *Where's My Truck?*

Peppe, Rodney. *Little Wheels*

Piper, W. *The Little Engine That Could*

Politi, Leo. *Mr. Fong's Toy Shop*

Psier, Peter. *Crash! Bang! Boom!*

Rice, Eve. *New Blue Shoes*

Rockwell, A., and Rockwell, F. *The Tool Box*

Russell, Betty. *Big Store, Funny Door*

Scarry, Patrica M. *Sweet Smell of Christmas*

_____ . *Christmas Mice*

_____ . *The Best Christmas Book Ever*

Simon, Norma. *Hanukkah in My House*

Stecher, Miriam, and Kandell, Alice. *Max, the Music Maker*

Steiner, Charlotte. *Pete and Pete*

Stephenson, Dorothy. *The Night it Rained Toys*

Thelen, Gerda. *The Toy Maker*

Walsh, Ellen Stoll. *Brunus and the New Bear*

Wildsmith, B. *The Twelve Days of Christmas*

Wright, Betty. *Teddy Bear's Book of 1, 2, 3*

Wright, Dare. *Holiday for Edith and the Bears*

Zaffo, George. *The Giant Nursery Book of Things That Work*

Zinnemann-Hope, Pam. *Let's Go Shopping*

Zolotow, Charlotte. *William's Doll*

Evaluating December Concepts

Throughout the month, continue to update and record significant progress and/or changes made by the children. Use the checklists and individual logs.

Because toys are stressed in many of the activities in December, this is an excellent time to observe systematically children at play time. You can gain valuable information in forming a more complete picture about the total child. Play time provides clues about the child's interests, attention span, stage of play development, social skills (i.e., ability to share and take turns), ability to manipulate toys, and imaginative and creative use of toys. Keep observations objective and document any important data.

LANGUAGE AND VOCABULARY

1. Toys—naming, describing, classifying, and sorting
2. Instruments—naming, describing, playing, listening to, and comparing
3. Exposure to holiday vocabulary
4. Cooking experiences
5. Color—green
6. Directional and positional concepts—bottom and top

FINE MOTOR

Lacing, painting, cutting, gluing, bead stringing, play dough manipulation, tower building, woodworking center, path tracing, horizontal line

PERCEPTION

Same and different, draw a person, puzzles, copying block, peg and bead designs, patterning

GROSS MOTOR

Organized games, ball handling (throwing and catching), movement experiences, scooter boards

PREMATH

One-to-one correspondence, calendar activities, sorting, number and numeral 5, small, medium, and large, square

CREATIVE DRAMATICS

SENSORY EXPERIENCES

DECEMBER
Parent-child activities

SUN	MON	TUE	WED	THU	FRI	SAT
MAKE GREEN JELLO WITH YOUR CHILD.	PLAY WITH AN "OLD" FAMILIAR TOY IN A NEW WAY.	LOOK THROUGH A CATALOG. MAKE A WISH LIST TOGETHER.	HAPPY CHANUKAH!	VISIT THE LIBRARY. SELECT SOME HOLIDAY BOOKS.	PLACE WAXED PAPER OVER A COMB TO MAKE A KAZOO. HUM.	PRACTICE DECEMBER SONGS AND FINGERPLAYS.
CUT A SANDWICH INTO 4 SMALL SQUARES.	FILL GLASSES WITH DIFFERENT AMOUNTS OF WATER. TAP WITH A SPOON.	LOOK FOR GREEN FRUITS AND VEGETABLES AT THE GROCERY STORE.	FIND AND NAME 5 GREEN THINGS IN THE HOUSE.	READ HOLIDAY STORIES TOGETHER. ANSWER "WH" QUESTIONS.	NAME AS MANY TOYS AS YOU CAN THINK OF.	FILL BALLOONS WITH DIFFERENT SUBSTANCES: RICE, SALT, ETC. SHAKE.
COLOR A PICTURE FOR SOMEONE SPECIAL.	SORT TOYS BY SIZE—LARGE, MEDIUM, AND SMALL.	SPRAY SHAVING CREAM IN THE BATH TUB. DRAW A PERSON MAKING DESIGNS.	CUT OR SNIP SCRAPS OF WRAPPING PAPER.	NAME ORNAMENTS FOUND AT THE TOP OF THE TREE.	WRAP A PRESENT. TALK ABOUT WHAT YOU DO FIRST, NEXT, AND LAST.	LET YOUR CHILD ASSIST WITH HOLIDAY BAKING.
TAKE A WINTER WALK. LOOK AT HOLIDAY DECORATIONS.	COUNT GIFTS UNDER THE TREE.	PREPARE A SNACK TO LEAVE FOR SANTA. LEAVE A SQUARE NAPKIN.	MERRY CHRISTMAS!	MAKE HOT CHOCOLATE TOGETHER AND STIR WITH A CANDY CANE.	PLAY A GAME WITH THE WHOLE FAMILY.	CLEAN OUT THE TOY BOX. WHAT'S AT THE BOTTOM?
PLAY WITH PLAY DOUGH AND COOKIE CUTTERS.	LISTEN TO MUSIC. MARCH, TAP, OR CLAP TO THE RHYTHM.	TALK ABOUT A NEW YEAR. DISPLAY A CALENDAR.				

JANUARY

CONCEPTS FOR JANUARY

LANGUAGE AND VOCABULARY

1. Winter—weather and nature's changes, clothing, activities, and vocabulary
2. Pets—naming, describing, comparing, sounds pets make, pet care, safety with pets
3. Library—jobs of the librarian, things we read
4. Go Togethers—matching things that go together and explaining why, e.g., hand—mitten
5. Color—white
6. Directional and Positional Concepts—over and under

Suggested field trips/classroom visitors: Visit a pet store or the library. Ask a veterinarian to visit class. Parents can bring pets to school on Pet Day.

FINE MOTOR: 1. MANIPULATION, AND 2. PREWRITING

Lacing, painting, coloring, gluing, play dough manipulation, cutting, block tower building, woodworking center, path tracing, *H* stroke and cross +

PERCEPTION

Same and different, draw a person, puzzles, copying block, peg and bead designs, patterning

GROSS MOTOR

Organized games, ball handling (bouncing, running), relays, standing on one foot, hopping

PREMATH

One-to-one correspondence, calendar activities, sorting, number and numeral 6, few and many, ordering numbers 1 through 6, rectangle

SENSORY EXPERIENCES

Sense of touch at the exploration table; float or sink experiences

CREATIVE DRAMATICS

- Pet Store
- Library
- *Three Little Kittens*

RECIPES

Things to make us warm

SNACK

Foods that are white, rectangular shaped, pet shaped, and foods that go together

SELF-HELP

Focus on boots, scarves, hats and mittens, continue outerwear

REVIEW

All previous concepts

ACTIVITIES FOR JANUARY

LANGUAGE AND VOCABULARY

1. WINTER

Weather Spinner. Talk about the changes in the weather that come with winter. Discuss that even though it's cold the sun still shines. Make a large weather spinner out of a pizza cardboard. Divide it into four sections that pictorially show various weather conditions—sunny, cloudy, snowing, raining. Each day discuss the weather and give children turns to place the spinner on the appropriate weather condition. A variation is to have children make their own spinners and change the weather daily.

Summer-Winter Sorting. Gather several pictures depicting typical winter and summer activity scenes (children building a snowman, children sledding, children building a sand castle, children swimming, etc.). Have children sort the pictures into categories: winter and summer or winter and not winter.

Clothing Sort. Provide various articles of clothing appropriate for summer or winter. Using two laundry baskets, sort clothes into winter or summer categories. Expand language by having children label clothing, decide who would wear it, and for what activity it might be worn. This activity could also be done with pictures, preferably following the activity with concrete clothing samples.

Flannel Board. Assemble a person at the flannel board. Review body parts while doing so. Once assembled, dress the person for winter weather. Label clothing pieces as they are put on the person.

Class Story. Tell a winter class story. Begin the story, and children take turns adding to it. Write the story on chart paper and read it at story times. Have children illustrate the story.

What Will I Wear?. Cut out pictures of seasonal clothing from catalogs and magazines. Children can name the article of clothing and tell what body part is covered by the clothing. Make a winter clothing collage.

135

Winter Walk. On a snowy day, take a walk around the school neighborhood. Talk about how the blanket of snow protects plants and animals against the winter wind. Look for tracks in the snow. Talk about who could have made the tracks. When back in the classroom, read a story about animals who make their winter homes in the snow.

2. PETS

Introduce Pets. Introduce one or two pets at a time; display a picture of each. Elicit as much information from the children as possible. Talk about the size and color of each animal, what covers its body (e.g., fur, feathers, scales), how it moves, what sound it makes, what it eats, etc. This activity can extend over several days.

Closure Activity. This auditory closure activity can be done with or without pet pictures cues. Children supply the missing word to tell correctly a characteristic about a pet. Some examples include:

> A fish swims, a dog _____ .
>
> A dog has fur, a bird has _____ .
>
> A cat meows, a dog _____ .
>
> A dog has four legs, a fish has _____ .

Veterinarian. Introduce veterinarian (vet) as a doctor who takes care of all kinds of animals. Let children share any experiences/knowledge they have about taking their pet to a veterinarian. Concepts to include: a vet can help a pet feel better by giving it medicine, bandaging its wounds, or performing an operation. Be sure to have a vet visit class if possible.

What's a Pet?. Talk about what a pet is. Stress that a pet is a friendly animal that you can play with, care for, and keep in your home. Use pictures of animals that could or couldn't be pets. Name them, then divide them into two groups. Expand on the activity by sorting animals into various categories: pets, farm, forest, or zoo animals.

Class Pets. If your class doesn't have a pet such as fish, hamsters, gerbils, etc., consider purchasing or borrowing one. This teaches even the youngest of children responsibility for feeding and caring for pets.

Pet Visitors. Allow children to bring their pets to the classroom. Children can introduce their pet, talk about what it eats, where it sleeps, sounds it makes, how it likes to play, and how they care for it.

Pet Book. Ask children to draw pictures of a pet they own or would like to own. Write the pet's name, or other information dictated by the child, on the picture. Staple the pictures together to make a class book of pets.

Pet Party. Ask children to bring their favorite stuffed pet to school. Have a party for the pets. Serve animal crackers and other treats. Encourage pets to "talk" to each other. Give children the opportunity to tell the class about their special pet.

What Would You Feed It?. Cut out pictures of pets and foods they eat (milk, bones, carrots, etc.). Have children take turns matching each pet to the food it eats.

Mother and Baby Pets. Display commercially prepared pictures or mounted magazine pictures of mother and baby pets. Talk about the pictures and have the children match the mothers with their babies. Help them learn the names of mothers and babies.

Pet Sounds. Prepare an audiotape of pet sounds, barking dogs, meowing cats, singing birds, etc. Play the tape for the children and discuss and label the sounds the animals make. Play the tape again and ask children to identify the sounds.

What Doesn't Belong?. Place pictures of three animals on the table (two pets, one farm or zoo animal). Have children name the animals, tell which one is not a pet, and tell why it doesn't belong.

3. LIBRARY

Mystery Box. Use your mystery box to introduce the library theme. Place a variety of reading materials in the box, including books, magazines, and newspapers. Give the children clues regarding one item at a time. When all the reading materials have been introduced and labeled, ask children where they could find all of these materials. If your class is familiar with the children's room at the library, include other materials found there, such as puzzles, tapes, records, headsets, videotapes, etc.

Sorting Game. Provide children with a variety of materials, some you read, others you don't read. Sort them into two groups. This activity can be followed up using pictures depicting things you do or don't read.

Play Library. Use the library set up for creative dramatics (see p. 151). Role-play a visit to the library. Children can alternate being the librarian or person checking out books. Children can select materials and present the librarian with a library card. Librarian can stamp cards when checking out books. Encourage the use of language throughout the activity. Help children understand the importance of talking quietly in a library.

Book Writing. Make class books to add to your own class library. Children enjoy finding pictures they've drawn with their own words written on them. Books can also be created with photographs and captions. Photograph events to use in class picture books, when on field trips, or during special class activities.

The Librarian. Role-play various job tasks, such as those of a waitress, builder, doctor, dentist, and librarian. The children guess which tasks go with the librarian. Some examples are putting books away, stamping library cards, reading stories. This activity should be preceded with a discussion about jobs of the librarian.

Storytellers. Have children select a favorite, familiar story from school, or bring one from home. That child can share his/her story with classmates by telling the story from pictures or simply by naming objects found on each page.

Books. Children will develop a love of reading by handling and looking at books. Spend time talking about the parts of a book (i.e., cover, front, back, spine, pages). Demonstrate careful page turning and use of a bookmarker to keep the place.

4. GO TOGETHERS

Go-Together Foods. Because food is concrete and very meaningful to children, it is often a good way to introduce new concepts. Display a variety of foods, each one having a match, or something that goes with it. Some examples include peanut butter and jelly, pancakes and syrup, Cheerios™ and bananas, bread and butter, hamburgers and french fries, cake and ice cream. Through discussion, lead children into finding the go togethers. Talk about why they go together, why other combinations don't go together, and other foods that might go with the pairs. This activity can be done with pictures or followed up with pictures.

Go-Together Clothes. Use either the flannel board or a doll for this activity. Provide articles of clothing and give children opportunities to tell which part of the body the clothing goes with. Some examples are hats, mittens, socks, shoes, pants, shirts, and boots. Talk about why the clothing goes with a particular body part and when you would wear it. Have the children put the clothing on the doll or flannel board person.

Common Object Go Togethers. Provide a display of common objects. Make sure each object goes with at least one other object. This activity becomes more difficult when the number of go togethers increases. Some common objects to display are forks, knives, spoons, cups and saucers, shoes and socks, paper and pencil, record and record player. Discuss why objects go together, what they are used for, and when they are used.

Picture Go Togethers. Following go-together activities using concrete objects, use picture go togethers. The use of pictures expands the number and type of concepts to be discussed/reinforced. For example, with pictures you can show how cow, horse, and pig go together with a farm. Use pictures depicting various seasons and pictures of children dressed for the season or engaging in activities particular to the season. Use pictures of various vehicles which go on land, air, or water and pictures of train tracks, road, water, or sky.

Go-Together Sounds. This activity requires recorded sounds and pictures which go with the sounds. Children determine which sound goes with each picture or pictures. Examples include animals and animal sounds, various musical instruments and their sounds, people and voices, and vehicles and their sounds.

5. COLOR—WHITE

Mystery Box. Introduce the color white using the mystery box. The box should be filled with familiar white items. Give clues to the children about individual items, always using color as a descriptor. Children guess what's inside. Reinforce the color white throughout all curriculum areas and whenever possible throughout the day.

White Collage. Provide winter shapes for gluing pictures on, such as: snowflakes, snowmen, hat or boot shapes. Have children find pictures of white objects in magazines or bring them from home. Make a collage with the pictures.

6. DIRECTIONAL AND POSITIONAL CONCEPTS—OVER AND UNDER

As with all prepositions and language concepts, the best way for children to learn and internalize concepts is to use them naturally in everyday experiences. Point out things that are over and under familiar classroom objects. Try to incorporate these words into activities across the curriculum.

Direction Draw. Draw a horizontal line across the chalkboard. Give children directions such as "Draw a circle over the line," "Make a plus sign under the line," etc.

Flannel Board. Place a piece of masking tape across a flannel board. Randomly put flannel cutouts on the board. Children practice their expressive skills as they tell where each cutout is in relation to the masking tape line.

Action Directions. Using concrete objects, give directions involving as many steps as children can follow. For example, "Put the book over your head, put the scissors under the table, and put the box under the slide."

Snowmen. Have children make snowmen out of three styrofoam balls glued together. Use the snowmen for directions with over and under. For example, "Put the snowman over the book," "Put the snowman under the pillow."

FINE MOTOR

1. MANIPULATION

Lacing. Many winter shapes lend themselves to lacing. Some of these include mittens, boot shapes, hats, and snowballs. Cut the objects out of heavy tagboard. Use a hole punch to punch holes around the shapes. Cut yarn, tape around one end of it to make it stiff, and lace around the shapes.

Bird Feeders. Provide each child with an orange cut in half. Let him/her squeeze the juice out using a juice squeezer. Use the remainder of the orange to make a bird feeder. Using a spoon, have children remove the remaining pulp. Poke three holes evenly around the top of the orange halves. Tie equal lengths of string to each hole and bring other ends together to tie at top. Fill feeder with bird seed and tie to a tree.

Popcorn for the Birds. Pop popcorn to eat for snack. Have children use the remaining popcorn to make gifts for the birds. Give each child string attached to a blunt needle. Children will string the popcorn and hang it from a tree for birds to eat.

Class Picture. Have the children work together to make a large class picture or bulletin board. Cut a long sheet of roll paper 4 to 6 feet in length and add to the picture daily. *Day one:* Have children cut trees (large green triangles) and glue to the paper. *Day two:* Children add snowmen, made by cutting out two to three white circles, gluing them together, and decorating. *Day three:* Children draw or paint themselves on the picture, dressed for the winter weather. *Day four:* Each child brings in at least one winter picture cut from a magazine at home, which depicts a winter activity (sledding, skiing, making snowmen, etc.). Children glue magazine pictures to the large picture. *Day five:* Add snow to the picture using cotton or cotton balls.

Play Dough Snowmen. Make snowmen from play dough by rolling three balls, small, medium, and large. Sequence the balls, large on the bottom, medium in the middle, small on top. Provide buttons for the face.

Fasteners. Practice zipping, buttoning, and snapping skills using winter outer garments, dolls, doll clothes, commercial dressing boards, or toys which are specifically designed for those tasks.

Paper Plate Puppy Puppets. Each child colors a small paper plate, cuts long droopy ears, and attaches them to the plate with brad fasteners. Facial features can be added using paper scraps. Staple the puppy to a tongue depressor.

Ivory Snow. Pour some Ivory Snow soap flakes into a large bowl. Children can add water and beat the mixture with an eggbeater. Pour mixture into the sensory table.

Comb Painting. Have children finger paint faces on a hard surface. Let them use old combs to "comb hair" around the face.

Bird Feeders. Punch a hole in a toilet tissue tube. Have children spread peanut butter on the tube, then roll into birdseed. You can add yarn for hanging.

Sponge Painting. Add white detergent to white tempera to make "fluffy white" when children sponge paint a snowman. Paint on a black hat and buttons and add a face.

Snow Painting. Go outside on a snowy day. Give each child a paintbrush to paint the snow. Some may want to dribble or spatter paint on the snow. Different effects will be achieved according to how wet, powdery, or frozen the snow is.

Easel Painting. Supply white paint at the easel. On alternating days, supply other colors for review and reinforcement. Allow children to mix white with the other colors. Talk about the results. Draw winter or pet outlines on easel paper or cut out those shapes for negative space painting. Children can experiment with the shapes and colors. Draw rectangles on easel paper or cut them out to make interesting rectangular-shaped pictures.

Paper Tearing. Provide pet-shaped outlines. Have children tear paper and glue onto shapes.

Bookmarks. Make bookmarks. Have children cut out rectangular shapes and decorate them to use as bookmarks.

Finger Painting. Use white finger paint on the table top. When finished, press dark paper on top of the paint. The design will appear on the paper.

Styrofoam Sculptures. Give children different sized pieces of styrofoam, from small, s-shaped pieces to large packing pieces. Invite them to stack and glue the pieces together in creative ways.

Winter Sewing. Children can string varied styrofoam packing pieces using heavy thread or yarn on craft needles.

Painting Winter. Children paint with white tempera on dark colors of construction paper. They can sprinkle salt or glitter on the wet paint to make their snow pictures sparkle. Shake off the excess.

Blot Prints. Have children fold paper, paint on one side of the fold, press and blot onto the other side. Use tempera or watercolors.

Coupon Clips. Have children practice cutting square and rectangular shapes by cutting coupons.

String Painting. Dip ends of string into various colors of tempera paint, one at a time. Drag wet string across the paper. For variety, dip short pieces of string into paint. Drop the entire string at random onto the paper. Place another paper on top and pat gently.

Straw Painting. Pour a small amount of white paint on dark construction paper. Blow the paint around with a straw to make designs.

Rectangle Prints. Cut pieces of sponge into different sized rectangles. Dip into white paint and then dab on dark-colored construction paper.

Snowflakes. Have children fold paper into quarters and cut out designs or simply snip the folds and around the edges of the paper. When the paper is unfolded, a snowflake design will emerge. Hang snowflakes from the ceiling or in the windows.

Shiny Fish. Give each child an outline of a fish shape. Let them decorate the fish with snips of shiny vinyl wallpaper, shiny paper, or with sequins.

Paper Punch. Allow children to use a paper punch to punch holes in white paper. Use as snowflakes or snow on pictures and in collages.

Clothespins. Hang up a clothesline. Provide winter doll clothes, clothes cutouts, or winter hats and mittens for children to hang on the line with "pinch together" clothespins.

Pet Prints. Dip pet-shaped cookie cutters into paint, then print on paper.

Turn, Turn. Have children practice turning the pages of a book one page at a time.

Magazine Folds. Give each child an old magazine. Have children fold each page in half, press the edges with their fingers, and tuck into the center.

Fine Motor Center. Many concepts can be reinforced and expanded at the January fine motor center. Supply white crayons, paper, and chalk for drawing. The language concepts over and under can be reinforced. Provide paper with a horizontal line drawn on it. Children can glue, paint, or draw over or under the line.

Set out cookie cutters shaped like pets or familiar winter objects for use with play dough. Snowballs and snowmen can be made with play dough. The prewriting strokes for the month, + cross and H stroke, can be made from play dough.

Winter and pet shapes cut from cardboard can be used as stencils for children to trace around. White collage materials should be available along with white foam meat trays. White tissue paper glued on winter shapes make exciting snowmen or snowballs. Small white pieces of styrofoam (packing material) also fit the winter theme.

2. PREWRITING

Connect the Dots. Connect dots to make a variety of winter objects including snowmen, boots, mittens, hats, sleds, and skis.

Path Tracing. Make paths for tracing hats to snowmen, mittens to hands, boots to feet, and jackets to children.

Chalk Drawings. Use white chalk on the chalkboard or dark paper to practice making circles, horizontal and vertical lines, + crosses and H stroke.

Stencils. Have children trace around rectangle stencils. If interested, they can decorate and cut out the rectangles.

Prewriting Center. Use the prewriting center (see October) to practice the strokes being stressed this month. Provide samples of strokes for children to trace or copy, or make strokes with the child present, to imitate.

H and +. Practice making the *H* and + shapes with children's bodies. A + can be made easily by standing straight with arms out at the sides, or have children lie on the floor with arms straight out. Make an *H* with three children. Two of the children lie parallel on the floor while a third child lies perpendicular between the other two.

Ribbon Strokes. Use wide ribbon to make *H* strokes and + crosses. Have children spread glue on paper or use a glue stick to make the appropriate stroke. Children place ribbon over the sticky area.

Air Strokes. While playing background music, practice making the + and *H* strokes in the air.

Highways. Make highways on the floor in +, *H*, and rectangle shapes. Have children drive their cars and trucks around the strokes/shapes.

PERCEPTION

Mitten Match. Prepare matched pairs of mittens from construction paper. Mittens can differ by extreme characteristics such as color, or more subtly by designs, depending on the level of students. Children find the matching mittens.

Mitten Match 2. Bring in pairs of mittens and mix them up in a basket. Children will find the pairs and use clothespins to keep them together.

How I Look in January. Add to your books by having children draw themselves in January. They may choose to dress themselves in winter clothes or add snow or snowmen to their pictures.

What's Missing?. Use either stuffed animal pets or pictures of pets. Present four or more animals or pictures to children. Ask them to label the pets. Have children close their eyes and you remove a pet. When children open their eyes, they guess what's missing.

Finish the Pet. Supply pictures of pets with one or more missing parts (e.g., tail, ear, eye). Children guess what's missing and draw, glue, or paint it on.

Fish Match. Prepare five to ten pairs of tropical fish. The pairs can differ in size, color, or design. Children find the pairs that go together.

Go Fish. Play a go fish card game. Children fish for matching pairs. In the commercial Go Fish™ game, children match the same colored fish. The game can be altered by matching numerals, shapes, etc., drawn on fish shapes.

Perception Center. Throughout the month, alternate perceptual activities and materials. Try to provide puzzles which depict the monthly themes of pets, winter, library, and things that go together. Simple puzzles can be made by mounting pictures on cardboard, then cutting them into pieces. Pegboards and pegs, and blocks for block designs, should be alternated.

Touch and Match. Using pairs of familiar objects such as scissors, paper cup, and saucer, display one of each pair for children to see. Put the other object from the pair into a feely bag. Children use their sense of touch to determine what the object is and which object outside the bag it goes with.

Tape Pictures. Give each child a piece of double-faced tape approximately one foot long. Using precut shapes, create a pattern on a sample length of tape, e.g., red rectangle, white circle, orange +, etc. Continue placing down the length of the tape. Using visual clues and/or auditory directions, have children match their pattern to the sample.

Guess the Pet. Cover pictures of pets with construction paper with lines cut up the paper to within 2 inches of the top. Each paper should have four or five sections cut. Open one section at a time. Children try and guess the pet before all the doors are open.

Flannel Board Snowman. Assemble a snowman at the flannel board. Have children add balls, faces, hats, buttons, etc. Use this opportunity for reviewing body parts.

Pet Pattern Parade. Use cutouts of pets or small plastic pet sculptures (purchased at the dime store). Set up a pet pattern for children to continue, e.g., cat, dog, rabbit, cat, dog, rabbit, etc.

Wallpaper Match-Up. Cut out different sized rectangluar pieces of wallpaper of various colors and textures. Children can sort the wallpaper pieces according to size, color, texture, pattern, etc.

Listening Walk. Go on a winter walk and have children listen for sounds of the season, e.g., teeth chattering, ice breaking, cars' engines stalling, snow crunching underfoot, snowplow plowing, etc.

Library Sorting. Have children sort the classroom library books by color, shape, and size.

Visual Memory. Show children a colorful illustration from a book for a few moments. Then have children tell everything they can remember without looking.

Touch a Pet. Have children touch a variety of fabric swatches, craft feathers, sequins, cotton balls, etc. Children can tell what pet they think would feel like each sample they touch.

GROSS MOTOR

Snow Play. Dress for the weather and go outside to play in the snow. Push and pull sleds. Roll balls to make snowmen or other snow sculptures.

Bean Bag Toss. Make a large snowman out of cardboard. Cut a large hole for his mouth. Toss bean bags into the hole.

Pet Moves. Provide pictures of a variety of pets such as birds, fish, snakes, cats, and dogs. One at a time, each child moves like one of the animals. The other children try to guess which pet is moving.

Bounce Counts. Provide each child with a ball. Have him/her practice bouncing and catching the ball. Then have him/her count how many times she/he can bounce and catch the ball.

Run Mice, Run!. Play a variation of the running game, tag. One child is the cat and others are the mice. The cat tries to catch a mouse by tagging him/her. The first mouse tagged becomes the new cat.

Snow Walk. Have children pretend they are trudging through snow wearing their winter boots. Then go outside on a snowy day and have children experiment with different movements in the snow; walk, hop, jump, etc.

Bunny Rabbit Relay. Draw chalk lines approximately 10 feet apart or use masking tape on the floor. Children pretend they are bunny rabbits and jump on two feet from line to line. Children with more developed gross motor skills can hop on one foot from line to line.

Farmer in the Dell. Play "Farmer in the Dell." Have children think of names of different pets to use in the game

Cold Snowball. Play this group game much like hot potato, but substitute a cold snowball. Use a small-sized ball and pass it around the circle while music is playing. When the music stops, whoever is left holding the cold snowball becomes a snowman on the outside of the circle.

Doggie Doggie, Where's the Bone?. In this circle game, one child is chosen to be the "doggie." The "doggie" leaves the room, while another child, "It" (the previous "doggie"), delivers the "bone" to a child sitting in the circle. To do this, all of the children in the circle sit with hands behind their back. "Doggie" comes back to the room and tries to guess who has the bone. In some versions of the game the number of guesses is limited to three. Upon guessing who has the bone, "Doggie" becomes "It", the child with the bone becomes "Doggie," and "It" goes back into the circle.

Fish, Fish, Bird. This game is played like duck, duck, goose. One child, "It," walks around the circle lightly tapping each child's head and saying "fish." When "It" comes to the child she/he wishes to be chased by, "It" says "bird." That child chases "It" around the circle and back to the vacated place. Play continues with "Bird" becoming "It."

Kitty Says. This game is played like Simon Says. You may wish to be "Kitty" so that you can reinforce skills to be focused on. Kitty might say to stand on one foot, hop, jump, or run. If you give the direction without saying "Kitty says," the children should not perform the action.

Basketball. This activity is excellent for children just beginning to bounce balls. Children sit on their bottoms with their two feet touching each other. Their legs are to be rounded like a basketball hoop. Children practice dropping the ball and catching it in the hoop.

Ball Toss. Children practice eye tracking skills by tossing the ball slightly into the air and then catching it.

Numeral Bounce. Draw or tape a very large, ladder-shaped rectangle on the floor. Divide it into six to ten sections. Number each section beginning with one. Children first bounce the ball into section 1, 2, and so on.

Throw and Catch. Supply each child with a ball and ample wall space. Let him/her throw the ball against the wall and catch it.

Pet Relay. Divide the class into teams of three or four children. Give each child a pet label such as dog, cat, rabbit, hamster, etc. Tape a picture of pet food to the wall or place a bowl on the ground. One child from each team runs to the pet food and back. The relay continues until all pets have been "fed."

Snow Angels. Have children lie on their backs in the snow or on the floor with arms and legs at their side. Move arms up and down in the snow to make wings. Legs move out and in to make the angel's robe. Have children try and move arms and legs at the same time. You may try having children move right arm and leg or left arm and leg.

Animal Moves. Play instrumental music. Each child moves like a pet (jumps like a cat, runs like a dog, swims like a fish, flies like a bird, hops like a rabbit, etc.). When the music stops, the children must each move like another animal Continue until each child has moved like three or four different animals.

SENSORY EXPERIENCES

Whipping Snow. Pour a small amount of water into Ivory Flakes™ and beat (approximately 1/2 cup water to 1 cup flakes). Children can scoop, mound, finger paint, etc., in the "whipped snow" at the exploration table.

Bring Winter In. Bring in clean, freshly fallen snow to put in the exploration table. Children can play in the snow, making snowballs, snowmen, small snow forts, etc. They might enjoy burrowing plastic animals like snakes, turtles, frogs, skunks, etc., under the snow. Also provide a variety of plastic containers and spoons for inside snow play. The children would enjoy adding drops of food coloring to the snow.

Sink or Float. Place warm water in the exploration table. Provide a tray filled with objects the children can put in the water (marbles, ping pong balls, golf balls, feathers, colored ice cubes, stones, pennies, styrofoam packing, blocks, sponges, balloons, straws, etc.). Lead children to notice that some things sink and some float. Challenge children to find other objects in the room and have them predict if they will sink or float. They can easily check out their predictions. Some children might be interested in sorting the objects into the two categories after water play is completed.

PREMATH

Goldfish. Cut out goldfish from construction paper or cardboard. Put six or more fish in a goldfish bowl and have children count the fish.

Fish Math. Use six small goldfish bowls. Label each with a numeral one to six. Using cutout goldfish, have children put the correct number of fish in the fish bowl.

Bird Feathers. Provide cutouts of birds without feathers. Put a numeral one to six on each bird. Have children put the correct number of feathers on the birds.

Bird Houses. This activity is similar to Fish Math. Cut bird cages from construction paper or cardboard. Label each with a numeral one to six. Provide cutouts of birds. Children put the appropriate number of birds in each cage.

Count the Snowmen. Put snowmen on the flannel board and have children count them. To vary the activity, have children count sets of snowmen and match them to the corresponding numeral on the flannel board. Use sets of up to six.

Dress the Snowmen. Provide cutouts of snowmen with a numeral from one to six written on each. Children put the correct number of buttons on each snowman.

Ice Cube Sort. Use an ice cube tray for counting sets. Label each section with a numeral one to six or higher depending on students' ability levels. Sort small objects into the ice cube trays corresponding to the numerals.

Flannel Board. Display six flannel board snowmen, each wearing a numeral one to six in random order. Have children put the snowmen in numerical order.

Tall Snowmen. Using precut snowballs or snowballs cut by the children, make a six-ball snowman with each snowball having a numeral on it from one to six. Children assemble the snowmen in numerical order.

Book Assemble. Upon completing individual books or a class book, write page numbers on each page. Children assemble the books in numerical order.

Pet Parade. On the day that children bring in their stuffed pets from home, assign each pet a number from one to six. Have pets and owners line up for the parade in numerical order.

Goldfish Bowls. Using goldfish bowls and cutout fish, put a few fish in one bowl and many fish in another bowl. Children decide which bowl has a few and which has many. Transfer fish from bowl to bowl so the bowl with a few and many changes.

Bunny Baskets. On the flannel board, display baskets and cutout bunnies. Give directions to the children to put a few bunnies in the basket or put many bunnies in the basket.

Snack Time. During daily snack time, alter the amount of snack so children get a few or many pieces. For example, on popcorn day children get many kernels. On cracker with cream cheese day, children get only a few.

Snowflakes on Trees. Provide each child with a simple tree sketched on paper and cotton balls. Direct the children to glue a few cotton balls on one tree and many on the other.

Library Books. When playing in the classroom library, suggest to children that they check out either a few or many books.

Calendar. Give each child the opportunity to put the appropriate numeral on the calendar. Expand concepts at calendar time by questioning such as, "Count how many days until Friday." "Count the days in the week or month." Talk about what happened yesterday, or what special thing is going to take place tomorrow. Use cutouts of the monthly themes for representing each day. Pattern pets: dog cat, cat, dog, cat, cat, or winter clothing: boot, mitten, boot, mitten, etc., on the calendar.

Shape Sort. Use shoeboxes labeled pictorially with a triangle, circle, square, or rectangle. Using those shapes cut out of different colors, textures, and sizes, sort the shapes into the appropriate boxes.

Rectangle Walk. Take a walk around the classroom, school, or block. Find as many rectangles as possible. Either collect them or make a list of what was found. Count how many were found upon returning from the walk.

Rectangle Attributes. Talk about the attributes of a rectangle: four corners, two long sides, and two short sides. Present various four-sided shapes and sort rectangles and not rectangles. Have children tell why shapes are/are not rectangles.

Rectangle Pictures. Give students paper with a rectangle drawn somewhere on it. Have them add to the pictures. See how many different things can be made from a rectangle, e.g., a wagon, a ladder, etc.

SONGS AND FINGERPLAYS

Winter Weather (tune: "Are You Sleeping?").

Winter weather, winter weather.
Cold and ice, snow is nice.
Put your coat and boots on.
Put your hat and scarf on.
Let's go out to play!
Let's go out to play!

Snow Is Falling (tune: "Mary Had a Little Lamb").

Snow is falling from the sky, from the sky, from the sky
Snow is falling from the sky, right in my backyard.
Yeah!

Ten Little Snowmen (tune: "Ten Little Indians").

One little, two little, three little Snowmen,
Four little, five little, six little Snowmen,
Seven little, eight little, nine little Snowmen,
Ten little Snowmen bright.

(Sing the song and substitute names of favorite pets.)

Five Little Snowmen (Point to each finger).

Five little snowmen, sitting by the door; out came the sun and
then there were four.
Four little snowmen, sitting by the tree; out came the sun, and
then there were three.
Three little snowmen, sitting by the zoo; out came the sun, and
then there were two.
Two little snowmen, sitting just for fun; out came the sun, and
then there was one.
One little snowman, wishing he could run; out came the sun and then
there were none.

Snowman Poem.

I am a snowman round and fat, (Stretch arms out.)
Button eyes and tall black hat. (Point to eyes and head.)
When the sun comes out you'll see, (Point to sky.)
That will be the end of me. (Melt to the ground.)

Bingo, the Dog.

There was a boy who had a dog and Bingo was his name O
B-I-N-G-O, B-I-N-G-O, B-I-N-G-O, and Bingo was his name O
There was a boy who had a dog and Bingo was his name O
(clap) I-N-G-O, (clap) I-N-G-O, (clap) I-N-G-O and Bingo was his name O.

(Continue leaving out a letter in each verse and replacing it with a clap, until
you clap out the name *Bingo*. Last verse same as first.)

My Next-Door Neighbor (tune: "Old McDonald").

My next-door neighbor has some pets
E-I-E-I-O
And at his house he has a cat.
E-I-E-I-O
With a meow-meow here, and a meow-meow there
Here a meow, there a meow, everywhere a meow-meow
My next door neighbor has some pets
E-I-E-I-O!

(Substitute the name of other pets and the sounds they make: dog—bark or
bow-wow, bird—chirp, chirp.)

RECIPES

Animal Crackers (recipe from Kinder Krunchies by Karen S. Jenkins, 1982, Distributed by Discovery Toys).

1. Grind 1/2 cup oatmeal until fine.
2. Add:

    2 teaspoons honey

    1/4+ 1/8 teaspoons salt
    3/4 cup flour

3. Cut in 1/4 cup butter.
4. Add 4 tablespoons buttermilk.
5. Roll very thin—cut with pet-shaped cookie cutters.
6. Bake at 400 degrees until brown (10–12 min.).

ABC Soup.

4 cups beef bouillon (4 cubes)	1/4 cup diced onion
1/2 cup diced potato	1 cup alphabet noodles
1/2 cup diced carrot	

Melt bouillon in water and simmer. Dice vegetables on cutting board and add to broth. Cover pot and simmer for 30 minutes. Add noodles and cook for five more minutes.

Soft Pretzels.

1 package yeast disolved in	4 cups flour
1 1/2 cups warm water	1 egg
1 teaspoon salt	
1 tablespoon sugar	

Combine all ingredients except egg. Mix and knead dough. Form into individual balls. Have children roll into H's, +'s, and rectangles, or other shapes. Brush with egg and sprinkle with salt. Bake at 425 degrees until brown.

Individual Pizzas (tastes good on a cold day).

    English muffin halves
    Pizza sauce
    Grated mozarella cheese

Give each child 1/2 of an English muffin. Spoon sauce over muffin. Top with grated cheese and broil or bake until cheese is melted.

JANUARY SNACKS

Snowmen. Make snowmen from marshmallows held together by toothpicks. Use raisins, chocolate chips, or licorice for decorations.

Animal Crackers. Serve either animal crackers from the grocery store or home-made (see recipe).

Pet-Shaped Cookies. Make your favorite rolled cookie recipe. Use pet-shaped cookie cutters to form cookies. Bake and eat.

Pet- or Winter-Shaped Breads and Spreads. Cut bread with pet- or winter-shaped cookie cutters. Spread with favorite toppings such as peanut butter, jelly, cream cheese, etc.

White Snacks. Eat things that are white. At the beginning of the month, brainstorm white snacks with the children, and serve their suggestions throughout the month. Some examples are white milk, popcorn, vanilla pudding, vanilla ice cream, crackers with cream cheese, and cottage cheese.

Rectangular Snacks. Eat snacks that are rectangular in shape. Brainstorm ideas at the beginning of the month with the children. Some examples are graham crackers, granola bars, bread and spreads cut into rectangles and Long Johns.

Snacks to Make Us Warm.

> Hot chocolate—add white marshmallows
>
> Hot cereals such as oatmeal or cream of wheat
>
> Hot pudding
>
> Warm muffins
>
> Warm soups

Go-Together Snack.

> Toast with butter, jam, cinnamon, etc.
>
> Pancakes, waffles, or french toast with syrup
>
> Peanut butter and jelly
>
> Eggs and toast
>
> Cake and ice cream
>
> Cereal with bananas and milk
>
> Bagels with cream cheese
>
> Ice cream and ice cream cones
>
> Vegetables and dip
>
> French fries with ketchup
>
> Celery with cream cheese spread on top
>
> Cheese and crackers

CREATIVE DRAMATICS

Pet Store. Set up a pet store in your creative play area. Ask children to bring in stuffed animals that might be found in a pet store. If possible, use real pets (e.g., goldfish, gerbils, hamsters, etc.). Props might include a cash register, play money, pet food, pet care products, and pet accessories such as cages, toys, and beds. Children can "buy" pets and supplies and practice caring for them. Use the area for free independent play, with a teacher to elicit language, or for structured, teacher-directed activities.

Library. Set up a library in your classroom. The book area is the ideal place for this. Provide books, tapes, records, magazines, and newspapers. Supply index cards to use as library cards and a stamp pad for checking books out and in. Children can review large, medium, and small by sorting books according to size. The "librarians" can sort books into categories of winter stories and pet stories by looking at the cover or the pictures inside. Provide times for independent play as well as times for more structured, teacher-directed activities.

Three Little Kittens. Read one of several versions of the story *Three Little Kittens* to the children until they are familiar with it. The children can choose to be the mom cat or one of the kittens. By looking at pictures in the story, have children brainstorm props they would like to gather and use to help tell the story (pairs of mittens, yarn tied on the back of two chairs for a clothesline, play dough pies, etc.). The children might enjoy cutting tails, ears, and whiskers they can wear when acting out the story. Make sure to leave the props and story out for children to use during their free time.

CHILDREN'S LITERATURE

Adelson, Leone. *All Ready for Winter*

Batherman, Muriel. *Some Things You Should Know about My Dog*

Bonsall, Crosby Newell. *The Case of the Cat's Meow*

Bridwell, Norman. *Clifford's Family*

———. *Clifford's Kitten*

———. *Clifford Takes a Trip*

———. *Clifford the Big Red Dog*

———. *Clifford the Small Red Puppy*

Briggs, Raymond. *The Snowman*

Brown, Margaret Wise. *Goodnight Moon*

———. *Winter Noisy Book*

Bruna, Dick. *Miffy in the Snow*

Buckley, Helen Elizabeth. *Josie's Buttercup*

Bunting, Eve. *Winter's Coming*

Burningham, John. *The Snow*

Burton, Virginia Lee. *Katy and the Big Snow*

Calhoun, Mary. *Cross Country Cat*

Carrol, Ruth Robinson, *What Whiskers Did*

Charles, Donald. *Calico Cat Looks Around*

Claude-Lafontaine, Pascale Monsieur. *Bussy, the Celebrated Hamster*

Concover, Chris. *Six Little Ducks*

Eckert, Horst. *Dear Snowman*

Elkin, Benjamin. *Six Foolish Fishermen*

Flack, Marjorie. *Angus and the Cat*

———. *Angus and the Ducks*

———. *Angus Lost*

Freeman, Don. *Ski Pup*

Gag, Wanda. *Snow White and the Seven Dwarfs*

Hoff, Sydney. *Katy's Kitty: Three Kitty Stories*

Jeffey, Susan. *Snow White and the Seven Dwarfs*

Kahl, Virginia Caroline. *The Habits of Rabbits*

Keats, Ezra Jack. *Pet Show*

———. *Snowy Day*

Knotts, Howard Clayton. *The Winter Cat*

Krauss, Ruth. *The Happy Day*

Lathrop, Dorothy Palis. *Puppies for Keeps*

Marzallo, Jean. *Three Little Kittens*

Pursell, Margaret Sanford. *Polly the Guinea Pig*

Rey, Margret Elisabeth Waldstein. *Pretzel and the Puppies*

Ricciuti, Edward R. *An Animal for Alan*

Sandberg, Inger. *Nicholas' Favorite Pet*

Selsam, Millicent Ellis. *How Puppies Grow*

Shaw, Charles Green. *It Looked Like Spilt Milk*

Tobias, Tobi. *Petey*

Tresselt, Alvin R. *The Mitten*

——— . *White Snow, Bright Snow*

Turner, Nancy Byrd. *When it Rains Cats and Dogs*

Viorst, Judith. *The Tenth Good Thing about Barney*

Welber, Robert. *Winter Picnic*

——— . *The Winter Wedding*

Wong, Herbert H., and Vassel, Matthew F. *My Goldfish*

Wyse, Lois. *Two Guppies, a Turtle and Aunt Edna*

Zion, Gene. *Harry and the Lady Next Door*

——— . *The Summer Snowman*

Evaluating January Concepts

Throughout the month, continue to update and record significant progress and/or changes made by the children. Use the checklists found in the Appendix in the areas of fine motor, perception, math, gross motor, etc. Observe children's use of winter vocabulary in structured lessons and during play. Assess their ability to match go-together objects and pictures.

During January, you should carefully observe each child's ability to attend to the wide variety of tasks and activities presented throughout the day. Objectively record what activities the child finishes and which are left incomplete. You may begin to see a pattern developing in attending related to individual interests and abilities. This may help you know when to encourage and/or assist the child to task completion.

LANGUAGE AND VOCABULARY

- Winter—weather and nature's changes, clothing, activities, and vocabulary
- Pets—naming, describing, and comparing, pet care and safety
- Library—jobs of the librarian, things we read
- Go togethers—matching things that go together
- Cooking experiences
- Color—white
- Directional and Positional Concepts—over and under

FINE MOTOR

Lacing, painting, coloring, gluing, play dough manipulation, block tower building, cutting, woodworking center, path tracing, *H* stroke and +

PERCEPTION

Same and different, draw a person, puzzles, copying block, peg and bead designs, patterning

GROSS MOTOR

Organized games, ball handling (bouncing, running) relays, standing on one foot, hopping

PREMATH

One-to-one correspondence, calendar activities, sorting, number and numeral 6, few and many, ordering numbers 1–6, rectangle

CREATIVE DRAMATICS

SENSORY EXPERIENCES

JANUARY
Parent-child activities

SUN	MON	TUE	WED	THU	FRI	SAT
HAPPY NEW YEAR!	PRACTICE HOPPING AND STANDING ON 1 FOOT.	FIND THINGS AROUND THE HOUSE THAT ARE WHITE, NAME THEM.	LOOK THROUGH THE HOLIDAY CARDS. FIND THOSE SHAPED LIKE RECTANGLES.	READ SOME STORIES ABOUT WINTER.	MAKE HOT CHOCOLATE TOGETHER. ADD MARSHMALLOWS. WATCH WHAT HAPPENS.	MATCH FAMILY GLOVES OR MITTENS.
CUT A HOLIDAY CARD INTO PIECES TO MAKE A PUZZLE.	PRACTICE DESIGN COPYING: 0, —, 1, H, AND +. USE CRAYONS OR MARKERS.	LOOK THROUGH A MAGAZINE OR CATALOG FOR WINTER CLOTHING.	SING WINTER SONGS.	FINGER PAINT WITH WHITE SHAVING CREAM. DRAW A PERSON.	MAKE ANGELS IN THE SNOW.	PLAY A GAME OR PUT A PUZZLE TOGETHER.
CUT WHITE PAPER. MAKE SNOWFLAKE SNIPS.	PRACTICE PUTTING ON WINTER CLOTHING.	VISIT THE LIBRARY. GET A LIBRARY CARD.	MAKE A TINY SNOWMAN. BRING INSIDE. WATCH WHAT HAPPENS.	CUT AND GLUE PICTURES TO MAKE A PET COLLAGE.	FEED THE BIRDS. COUNT THEM IN YOUR YARD.	FOLD NAPKINS INTO RECTANGLES.
FIND THINGS IN THE HOUSE THAT GO TOGETHER. DOG—BONE HAT—SCARF BED—SHEETS	READ SOME BOOKS ABOUT PETS.	PICK UP WHITE COTTON BALLS WITH TWEEZERS OR CLOTHESPINS. COUNT THEM.	MAKE A SNOWMAN WITH MARSHMALLOWS.	SELECT WHITE OBJECTS TO SHOP FOR: BREAD, CAULIFLOWER, CHEESE, ETC.	MAKE SETS OF BUTTONS, SOME WITH FEW AND SOME WITH MANY.	BLOW A BALLOON. BAT IT OVER AND UNDER OBJECTS.
PLAY IN THE TUB. WHAT SINKS? WHAT FLOATS?	FIND THINGS IN THE HOUSE THAT KEEP US WARM—BLANKETS, JACKETS, HOT CHOCOLATE, ETC.	SORT THE SILVERWARE.				

FEBRUARY

CONCEPTS FOR FEBRUARY

LANGUAGE AND VOCABULARY

1. Rooms of the House—kitchen, bedroom, bathroom, living-family room: naming, sorting, and classifying household objects
2. Dental Health—job of the dentist, dental health: daily care, good foods to eat, sense of taste, vocabulary
3. Mail Carrier—job of the mail carrier, my address, vocabulary
4. Valentine's Day—theme of friendship and sharing
5. Colors—red and pink
6. Directional and Positional Concepts—high and low

Suggested field trips/classroom visitors: Visit the post office. Have a dentist or hygienist visit the class.

FINE MOTOR: 1. MANIPULATION AND 2. PREWRITING

Lacing, painting, coloring, gluing, play dough manipulation, cutting, block tower building, bead stringing, centers, path tracing, diagonals \ and /, and ∨ stroke

PERCEPTION

Same and different, draw a person, center activities: puzzles, copying block, peg, and bead designs, patterning and sorting

GROSS MOTOR

Organized games, movement activities, gymnastic activities: side-to-side rolling, forward rolls, and other mat activities

PREMATH

One-to-one correspondence, calendar activities, sorting, number and numeral 7, empty and full, heart shape

SENSORY EXPERIENCES

Exploration table, sense of taste

CREATIVE DRAMATICS

- Housekeeping
- Mail Carrier—Post Office
- *The Three Pigs*

RECIPES

Foods to share

SNACK

Food related to monthly concepts and themes

SELF-HELP

Continue working with fasteners, meeting children at their developmental levels

REVIEW

Any previous concepts

ACTIVITIES FOR FEBRUARY

LANGUAGE AND VOCABULARY

1. ROOMS OF THE HOUSE

Home Sweet Home. Begin the unit by showing children pictures of different homes. Try to include a single-family home, an apartment building, a mobile home, a houseboat, and a farm house. Have children describe each and try to label the parts some have: attic, basement, windows, roof, doors, porch, chimney, etc. A discussion of neighbors and the neighborhood might follow.

Before beginning to teach about the rooms of the house, establish a list of five to fifteen objects/vocabulary words to be focused on for each room of the house. You can develop a picture file by cutting out the objects from magazines, old workbooks, catalogs, etc., mounting them on construction paper, and laminating them.

These pictures form the basis for lessons and later evaluation of the children.

Introduce Rooms. Introduce each room of the house on a separate day. Show picture cards to the children. They name the object, tell how it looks, and what room it is found in. Ask children a variety of "wh" (who, what, where, when, why) questions based on the individual goals and levels of the students. Using a doll house with people and furniture is a good way to help children see parts of the whole at a child-size level.

Where Does It Happen?. Have a doll house on display for children to see. Name familiar activities and have children name the room where the activity takes place. Examples could include eating breakfast, taking a nap, taking a bath, washing the dishes, watching TV, brushing teeth, playing a game, listening to music. Help children understand that there may be more than one room where an activity can take place.

Fast Naming. Name a room of the house, and children brainstorm as many objects as they can think of that go in the room.

Moving Day. Read the story *Moving Day* by Leone Anderson, or tell a story about a family moving to a new house. Fill a large toy truck with pieces of play furniture that the movers must put in the correct room. Each child gets a chance to take a piece of furniture from the truck, name it, and put it in the correct room of the doll house.

Memory Game. Play a game called "Cleaning Day." Say, "On cleaning day, Mom dusted the dresser, the nightstand, and the end table." Children must remember and name the objects dusted. Try other examples: "On cleaning day, Dad vaccumed under . . ." "On cleaning day, Mom washed . . ." Vary the number of objects children are to remember based on their level.

What I Need. Name a familiar household activity and have children identify objects needed to perform the activity. Try this activity with and without picture cue cards. Examples could include take a bath—bathtub, water, soap, washcloth, toys, sponge, towel, etc.; make the bed—a bed, sheets, pillow, pillowcase, blanket, spread, etc.

Classification in the House. Place about six objects on the table at a time. Children name each object and take turns answering questions: What things are big—small? red—brown? shaped like a square—rectangle? hard—soft? heavy—light? used together? made of wood—metal?

The list of questions is limitless. This is a good opportunity to reinforce previous concepts taught.

Riddle Time. Give children riddles about objects found in the house. Children guess the name of the object. You can vary the number of clues given and stop before all are given so children can begin guessing.

EXAMPLE:
1. You find me in the bedroom.
2. I am a piece of furniture.
3. I am hard and soft.
4. You sleep on me. (bed)

Children will see how logical answers change as more clues are given.

What Do You Do First?. Name two actions, and children say what they would do first. *Examples:* make the bed and go to sleep, set the table and eat breakfast.

Language Experience. Children can dictate a variety of stories about the house theme. Some might include the jobs I have at my house, the favorite toy in my bedroom, etc.

2. DENTAL HEALTH

Smiling Faces. Begin the unit on dentists and dental care by having children stand in front of a large mirror. Have them name and touch all the parts: lips, mouth, tongue, teeth, and gums. Have children try to smile without opening their mouths. Ask how teeth help our faces show happy, sad, scared, etc. Make these faces in the mirror. Help children to understand that our teeth shape our faces and show others how we feel.

Teeth for Eating. Give each child a saltine cracker. Have them try to eat their crackers without using their teeth. Show pictures of food like apples, corn on the cob, candy bars, etc. Have children name the food and tell if they think they could eat the food easily without having teeth. Using a mirror, show children the teeth used for biting, tearing, and chewing. They will begin to understand how our teeth help us to eat.

Teeth for Talking. With the children, take turns trying to say "these three teeth" without letting the tongue touch the teeth. Try saying other words with and without tongues touching teeth. Lead children to understand that teeth help us talk more clearly. Provide a mirror for children to look at when they are talking.

Healthy Teeth. Teach children three things to help keep teeth healthy:

1. Brush with a toothbrush and toothpaste, floss, swish and swallow;
2. Eat the right food—not too much sugar; and
3. Visit the dentist.

Bring in a toothbrush, toothpaste, and floss, or ask for samples from a local dentist. Children name objects. If possible, give children an opportunity to brush properly at school with the help of you, an aide, or parent volunteer after snack time. Practice swish and swallow. Explain to children that brushing and flossing removes food and sticky plaque they can't see, to keep teeth strong and healthy.

Eating Right. Talk about the importance of eating healthy foods. Explain that eating too much sticky, sugary food can make holes only the dentist can fix. Show pictures and have children brainstorm foods that have a lot of sugar. Show pictures and brainstorm foods that are crunchy and healthy for teeth.

Tooth Collages. Cut pictures from magazines and grocery ads that show healthy foods and those not so healthy. Children take turns choosing a picture, naming it, and deciding if it makes teeth happy or sad. They glue the picture on a large tooth cut from kraft paper that is either smiling or frowning.

The Dentist. Have children share any experiences they may have had when visiting the dentist. Explain that people can go for a check-up if teeth hurt or even if they feel fine. Talk about what might happen during a check-up: Dentist uses instruments to count, check, clean teeth, and fill holes called cavities, the dentist may take a little picture of teeth called an X-ray, the dentist may give you something to drink to help keep teeth strong.

Lost Tooth. Read or tell a story about children losing baby teeth. Have children share experiences of their older brothers or sisters.

Language Experience. After a classroom visit from a dentist or hygienist, have children dictate a story about the visit and everything they have learned about health care.

Rhyme Time. Teach children a simple rhyme:

Even if you're in a rush,
Don't forget to swish or brush!

3. MAIL CARRIER

Mail Carrier. Talk about the mail carrier's uniform, truck, and job. Make a bag that resembles one used by a mail carrier. Fill it with letters, newspapers, cards, postcards, magazines, etc. Have children name and tell about each thing a mail carrier can bring. Add information, if necessary.

Letter. Show a letter. Talk about the sequence of events needed to get the letter from one place to another: Write a letter, put it in an envelope, put on a stamp and an address, put it in the mailbox. Have children dictate a class letter to someone, talking through the process with children. Walk to a mailbox and mail the letter.

Learning Addresses. Talk about what an address is and how it helps the mail carrier deliver mail. Prepare a letter or card for each child. Include names and addresses. Put cards in the mail carrier's bag. Pretend to be the mail carrier. Take a card out of the bag, read the address as children listen for their home address to claim their mail. You can ask children to recite all or part of their address back to the mail carrier.

Post Office. Some children may understand that mail from boxes is sorted at the post office before it will be delivered to people's homes. A visit to the post office may help them understand this step in getting mail from one place to another.

4. VALENTINE'S DAY

Friends. Help children brainstorm ways they show friendship to others, e.g., share toys and food, help with jobs, say nice things, etc. Talk about the special act of showing love and friendship by sending valentines on Valentine's Day.

Love Letter. Children dictate sentence stories about why they love Mom and Dad, why they are special, etc. They can draw a picture on their "story letter." Children help prepare the letter for mailing by putting on the stamp and telling any part of the address they know. The class mails the story letters.

5. COLORS—RED

Introduce Colors. Introduce the colors red and pink on separate days using the mystery box. Make a game of having children tell as many things as they can about each item in the box.

Riddles. Give riddles about objects found in the mystery box. Children try to name the object. Do with both red and pink objects.

Lollipop Sharing Game. Prepare three large circles for each color and staple a tongue depressor on each circle to make a lollipop. Pass a colored lollipop to each child. Children sit in a circle holding their lollipop in front of them. Then give one direction at a time for each child to follow (e.g., "share red to pink," etc.). The child with the red lollipop gives his/her candy to the child holding a pink lollipop and returns to his/her place. The game continues as children share colored lollipops with their friends.

Fishing. Use the fishing game. Fish for red and pink fish.

6. DIRECTIONAL AND POSITIONAL CONCEPTS—HIGH AND LOW

High-Low. Children help put classroom toys and materials away on shelves and in drawers. Give directions, e.g., "Put the truck on the high shelf. Put the dolls in the low drawer," etc.

Fill the Closet. Prepare a paper model of a closet—one large closet for the class, or a small closet for each child. Children open the doors to an empty closet that has only a clothing rod across the top. Tell children they must fill the closet by gluing pictures where they belong—up high or down low. Give children pictures cut from magazines and catalogs. Include pictures of shoes, slippers, boots, toys, games, coats, shirts, pants, dresses, etc.

High-Low Walk. Go for either an inside or outside walk with the children. Divide children into two groups. Tell one group to look for things that are up high and the other group to look for things that are down low. Upon returning, list the items the children noticed on a large sheet of paper. List the high items up high and the low items down low.

FINE MOTOR

1. MANIPULATION

Lacing. Cut a heart shape from a large, styrofoam meat tray. Punch holes around the edges. Children can lace around the heart shape with red or pink yarn.

Fill My Heart. Give each child a large heart shape. Children can fill in their heart by snipping and gluing red and pink paper, shiny paper, yarn, and other collage materials.

Valentine Bag. Provide a white, bakery-sized bag for each child. Using heart-shaped sponges, children decorate their bag by sponge painting red, pink, or lavender hearts on the bag. Children can glue or staple a handle on the bag. This makes a perfect valentine card holder.

Fold It. Have children practice folding paper to fit into different sized envelopes.

Make Valentines. Provide glitter, lace doilies, paper heart shapes, rickrack, stickers, and other materials. Children will enjoy making valentines for their friends and dictating sentence stories for you to write inside the cards.

Mystery Pictures. Cut out six heart shapes from heavy tagboard. Attach hearts to the table top with double-faced tape. Tape a piece of 12- by 18-inch paper over the hearts. Children rub over the hidden shapes with the side of their crayons. The mystery hearts will appear.

Dip It, Cut It. Dip heart-shaped cookie cutters into paint. Make heart prints. Cut bread, cheese, lunch meat, cookie dough, or play dough with heart-shaped cookie cutters.

Popsicle™ Pictures. Fill an ice cube tray with a mixture of water and food coloring or water and tempera paint. Place in the freezer. When the mixture begins to set, put a Popsicle™ stick into each section. Children can paint with their "popsicles" (not edible!). Finger paint paper works best.

Kitchen Kapers. Provide opportunities for children to use and manipulate a variety of kitchen utensils: rolling pin with play dough, egg beater with water and detergent, potato masher with soft dough, grater with modeling clay, flour sifter with fine sand, and garlic press with play dough, etc.

Friendship Collage. Make a class friendship collage on a huge heart shape cut from kraft paper. Children cut pictures from magazines and catalogs that show toys, food, etc., that they might share with a friend. Glue pictures on the heart.

Tooth Prints. Cut chunks of potato into pieces that resemble the shape of a tooth. Children can dip the potato into white paint and make tooth prints on dark-colored construction paper. Children might also enjoy making cavities by dabbing black paint on the tooth print with a Q-Tip.™

Snow Spraying. Take several spray bottles and fill halfway with water and several drops of food coloring. Go outside and have children spray the snow. They can also make new colors by spraying snow with different colors.

Dream House. Have children cut a variety of shapes—squares, circles, rectangles, and triangles—in different sizes. They glue the pieces down to create their dream house.

Friendship Necklace. Children paint styrofoam packing pieces, some red and some pink. After the pieces dry, children can string the pieces on yarn or heavy thread. Tie ends together. Children can give the necklace to a friend.

Visual perception is strengthened if children pattern the red and pink styrofoam pieces on the necklace (red, red, pink, red, red, pink, etc.).

Rug Making. Show children pictures of different kinds of rugs. Give each child a large rectangle or oval piece of construction paper. Children practice snipping/ fringing around the paper to make a rug.

Making Garbage. Have children "make garbage" using only one hand at a time. Children take single sheets of newspaper and crumple them up into balls. They will have fun tossing their garbage into an empty round can or basket until it is full.

Pick-up. Use shortened pipe cleaners or straws. Drop them out of a can and have children pick up one at a time—trying not to move any other pieces.

Button Hop. Use large, flat buttons. Show children how to push one button down on the edge of another to make it hop.

Stacking. Children stack wooden blocks, poker chips, paper cups, etc., as high as possible.

House of Cards. Show children how to make a house using three cards from a deck. See how many they can make.

Diagonal Folds. Draw a diagonal line on scraps of tagboard or heavy paper. Children practice folding on the line and pressing down with their fingers.

Pick and Hold. Children see how many small objects (closed safety pins, raisins, buttons, etc.) they can pick up and hold in one hand before any drop out.

Poke It. Children poke toothpicks or pegs into a ball of modeling clay.

Two Hands Together. Place two cups in front of each child with a pile of small objects in the middle (dry beans, pegs, pennies, etc.). Children try to pick up the objects simultaneously with both hands and drop them in the cups.

Toothy Smile. Give each child a large pair of white lips that form a smile. Children color the lips red and glue on white snips or great northern beans to make a toothy grin.

Kitchen Prints. Children dip kitchen utensils such as a spatula, fork, or potato masher into paint and print onto paper.

Toothbrush Painting. Save old toothbrushes and clean in very hot water. Allow to dry thoroughly. Children dip the bristles into tempera paint and scrub and brush the paint on heavy paper.

Stamping. Children will enjoy pressing rubber stamps on stamp pads to press designs onto paper.

Mail Bags. Give each child a large, brown paper bag and attach a piece of yarn for the strap. Children can paint, color, stamp, or decorate the bag with collage materials.

Fine Motor Center. There are many ways to utilize the February themes at the fine motor center. Provide heart shapes for children to cut. The heart cutouts can be used for children to lace, or to glue onto paper to produce a collage. Supply other collage materials such as doilies or pieces of rickrack and a wide variety of other pink and red items.

Provide pink and red play dough, rolling pins, and heart-shaped cookie cutters. Provide paper and envelopes (junk mail can be used) for children to fold and stuff. Also provide unopened junk mail for children to open. Use stamps from Publisher's Clearinghouse-type contests for children to affix to envelopes, or use stickers that resemble stamps.

Supply magazines for children to cut houses and furniture to glue onto house-shaped paper to make collages. Encourage children to fringe (snip) rugs for their collage.

Supply paint and old toothbrushes for toothbrush painting. Old toothbrushes can be used to spread glue. Also supply toothpicks for children to glue together to form shapes or to use on collages.

2. PREWRITING

Dot to Dot. Prepare several dot-to-dot pictures for children to complete. Include simple household objects and hearts.

Path Tracing. Make diagonal and ∨-shaped paths for children to follow. They can draw between the lines to take a letter to a house, a toothbrush to a tooth, etc.

Follow That Line. Children use felt-tip pens or crayons to trace over diagonal lines and ∨ strokes predrawn on various textures of paper.

Copy Mine. Draw a diagonal or ∨ on a small chalkboard. Children copy the line on paper, on a small chalkboard, or in the air.

Glue It. Give children a large sheet of paper divided into thirds. Draw a diagonal \, /, or ∨ in each section. Children glue straws or toothpicks down to copy the line in each section.

Folding. Children fold straws or pipe cleaners to make the ∨.

Prewriting Center. Add pink and red markers, crayons, chalk, and colored pencils to the prewriting center. Provide heart-shaped stencils for children to trace. Also provide triangle, square, and rectangle stencils for children to trace and combine to form a house shape. Provide prepared paper-and-pencil activities for children. Examples include dot-to-dot pictures, paths, and mazes which reinforce the February theme.

PERCEPTION

Heart to Heart. Cut many pairs of hearts. Vary the size of heart pairs and shades of pink and red construction paper used. Children match hearts having the same size and/or color.

Break My Heart. Cut out large heart shapes from construction paper. Cut each heart into pieces. Children can assemble the heart puzzles.

Heart Matching. Cut out at least twenty-four hearts from construction paper. Decorate pairs of hearts in the same way. Children can match the hearts.

Heart Concentration. Using the heart pairs made for Heart Matching, children can play a memory/concentration game. Place two to four heart pairs on the table, with the design facing the table. Children take turns turning over two cards at a time trying to find a match. If the child makes a match, she/he keeps the hearts, if not, cards are turned over in the same place and play continues with the next child.

Draw a Person. Using crayons, chalk, or markers, have each child draw a person according to his/her ability. Save the picture for booklet.

Whose Letter?. Prepare an envelope for each child, printing first and/or last names on the front. Take one letter from a mailbox or mailbag and show it to the children. Children indicate who it belongs to.

Name Matching. Prepare a pair of cards or envelopes with the first and/or last name of each child in the class. Children match the name pairs.

Find the Hearts. Draw a simple scene on 8 1/2- by 11-inch paper, or use a picture from a coloring book. Then draw in complete or partially hidden hearts and copy the picture. Children must find and color the hearts on their paper.

Name Cups. Print each child's name on a styrofoam cup with a permanent marker. Print each letter of the child's name on a 1-inch piece of tagboard. Put the letters in the cup. Children shake the cup, spill the letters, and copy their names by matching with the name on the cup.

Kitchen Smells. Collect the small plastic canisters film comes in. Half-fill two canisters for each cooking item or spice (cinnamon, onions, basil, coffee, etc.) or pour one to three drops of extracts (lemon, peppermint, orange) on a cottonball and place it in the canister. Children can match smells, sort good and unpleasant smells, or identify one of three smells that is different.

What's in the Bag?. Place a familiar kitchen utensil in a feely bag, pillowcase or in the mystery box. Each child can reach inside, feel the object, and try to name it. Include a rolling pin, spoon, egg beater, spatula, etc. If the child is unable to name the object, ask the child to demonstrate how it could be used.

Build a House. Precut circles, squares, triangles, rectangles, etc., out of flannel or fabric interfacing to be used on a flannel board. Shapes should be of several colors and sizes. Make a house on the flannel board using the pieces. The children can take turns building their house to look like the sample, or provide small, individual flannel boards so all the children can build at once.

How Docs It Feel?. Collect a variety of fabrics that could be used for draperies or upholstery coverings. Cut two 2- by 4-inch pieces from each scrap. Staple or glue the fabric swatches on pieces of tagboard. Children can match the pieces that are the same, feel and find two of three that are the same, or feel and find one of three that is different. Children can cover or close their eyes, or put their hand into the side of an empty box for this tactile experience.

Household Sounds. Make a tape of household sounds or use one commercially prepared. Play the tape and have children identify what is making the sound (toilet flushing, vaccuming, doorbell ringing, etc.).

Look-Alike Houses. Prepare about twelve to fifteen house pairs. Pairs should differ in obvious ways: position of doors, chimney, and windows, number of doors and windows, etc. Children find and match houses.

House Puzzle. Prepare a model of a house on 18- by 24-inch paper for each child. Draw doors, windows, and a chimney on each. Vary the sizes and shapes on each house. Provide cutouts to match doors, windows, and chimney. Children match pieces and paste.

Room Sorting. Prepare a large house shape from kraft paper and divide it into four sections. Children decide what room each section should represent. Children take turns selecting pictures of furniture and household objects precut from catalogs and magazines and glue the picture in the appropriate room.

Like a Mirror. Tell children to pretend that they are looking at a mirror in the bathroom or in their bedrooms as they watch you. Children copy the actions they see "in the mirror" (combing hair, drying dishes, brushing teeth, etc.).

Patterning. Have children copy and continue patterns using hearts and other shapes cut from construction paper.

Sorting. Children sort a deck of cards into suits.

Envelopes. Children sort envelopes by size.

Mail Carrier Sorting. Children sort pictures of items related to the mail carrier and his/her job from those that aren't.

Perception Center. Children can copy peg designs such as heart shapes, house shapes (made from a triangle, square, and rectangle) letter/envelope shapes, and tooth shapes. Shapes can be drawn on the pegboards with washable markers, or you can prepare examples for children to copy. Heart shapes, letters, and envelopes can be cut apart for children to assemble as puzzles. Children can practice matching skills by finding valentine cards that are the same, envelopes with the same name written on them, or letters written with the same colored ink. If possible, provide commercial puzzles that follow the themes of sharing, dentist, mail carrier, or rooms of the house.

GROSS MOTOR

Skating. Show children how to "ice skate" by sliding their feet on the floor. "Skating" in stocking feet works best. Children can skate forward, backward, sideways, or in simple formations. Gliding to waltz music adds to the movement experience.

Remember the Moves. Depending on the memory skills of the group, give children two to four movements to remember. At a signal, they try to perform all the movements in order (hop, twist and jump or bend, wiggle and walk, etc.).

Up High, Down Low. Prepare two large signs on tagboard, one sign showing an arrow pointing up high, and the other showing the arrow pointing down low. Children move around freely. When a whistle blows, they look at you holding one of the signs. Children move stretched on tiptoes with arms held high if the sign points up high. They crawl or creep down low if the arrow points down low. When the whistle blows again, free movement continues. Moving up high or down low continues at another whistle signal.

Carpet Relay. One child from each of two teams sits on a carpet square and moves to and from a given location. The first team to complete the relay wins.

Cracked Ice. Place several carpet squares on the floor at varying distances apart. The floor is cracked ice and the carpet squares are frozen solid. The children move carefully to cross the river without falling through the cracked ice.

Can You?. Children sit in a semicircle with you facing them in the middle. Give directions that involve paired body parts or opposite-side body parts. The children try each movement (e.g., Can you touch your shoulders? Touch your nose to your knees? Grab one ankle with both hands?).

Shape Pick-up. Place three of two or more shapes (heart, circle, square, triangle, or rectangle, etc.) around the room. Children take turns picking up all three of a specified shapes while moving around the room on a scooter board.

Obstacle Course. Place cardboard boxes or traffic safety cones around the room. Children propel their scooter boards in a prone, kneeling, or sitting position and move around the obstacles without touching them.

Moving Down Low. Place several pairs of traffic safety cones (about 24 inches apart) around the room and top each pair with a yardstick. Children take turns creeping, crawling, or moving on a scooter board down low through the cones without knocking down the yardstick.

Letter, Letter, Mail Carrier. Children sit in a circle. One child holds a letter in an envelope and walks around the outer edge of the circle saying, "Letter, letter, letter, . . . mail carrier!" When the child says *mail carrier,* he/she drops the letter behind the child tapped. The child chases the other around the circle back to the original space. Then that child walks around with the letter and the game is repeated.

Flossing Teeth. Children make two lines of "teeth" by standing close together with feet about 12 inches apart. Children take turns crawling and "flossing" between the holes of the teeth made by the children's legs.

Mat Activities—Rolling. Children can experience various rolling activities on a mat. Ask them to lie flat on their stomachs and:

> roll with arms extended over the head, keeping feet together, reverse direction.

roll with arms extended over the head, holding a small ball or bean bag, reverse direction.

roll with arms held at the sides of body, reverse direction.

roll with one arm extended over the head and one arm held at the side, reverse direction.

Mat Activities—Crawling. Children crawl across the mat:

GI Joe style—arms bent toward the chest, pulling forward, keeping legs flat on the mat, dragging behind

Alligator style—bend arms and legs to move while laying flat on stomach

Mat Activities—Creeping. Children move across the mat creeping forward on hands and knees using alternating motions. Children reverse and creep backward.

Doggie Walk. Children bend down in a dog-like position balancing their bodies evenly on both hands and feet. They move across the mat on all fours doing the "doggie walk."

Monkey Walk. Children bend over and hold their ankles loosely with their hands. Bending knees slightly, children move across the mat like monkeys.

Frog Jump. Children get in a squatting position on the mat, placing hands flat between their knees. They jump forward on all fours like a frog and move to the end of the mat.

Crab Walk. Children sit on a mat with knees bent and hands placed behind their backs, under their shoulders. By pushing their bodies up off the mat, children make a crab. They move carefully in either direction.

Forward Rolls. Children squat down on their heels, keeping hands flat on the mat. Keeping their chins tucked against their knees, children raise bottoms up and push off with toes. Lead body over on a roll, keeping head tucked against knees. Children can roll to the end of the mat.

Body Awareness. Children spread out on mats, preferably two children to a mat. Call out different body parts, and the children must move positions so that part touches the mat (shoulder, back, stomach, elbow, etc.).

SENSORY EXPERIENCES

Kitchen Kapers. Fill the exploration table with water, oatmeal, rice, cornmeal, dried peas, etc., when learning about the kitchen and objects found there. Children will enjoy washing, pouring, measuring, filling, emptying, sifting, and ladling at the table. Provide a variety of objects for children to manipulate that reinforce kitchen experiences. Include plastic dishes, measuring spoons and cups, ladles, sifters, funnels, salt shakers, etc.

Tub Time. When learning about the bathroom, let children enjoy playing with warm, soapy water in the exploration table. Provide sponges, washclothes, towels, small bars of soap, plastic dolls, cars, and trucks. Children will enjoy being in charge at "bathtime."

Clean Mud.

Six rolls of white toilet paper
Two small bars of Ivory™ soap
1 1/2 cups of Borax™
Lots of water

Have children unroll the toilet paper into a large plastic tub. Add cups of water until covered with water and let set a few days. Grate the soap and add that along with the Borax™ to the soaking paper. If it is still too wet, drain over a fine screen or cheese cloth (do not squeeze). Put clean mud out in a large plastic tub or pan to manipulate, mold, shape, and have fun with. It should last for weeks, slowly becoming firmer and eventually hardening.

Taste and Compare. Provide a variety of sensory experiences that encourage children to taste and compare. Ask what tastes good and what doesn't. Some children may be ready to discriminate tastes using the words *sweet, sour,* and *salty*.

Things that look the same:
salt vs. sugar
vanilla vs. soy sauce
flour vs. sugar
Things to sip:
Kool Aid™
lemonade
salt water
Things sweet: cookies, candy
          sour: lemons, pickles
          salty: pretzels, popcorn
Make popcorn, taste it with and without salt.
Squeeze fresh lemons to make lemonade, taste it with and without sugar.

PREMATH

Bean Bag Toss. Prepare seven large heart shapes and number them from one to seven. Laminate the shapes. Scatter the hearts on the floor. Each child tosses a bean bag on a heart and names the numeral. Children can also work on ordering the hearts from one through seven.

Mend My Heart. Cut out seven large hearts from construction paper. Cut each heart in half making sure that hearts are all cut differently. On one side of the hearts write the numbers one through seven, and on the other, draw sets of objects to match the numbers. Pass out pieces to the children. The children move around the room trying to match a numeral with its set. If the heart pieces fit together, the heart is mended!

Cut and Count. Have children make a flat pizza shape from play dough. They can cut the pizza into seven pieces with a dull knife or pizza cutter to share with a friend.

How Many?. Fill the classroom doll house with the furniture, household objects, and people available. Children take turns counting the windows, the beds, the doors, the tables, the number of people in the kitchen, in the house, etc.

Sort and Count. Children sort and count the spoons, cups, and napkins used at snack time.

How Much Furniture?. Children touch and count the furniture found in the room: tables and chairs, desks, etc.

Cabinet Count. Have children touch and count objects kept up high and down low in classroom cabinets, on shelves, etc.

Shape Game. Prepare large shapes cut from construction paper (circles, triangles, squares, hearts, etc.). Laminate pieces. Children begin the game by standing in a circle. Give a shape to each child. Then begin giving directions (e.g., "Circles sit down. Hearts turn around. Squares hop." etc.). Midpoint in the game, have children get a new shape. This is an excellent listening activity.

Flannel Board Story. Tell a simple story. Provide teacher-made or commercial flannel board cutouts (stars, flowers, snowmen, animals, etc.). As you tell the story, the children take turns adding and removing the correct number of pieces on the flannel board. ("Joe walked to John's house. On the way he saw three snowmen. The children in front of John's house were building one snowman, too. On the way to the park the boys saw two more snowmen . . ." Continue on.) Several times throughout the story, stop and have children touch and count objects on the flannel board to find out "how many _____ are there now?"

Seven Jump to Heaven. Seven children sit in a circle and pass a bean bag to the person next to them. As children get the bean bag, they count their number out loud from 1 to 7. When the bean bag has traveled around the circle through 7, children all "jump up to heaven" and shout 7.

Heart Cards. Remove the face cards from a deck of cards. Children find and count how many cards have hearts on them.

Hearts in Order. Remove the heart cards from 1 through 7 from a deck. Children put the cards in order.

Go Fish. Pull the four suits of cards, 1 through 7, from a deck. Two to four children can play the game. Deal four cards to each player. The rest of the cards are placed face down on the table. The children try to make pairs of cards with matching numbers. Pairs are placed on the table. In a clockwise direction, children take turns asking each other for a card to make a pair. ("Do you have a 5?" etc.) If the child has the correct number, she/he gives it to the other, so a pair is made. If the child doesn't have the requested card, the asker must "go fish" by taking a card from the middle. The child keeps the card whether or not a pair is made. The next child takes a turn, etc. The winner is the first person to go out by having no more cards.

Cards in the Middle. Place the four suits of cards, 1 through 7, from a deck face down on the table. Children take turns picking up a card, naming the number, and counting the symbols on each card.

Moves through Six. Children take turns rolling a die. They must jump, tap, hop, etc., the same number of times as shown on the die.

February Calendar. Continue daily calendar activities with the children by adding a symbol each day. Calendar cutouts to pattern on the calendar could include red and pink hearts, toothbrushes and teeth, etc. Count how many days are in each week, how many days are left in the week, and how many days until a classmate's birthday or the next field trip. Count the numbers forwards and backwards on the calendar. Talk about events that happened yesterday, today, and will happen tomorrow. Clap the names of the days of the week.

Empty and Full. Bring several empty milk cartons to the snack table. When it's time to begin serving, show children the cartons, let them feel the cartons, and ask them what's wrong. Supply the word *empty* if the children are unable to. Ask several children to walk to the refrigerator to find cartons that are full.

Filling and Dumping. Give children opportunities to use a variety of cups, bottles, jars, and containers at the rice- or water-filled exploration table. Have children name containers that are empty and those that are full.

Sorting Empty and Full. Have children sort bottles, jars, baskets, vases, plates, cups, etc., that are empty and full.

Heart Game. Form a huge heart shape on the floor with masking tape. Children stand behind a line. If you say "full," children run to stand inside the heart. If you say "empty," they all scramble out.

Snack Time. Talk about the full cartons, packages, and so on at the beginning of snack. Talk about what's empty at the end of snack.

Letter Days. Use the calendar to count the days that the mail carrier delivers mail. Children can learn not to wait for the mail carrier on Sundays and holidays.

Snow White. Read *Snow White and the Seven Dwarfs.* Count the dwarfs. Make flannel board cutouts of the dwarfs. Give each dwarf a lunch box, flower, or other item to reinforce one-to-one correspondence.

SONGS AND FINGERPLAYS

The Valentine Song (tune: "Farmer in the Dell").

A valentine for you
To cheer you when you're blue
Heigh-ho, the derry oh,
A valentine for you.
I'll mail you a hug
And send you all my love.
Heigh-ho, the derry oh,
A valentine for you.

Friends (tune: "If You're Happy and You Know It").

If you have a toy, then share it
with a friend.
If you have a toy, then share it
with a friend.
If you have a friend and know it
and you really want to show it.
If you have a toy, then share it
with a friend.
(Brainstorm other objects or food items children would like to share. Substitute into the song for new verses.)

Counting Valentines (tune: "Ten Little Indians").

One red, two red, three red valentines,
Four red, five red, six red valentines,
Seven red, eight red, nine red valentines,
Ten red valentines.
(Sing again—substitute the color pink.)

Valentines (fingerplay)

Red valentines, pink valentines
How many do you see?
Red valentines, pink valentines
Count them with me.
One for father (Hold up thumb.)
One for mother (Hold up pointer finger.)
One for sister (Hold up ring finger.)
One for brother (Hold up little finger.)
And here is one for you. (Make heart shape with thumbs and index finger.)

Look in the Mailbox (fingerplay).

When you look in the mailbox,
What do you think you'll see? (Pretend to look in box.)
It might be a valentine,
And it might be from me. (Point to themselves.)
(Substitute postcard, package, letter, etc., for new verses.)

Clean Teeth (tune: "Mulberry Bush"—pantomime the actions).

This is the way we brush our teeth,
We brush our teeth, we brush our teeth.
This is the way we brush our teeth,
So early in the morning.
(Substitute other actions for new verses: floss our teeth, swish the water, chew
our food, and eat good snacks, etc.)

Oh My Bedroom (tune: "Clementine").

Oh my bedroom, oh my bedroom,
Oh my bedroom is a mess!
I have to clean my bedroom,
So it will look its best!
Make the bed,
Pick the toys up,
Gather all the dirty clothes!
I have to clean my bedroom,
So it will look its best!

All Around the House (tune: "Pop, Goes the Weasel").

All around our homey house
We look for the (teacher or children supply the name of a household item).
Where is the (household item named above)?
In the (children supply name of correct room—living room, kitchen, bedroom,
bathroom)

RECIPES

Winter Sweet Pizza.

Cream together: Add:

   1/2 cup of butter   1 1/2 cups of flour
   3/4 cup of sugar   1 teaspoon of cream of tartar
   1 egg   1/4 teaspoon salt
                1/2 teaspoon baking soda

Combine mixture and spread crust on a round greased pizza pan. Bake 10–12
minutes at 400 degrees until golden brown. Cool completely. Top with a
mixture of one eight ounce cream cheese and 1/4 cup honey. Arrange cut

winter fruits on top (apples, pears, bananas, oranges, and kiwis). Cut into pieces and share.

Heart Cake.

Grease and flour 1 square pan, 8 × 8× 2 inches, and 1 round layer pan, 8 × 1 1/2 inches.

Prepare 1 package of white cake mix as directed. Divide the batter between the square and round pans. Bake square pan 25 to 30 minutes, round pan 30 to 35 minutes or until wooden pick inserted in center comes out clean. Cool.

Place square layer on tray. Cut round layer in half. Place cut edge of each half against the top sides of the square to make a heart shape. Frost with pink buttercream frosting.

Buttercream Frosting.

6 tablespoons butter
1 1-pound package of confectioners' sugar, sifted (about 4 3/4 cups)
1/4 cup milk
1 1/2 teaspoons vanilla

Cream butter; gradually add about half the sugar, blending well. Beat in 2 tablespoons milk and vanilla. Gradually blend in remaining sugar. Add enough milk to make of spreading consistency. Add drops of red food coloring to get desired shade of pink.

Pizza Bread.

1 long loaf of French bread cut in half lengthwise
1 large can of pizza sauce
6–8 thin slices of salami cut into fours
1 small green pepper, diced
1 large package of mozzarella cheese
1 small can of mushrooms

Children assemble the pizza bread: Spoon sauce evenly over both halves of bread, put on salami, green pepper, mushrooms, and top with cheese. Bake in a 375-degree oven for about 20 minutes or until cheese melts on top.

Honey Nut Granola.

2 1/2 cups uncooked oats
1/2 cup firm brown sugar
1/2 cup sunflower seeds or chopped nuts
1/3 cup honey
1/3 cup melted margarine
1 teaspoon cinnamon
1/2 cup raisins

Preheat oven to 325 degrees. Combine all ingredients, except raisins; mix well. Bake in a lightly greased 13″ × 9″ pan for 20–25 minutes, stirring occasionally. Stir in raisins. Spread mixture onto an ungreased cookie sheet to cool. Makes 6 cups.

Red Knox™ Blocks.

> 4 3-ounce packages strawberry Jello™
> 3 envelopes Knox™ gelatin
> 4 cups boiling water

Mix jello and gelatin; add boiling water and stir until all is dissolved. Pour into a 9″ × 13″ pan and cool.

FEBRUARY SNACKS

Heart Tarts. Children cut two hearts from white bread using a heart-shaped cookie cutter. They spread cherry, strawberry, or raspberry preserves on one heart. Top with the second heart.

Crunch and Munch. Serve crunchy snacks that make teeth happy. Include apple slices, carrot sticks, celery sticks, green pepper sticks, popcorn sprinkled with cheese, and pretzel sticks.

Strawberry Shakes. Blend milk, banana chunks, and a package of strawberries to make pink shakes.

Yogurt Stir. Stir strawberry preserves into plain yogurt for a pink surprise.

Sweet Sundaes. On a special day, let children top a small scoop of frozen yogurt or vanilla ice cream with favorite toppings.

Negative Toast. Children cut a heart shape out of a slice of white bread with a cookie cutter. Toast the "negative space" bread. Top toast and heart cutout with red jelly, jam, or preserves.

Pink Fluff. Make any sugar-free red Jello™ according to package directions. Whip in a small amount of nondairy whipped topping.

Red and Yummy. Serve red foods such as apples, red peppers, red Jello™, tomato slices, strawberries, tomato soup, miniature hot dogs on a toothpick, and tart red cherries.

Pink and Juicy. Children watch and/or help peel a ruby red grapefruit. Separate into sections and share. Surprise! The red grapefruit is pink on the inside.

Apple Smiles. Give each child two slices of red apple. They spread on peanut butter to represent the gums and stick marshmallow teeth on the peanut butter gums.

CREATIVE DRAMATICS

The Three Pigs. Children enjoy dramatizing the folk tale *The Three Pigs*. All children are likely to participate in repeating the familiar lines, "Little pig, little pig, let me come in." "Not by the hair of my chinny chin chin!" "Then I'll huff and I'll puff and I'll blow your house in!"

When preparing props for retelling the story, children can be actively involved. With minimal help from you, an aide, or parent volunteer, children can build houses with blocks, straws, and sticks. All the little pigs can cut a circle to tape on their noses. The big bad wolf can fringe paper to make a tail.

Letter Carrier. Set up a post office and neighborhood mail route in the dramatic play area. The post office can be as simple as a table with a large sign that reads *Post Office.* Provide a wide variety of items for the postal workers to sort. Include newspapers, post cards, letters, and small packages.

The neighborhood postal route can be made using blocks, large cartons, or chairs as houses. Each house should have a simple address (e.g., a short sequence of numbers 1, 2, 3).

Envelopes can be prepared that match the house addresses. The children can take turns being mail carriers and house residents.

House. Children love to play house. They can alternate being Mom, Dad, or the children. In the dramatic play area, set up as many different rooms as possible. Include a kitchen, bedroom, laundry room, etc. Children can cook, wash dishes, clean, sort laundry, and sleep. Little prompting will be necessary since this is a familiar theme. Provide as many real objects as possible, e.g., kitchen utensils and dishes, a broom, real clothes, a sleeping bag and pillow, etc.

Dentist. Set up a dentist's office in the dramatic play area. Include a waiting room with a desk for the receptionist and a telephone and paper and pencil for message taking. Also set up an examination room with a "special" chair and an instrument table. Be sure to stress to children not to really put instruments in their mouths. Take advantage of the opportunity to discuss germs, hand washing, etc. Dental supplies might include floss, toothpicks, toothpaste, Q-tips™, paper cups, and rubber gloves. If possible, supply a toothbrush for each child.

CHILDREN'S LITERATURE

Adler, David A. *The House on the Rock*

Ahlberg, Janet and Allan. *The Jolly Postman*

Anderson, Leone Castell. *Moving Day*

Barrett, Judi. *I Hate to Go to Bed*
_____. *I Hate to Take a Bath*

Bate, Lucy. *Little Rabbit's Loose Tooth*

Becker, Edna. *Nine Hundred Buckets of Paint*

Bell, Norman. *Linda's Airmail Letter*

Berenstain, Stan and Jan. *The Berenstain Bears Visit the Dentist*

Brown, Myra. *Best Friends*

Burton, Virginia Lee. *The Little House*

Cohen, Miriam. *Bee My Valentine*

Disney, Walt. *Snow White and the Seven Dwarfs*

Drummond, Violet H. *The Flying Postman*

Du Voisin, Roger Antoine. *Crocus*

Geisel, Theodor Seuss. *Come Over to My House*

_____ . *In a People House*
Hader, Berta and Elmer. *The Little Stone House*
Haley, Gail Diana Einhart. *The Post Office Cat*
Hefter, Richard. *The Strawberry Book of Colors*
Heine, Helme. *Friends*
Hill, Eric. *At Home*
Hutchins, Pat. *The Doorbell Rang*
Jackson, Ellen B. *The Bear in the Bathtub*
Jaynes, Ruth. *The Biggest House*
Johnson, John. *This Is My House*
Keats, Ezra Jack. *A Letter to Amy*
Keeshan, Robert. *She Loves Me, She Loves Me Not*
Krahn, Fernando. *Little Love Story*
Lapp, Carolyn. *The Dentist's Tools*
Maestro, Betsy and Guilio. *Harriet at Home*
Maury, Inez. *My Mother the Mail Carrier*
Mayer, Mercer. *Little Monster at Home*
Miles, Betty. *A House for Everyone*
Minarik, Else Homelund. *A Kiss for Little Bear*
Modell, Frank. *One Zillion Valentines*

North, Carol. *The House Book*
Pluckrose, Henry. *Think about Tasting*
Richter, Alice, and Numeroff, Laura Joffe. *You Can't Put Braces on Spaces*
Rockwell, Anne. *The Awful Mess*
Rockwell, Anne and Harlow. *I Play in My Room*
Rockwell, Harlow. *My Dentist*
_____ . *My Kitchen*
Scarry, Richard McClure. *Is This the House of Mistress Mouse?*
_____ . *Richard Scarry's Postman Pig and His Busy Neighbors*
Schultz, Charles M. *Be My Valentine*
Schweninger, Ann. *The Hunt for Rabbit's Galosh*
Sendak, Maurice. *Where the Wild Things Are*
Silverstein, Shel. *The Giving Tree*
Thatcher, Hurd. *The Old Chair*
Tornborg, Pat. *Spring Cleaning*
Wantanbe, Shiego. *I Can Build a House*
Watson, Switzer and Hirschberg. *My Friend the Dentist*
Yoken, Jane. *No Bath Tonight*

Evaluating February Concepts

Throughout the month, continue to update and record significant progress and/or changes made by the children. Use the checklists found in the Appendix to assess concepts taught in February. Vocabulary assessment, both receptive and expressive, should focus on the list of household words you selected at the beginning of the month. You should continue to reinforce and review home addresses throughout the remainder of the year.

During February, you can observe each child's approach to activities. Does the child appear organized or disorganized? You might notice if the child is distracted excessively by extraneous visual or auditory stimulation during structured and unstructured activities. These observations can be briefly recorded in each child's "individual log." Behavior examples should be kept specific and objective.

LANGUAGE AND VOCABULARY

      Rooms of the house—naming, sorting, and classifying household objects

      Dental Health—job of the dentist, care, good foods

      Mail Carrier—job of the mail carrier, learning home address

      Valentine's Day—theme of friendship and sharing

      Cooking Experiences

      Colors—red and pink

      Directional and Positional Concepts—high and low

FINE MOTOR

      Lacing, painting, coloring, gluing, play dough manipulation, cutting, block tower building, bead stringing, path tracing, diagonals \\, /, and $\lor$ stroke

PERCEPTION

      Same and different, draw a person, puzzles, copying block, peg and bead designs, patterning and sorting

GROSS MOTOR

      Organized games, movement activities, gymnastic—mat activities

PREMATH

      One-to-one correspondence, calendar activities, sorting, number and numeral 7, empty and full, heart shape

CREATIVE DRAMATICS

SENSORY EXPERIENCES

FEBRUARY
Parent-child activities

SUN	MON	TUE	WED	THU	FRI	SAT
STRETCH UP HIGH AND CRUNCH DOWN LOW TO MUSIC.	FIND SOMETHING MADE OF GLASS, WOOD, METAL, AND PLASTIC IN THE LIVING ROOM.	LOOK FOR ADDRESSES ON THE HOUSES IN THE NEIGHBORHOOD.	LOOK FOR RED FOOD AT THE GROCERY STORE.	PRACTICE FEBRUARY SONGS AND FINGERPLAYS.	CUT OUT NEWSPAPER PICTURES.	REVIEW BODY PARTS AT BATH TIME. LET YOUR CHILD GATHER ALL SUPPLIES NEEDED.
FIND SOMETHING RED IN EACH ROOM OF THE HOUSE.	MAIL A LETTER OR PACKAGE.	MAKE A HEART-SHAPED SANDWICH. USE A COOKIE CUTTER.	WATCH FOR THE MAIL CARRIER TO ARRIVE. COUNT THE PIECES OF MAIL.	READ YOUR CHILD A BEDTIME STORY.	TRACE AROUND KITCHEN OBJECTS, PLATES, COOKIE CUTTERS, CONTAINERS, ETC.	HAPPY VALENTINE'S DAY! SAY NICE THINGS.
STACK ALL THE CONTAINERS IN THE CABINETS UP HIGH.	DISCUSS KITCHEN SAFETY—HOT STOVE, CLEANING SUPPLIES, SHARP OBJECTS, ETC.	COLOR A PICTURE; USE ALL THE COLORS.	WATERPLAY TODAY IN THE TUB OR SINK.	COUNT ALL THE PILLOWS IN THE HOUSE.	STRETCH YARN BETWEEN 2 CHAIRS. HANG UP SOCKS USING CLOTHESPINS.	HELP CLEAN YOUR BEDROOM DRAWERS AND CLOSET.
BLOW UP 2 BALLOONS, 1 RED AND 1 PINK. BAT THEM UP HIGH.	BUY A NEW TOOTHBRUSH. BRUSH TEETH THE RIGHT WAY.	FILL A PAPER PLATE WITH PICTURES OF GOOD FOODS TO EAT.	HELP MOM/DAD EMPTY THE DRYER AND FOLD THE WASHCLOTHS.	FOLD PAPER AND PUT IN OLD USED ENVELOPES.	PRACTICE FORWARD ROLLS ON A SOFT RUG.	PREPARE A HEALTHY SNACK TOGETHER: "ANTS ON A LOG"—CELERY WITH PEANUT BUTTER AND RAISINS.

MARCH

CONCEPTS FOR MARCH

LANGUAGE AND VOCABULARY

1. Transportation—naming and describing things that move, sorting and classifying
2. Doctor and Nurse—what they do, how they help us, things to do to stay healthy, vocabulary
3. St. Patrick's Day Theme—real and make-believe
4. Sequencing Stories, Pictures, and Events—what happens first, next, and last, beginning and end? What makes sense?
5. Color—yellow
6. Directional and Positional Concepts—first, middle, and last

Suggested field trips/classroom visitors: Visit a train station, bus station, or airport. Have a doctor/nurse visit the class. Have a pilot, train conductor, bus, or truck driver visit the class.

FINE MOTOR: 1. MANIPULATION, AND 2. PREWRITING

Lacing, painting, coloring, gluing, play dough manipulation, cutting, block tower building, bead stringing, centers, path tracing, design copying (square)

PERCEPTION

Same and different, draw a person, center activities: puzzles, copying block, peg and bead designs, patterning and sorting

GROSS MOTOR

Organized games, movement activities, bean bag activities

PREMATH

One-to-one correspondence, calendar activities, sorting, number and numeral 8, long and short, shamrock shape

SENSORY EXPERIENCES

Exploration table, sense of hearing

CREATIVE DRAMATICS

- Doctor–Nurse
- Transportation
- *The Gingerbread Man*

RECIPES

Healthy foods

SNACK

Food related to monthly concepts and themes

SELF-HELP

Provide activities at children's developmental levels

REVIEW

Any previous concepts

ACTIVITIES FOR MARCH

LANGUAGE AND VOCABULARY

1. TRANSPORTATION

Brainstorming. Give the children the opportunity to brainstorm things we ride in. Write all of their responses on chart paper or the chalkboard. Count how many different forms of transportation they name. Visual cues/pictures may be used.

Hide and Seek. Hide pictures or toy models of various forms of transportation around the room. Give the children clues regarding what type of vehicle to look for and where they can find it. For example, "It goes in the water." When the child has guessed that she/he is looking for a boat, give clues regarding where it is hidden, e.g., "It is under something to sit on."

Vehicle Classification. Using pictures or objects, sort vehicles from nonvehicles. Present the children with a variety of vehicles or various modes of transportation along with other categories of objects such as household or clothing items. Children name, then talk about and describe each item, decide if they are vehicles or not, and sort them into the appropriate group.

Transportation Sort. Present children with pictures or models of various modes of transportation that go either on the land, in the air, or in the water. Name, describe, and discuss each item. Sort them into categories of land, air, or water vehicles.

The Car. Take a walk to the parking lot to "visit" your car. Have the children look at the car and name the outside parts (hood, trunk, tires, doors, etc.). Allow one or two children at a time to go inside the car and label the parts (steering wheel, mirrors, seats, seat belts, etc.). Upon returning to the classroom, label a predrawn or model car with as many parts as the children can remember.

Car Safety. Review the car safety rules such as: Wear a seat belt, sit quietly in one place, use a quiet voice, don't touch door handles, etc. Discuss why each rule is important to remember. Following the review and discussion, make a class "car safety book." Write a safety rule on each page and have the children illustrate the pages. Laminate and assemble the book and place it in your class library.

Airplane Story. Make up a story about a family going on an airplane trip. Provide props and use children as actors in the story. Include all or part of the following sequence in the story, or make up another one: (1) Pack the suitcase, (2) drive to the airport, (3) check the baggage, (4) board the plane, (5) find seats, (6) fasten seat belt, (7) take off, (8) eat, (9) land, (10) unfasten the seat belt, (11) walk off the airplane. After going through the sequence a number of times, have children retell or act out the story in sequence. Younger children or children with more significant delays will need the number of steps in the sequence reduced.

Trains. Bring in pictures or models of passenger and freight trains. Discuss the differences between the two types of trains. Name the various cars on both the passenger and freight trains. Provide pictures or models of objects or people you might find on a passenger or freight train. Have children decide which train to put them on. Some examples include people, animals, tickets, dining room supplies, various freight items, etc.

Boats. Provide pictures of different kinds of boats. Include large and small boats, tugs, boats that use motors, sails, paddles, etc. Name the different kinds of boats. Talk about how many people would fit on the boat. Label the parts of the boats and encourage discussion about them.

School Bus. Ask your school bus driver to give the children a tour of the school bus. Ask him/her to label parts of the bus (wipers, horn, door opener, flashers, seats, etc.). School bus safety rules should be discussed and stressed. After the school bus tour, write a class story about "The School Bus" and mount it on a large cutout of a school bus.

Traffic Signs and Signals. The meaning of traffic signs and signals can be taught and stressed throughout this unit. Some ideas for teaching sign recognition and meaning follow.

Sign Walk. Go for a walk to look for signs and signals. Observe, describe, and label stop signs, yield signs, stop and go lights, train crossing signs and gates, pedestrian crossing signs, etc. Upon returning to the classroom, try to remember and list all the signs that were seen.

Signs in the Classroom. Use commercially made signs or make your own (see fine motor activities). Set up chairs and have children pretend they are riding in a car. Have them pretend to drive, then hold up a sign. Children can "read" the sign and follow the appropriate action.

Model Roadway. On large paper spread on the floor, make a map of a roadway. Draw signs on the map or use signs prepared in the fine motor activity section. Have children drive their cars, buses, or trucks on the map and follow the correct procedures for each sign.

Name It. Describe different vehicles discussed during the transportation unit. Have children identify the vehicle from the description and tell one more thing about it. Use visual clues if necessary.

Pedestrian Walk. Discuss that pedestrians must follow sign directions just as vehicles do. Go for a walk in the classroom, gym, or outside and follow the sign directions of teacher-made or posted signs.

2. DOCTOR AND NURSE

Mystery Box. Put real or play medical objects in your mystery box. Include the following: a stethoscope, a thermometer, Band-Aids™, a tongue depressor, cotton balls, a blood pressure guage, a medicine container, a syringe, and an otoscope. Have children remove objects; name one at a time, talk about each object, its use, and the children's personal experiences with the medical objects.

Keeping Healthy. Brainstorm with the children various things they do to keep healthy. Clues and leading questions may be necessary. Lead children into discussions on healthy foods, plenty of rest and exercise, bathing, tooth brushing, and regular check-ups with the doctor. If possible, find pictures to use as visual cues. Allow children the time to relate their own experiences. Make a list or write a language experience story based on the discussion. Illustrate the story with children's drawings or with magazine pictures which depict the various ways of keeping healthy.

What Does the Doctor Do?. Describe roles and responsibilities of doctors and nurses, as well as those of three or four other community helpers. Children must decide if the roles described are those of a doctor or nurse, or of other community helpers. Children enjoy catching you when you try to "trick" them with the other community helpers. Sample statements might include: "The doctor prescribes medicine when we are ill." "The nurse delivers our mail."

Role-Playing. Use the doctor's office setup in the dramatic play area for more structured role-playing. This will help foster language and concept development as they relate to this unit. Assign roles such as the parent, the patient, the doctor, and the nurse. Encourage language and prompt speaking and discussion between the characters when necessary.

Classroom Visitors. If possible, have a doctor and/or nurse visit the classroom. Ask them to talk about their jobs and how the job of the doctor and the nurse differ If it isn't possible to arrange the visit of a doctor and/or nurse, most hospital public relations departments will be happy to send a hospital representative.

Medicine Safety. Display various types and forms of medicine and the containers medicine comes in. Discuss the safety rules with the children. Reinforce that medicine is never taken unless prescribed by a doctor, and never taken unless under supervision of a parent or other responsible adult. Consider having a representative from a poison control center visit the class and talk about medicine safety and other issues of poison control.

3. ST. PATRICK'S DAY

Shamrock Hunt. Hide shamrocks throughout the room. Give children clues to help them "hunt" for the shamrocks. Review directional and positional concepts taught during preceding months when giving directions. This activity can be varied by hiding green and yellow shamrocks to reinforce color concepts. Count the shamrocks, and have children determine if there are more/less green or yellow shamrocks.

Secret Leprechaun. For a few days leading up to St. Patrick's Day, have a secret leprechaun visit the classroom. While the children are out, the leprechaun might leave materials for a special project, foods for a cooking project or snack, a special book to read, or a new game for the classroom. On St. Patrick's Day, he might leave a special treat or small gift (e.g., a sticker) for each child.

Real or Make-Believe? Present the children with a variety of situations that could be real and some that could only be make-believe. This activity can be done visually with pictures or as an auditory activity. Children must decide if the situations are real or make-believe. Some examples follow: (1) a cat climbing a tree, (2) a child wearing a swimming suit playing in snow, (3) a train going in water, (4) a child looking at a book, (5) an airplane flying, (6) a man walking upside-down in the air. Ask children why the situations are real or make-believe.

Four Leaf Clover Game. Prepare four leaf clovers with directions written on them. Put the clovers inside a "leprechaun's hat." Children take turns choosing a four leaf clover and following the directions on it. Vary the difficulty level of the directions based on the children's levels. Reinforce prepositions, colors, premath, and other concepts. *Example:* "Clap your hands eight times, walk to the table, put a book in the yellow box, and sit down on the chair."

4. SEQUENCING

Story Sequencing. Many of the favorite nursery stories lend themselves to sequencing activities. Stories such as *The Three Bears, The Three Pigs,* and *Little Red Riding Hood* follow a definite, predictable sequence. These stories are familiar to most children. Choose a story and read it or tell it using flannel board pieces. Follow by asking the children to retell it. Use the terms *first, next, last, beginning,* and *end* when the children are retelling the story. Provide the children with pictures or flannel board objects and ask them to put the pictures or objects in order. To simplify the activity, ask children to retell the story simply by using the pictures in the book that are already in proper sequence.

Activity Sequencing. Do a favorite activity that has a definite order and sequence. Simple cooking projects lend themselves well to this. When sequencing an activity, start with something simple that has only a few steps. For example, try making orange or apple juice from concentrate. First you open the can, next you pour the juice into a pitcher, then you add water, last you stir the juice. Provide teacher-made or Polaroid™ pictures of the activity for the children to sequence. Prepare children for the activity by sequencing what you will do. Follow the activity by asking the children to sequence what was done. Be sure to use the terms *first, next, middle,* and *last.*

Picture Recipes. When using March recipes, prepare "picture recipes." Children can follow these picture recipes and then review the activity by sequencing what they did. Draw each step of the recipe on a separate paper to make follow-up sequencing easier.

Dress the Leprechaun. Make a leprechaun for the flannel board and make flannel board clothes for dressing him. Have children take turns dressing the leprechaun and then telling what they put on him first, next, and last. Clothing examples include a green hat, green jacket and pants, and green leprechaun shoes.

School Day Sequence. Pictorially record a typical school day either with photographs or teacher-made pictures. At the end of the day, put the pictures in order of what happened first, next, and last, during the school day. Also discuss what happened at the beginning and end of the school day. Ask the children to tell about each picture and use their descriptions for captions. Assemble the pictures into a book to use in your class library or use the pictures to make a bulletin board.

5. COLOR—YELLOW

Mystery Box. Try varying the mystery box activity this month. Put only one item in the box. That will be used for a "yellow" introductory activity. Since cooking is motivating for most children, try putting a box of vanilla sugar-free pudding in the box. Give children clues so they can guess the mystery box item. Prepare the pudding together, following the directions on the box. Watch together as the pudding turns yellow.

Yellow Walk. Take a walk around the neighborhood looking for things that are yellow. Help children notice yellow lights, yellow houses and cars, yellow flowers, yellow curtains, etc. Upon returning, ask each child to draw something she/he remembers from the walk. Have the child dictate a sentence story about the picture. Assemble the pictures into book form and add to your class library.

Yellow Show and Tell. Ask the children to bring in only yellow objects for show and tell. Children will describe and tell about their yellow object. Follow by labeling objects and displaying them in a special place. Reinforce memory and listening skills by asking each child to tell about what one of his/her classmates brought to school.

Yellow Day. Choose a day in March to be "yellow day." On that day, everyone wears something yellow. Provide a yellow snack. Concentrate on activities that reinforce the color yellow at the fine motor and perception centers.

Yellow Box. Cover a box with yellow construction paper, label it "Yellow Box," and fill it with a variety of yellow objects. Have children take turns removing one item at a time from the box, and ask them to name and describe their object. Prompt them to describe physical characteristics, function, who would use it, when and where it would be used, etc.

6. DIRECTIONAL AND POSITIONAL CONCEPTS—FIRST, MIDDLE, LAST

Lining Up. When lining up throughout the day, let children alternate being first, last, or in the middle of the line.

Parade of Animals. Using stuffed animals or dolls, have children stage a parade. Discuss who is first, last, or in the middle of the parade.

Traffic Jam. Use toy vehicles to create a traffic jam at a stoplight or sign. Have children label vehicles as first, middle, and last.

Shamrock Designs. Have children cut shamrocks out of three different colors, for example, green, yellow, and blue. Give auditory directions to glue the shamrocks on their papers, putting green first, yellow in the middle, and blue last.

FINE MOTOR

1. MANIPULATION

Paper Airplanes. Give simple directions for folding paper airplanes. Accompany auditory directions with visual cues. Have children decorate their airplanes with crayons or markers.

Seat Belts. Bring an old seat belt to the classroom. Allow children to buckle and unbuckle the seat belt.

Easel Painting. Provide shapes of different vehicles at the easel. Alternate vehicles on various days. Include air, land, and water vehicles.

Transportation Bulletin Board. Divide a bulletin board horizontally into three sections: air, land, and water. Have children look through magazines and find pictures of vehicles appropriate to each of the three areas. Have children cut out the pictures and mount them on the appropriate section. The activity can be simplified by having pictures available and ready to be cut out.

Completer Pictures. Provide starter pictures of vehicles for children to complete. There is no right or wrong way to complete the picture. Starter pictures can be as simple as a shape (rectangle, square, oval) drawn on a sheet of paper. One child might turn a rectangle into a bus, while another might turn it into a space ship.

Creative Vehicles. Give children a variety of precut shapes. They can creatively assemble the shapes to make a new or familiar vehicle.

Milk Carton Trains. Clean and save half-pint milk cartons. Have children cut out wheels to glue onto the cartons. Attach milk cartons together with staples or string to make a train.

Sail Boats. Provide children with a predrawn or precut triangle and rectangle. Have them cut out the shapes. The triangle will be the sail and the rectangle the bottom of the boat. Use a tongue depressor or strip of construction paper for the mast. Boats can be mounted on construction paper or on the transportation bulletin board.

Sponge Painting. Cut pieces of a sponge into triangle, circle, square, and rectangle shapes. Have children dip the pieces of sponge into tempera paint and then print them on paper. Children can be encouraged to combine the shapes to create objects, such as cars, trucks, boats, etc.

Transportation Stencils. Use teacher-made or commercial stencils of vehicles. Children can trace around the stencils with markers or crayons. Assemble a book for each child by stapling together the pages. Ask children to label and tell about each vehicle. Write out their verbalizations for the "text" of the book. This activity can be completed over time, adding pages gradually.

Car Painting. Dip the wheels of small Matchbox-type cars into tempera paint. Then "drive" the cars on construction paper to make car tracks.

The Wheels on the Bus. Provide children with cutout school bus shapes. Have them cut a door that can "open and shut." Give them cutout strips to use or have them cut strips to use as wipers. Attach them to the windshield with brad fasteners. The children can make the wipers go "swish, swish, swish." Have them cut out wheels or give them precut wheels to attach with brad fasteners. The wheels on the bus can go "round and around." Allow children to think of additional verses and parts to add.

Traffic Signs and Signals. Children can make a variety of traffic signs to use while playing with vehicles or to decorate the bulletin board. Stop signs can be made by cutting out pretraced octagons and mounting them on tongue depressors. Stick the signs in play dough to make them stand up. Stop and go lights can be made out of rectangles and red, yellow, and green circles, mounted on a tongue depressor. A railroad crossing can be made from two tongue depressors formed into an X and glued together. Other traffic signs and signals can be made in similar fashions.

Syringe Painting. Use a syringe to squirt paint on paper. Provide a dish of thin tempera paint. Children suction up the paint and then squirt it on paper to make their "syringe paintings."

Tweezer Pick. This is an excellent activity for strengthening the pincer grip. Place small objects on a tray. Provide a tweezers for children to use for picking up objects from the tray and moving them to another container. Some examples of objects to pick up with the tweezers include erasers, cotton balls, small cubes, small beads, small wooden puzzle pieces, and other small 3D objects found around the classroom.

Yellow Water. Have children add yellow food coloring to water and use it for watercolor painting.

Picture Directions. At the fine motor table, provide picture sequence directions for making a shamrock. The directions should include: (1) Trace the shamrock, (2) color the shamrock, (3) cut the shamrock.

Band-Aid ™ *Fun.* Provide a box of different sized Band-Aids.™ Allow children to tear them open and bandage themselves, other children, and dolls. Vary the activity by using sterile tape. Have children measure and tear the tape and use it to bandage themselves, other children, and dolls.

Healthy Faces. Provide each child with a circle shape. Have them draw or glue a face on. Next have the children trace and cut their hands. Cut thin strips of paper for arms. Children then glue a tissue onto the hands, and glue the arms with the attached hands on to the head. Children can practice covering the nose and mouth with the tissue when they sneeze.

Stick People. Provide each child with five tongue depressors. Use them to make "stick" doctors and nurses. Have children draw on heads, hands, and feet. They can dress their people with scraps of fabric.

St. Patrick's Day Collage. Provide children with outlines of St. Patrick's Day shapes, e.g., four leaf clovers and shamrocks. Have them glue small squares of green tissue paper inside the outline.

Mixing Green at the Easel. Draw outlines of St. Patrick's Day shapes at the easel. Have children mix yellow and blue paint to make green. They can use the green paint to decorate the shapes.

Measuring Green. Give each child a measuring spoon and a baby food jar containing water. Have them measure equal parts of yellow and blue food coloring to make green. Use the green water for syringe painting.

Pipe Cleaner Art. Provide children with green pipe cleaners. Have them manipulate the pipe cleaners into various shapes. Four pipe cleaners can be used to make a shamrock, by making three circles which are held together in the middle by a green stem. Children also can make pipes or leprechaun hats.

Leprechaun Hats. Have children dress up on St. Patrick's Day in handmade hats. Give them the outline of a hat to cut out. Allow children to punch holes around the outside of the hat and lace the hats with green yarn. Attach a band to the hat which goes around the back of the children's heads, and secure the band with Scotch™ tape.

Yellow Collage. Provide children with yellow paper to use as the base for their yellow collage. Give each child an old magazine and have them look through their magazines for yellow pictures. If children are able, have them cut out the yellow pictures they find and glue them onto their paper. If necessary, cut out the pictures for the children.

Shamrock Prints. Cut pieces of sponge into various St. Patrick's Day shapes. Have children dip the sponges into green tempera paint and then print them on paper.

Straw Painting. Have children create designs by blowing paint on a paper through a straw. Place a teaspoon of thin tempera paint on a paper, give each child a straw, and have him/her blow the paint around on the paper.

Sock Puppets. Children can create their own puppets by sewing buttons on a sock for the eyes and nose and a piece of rickrack for a mouth. Use large needles and heavy thread or yarn for sewing. The children can pretend they're surgeons.

Long and Short Collage. Have children cut long and short strips of construction paper and glue them on another sheet of paper to make a long and short collage.

Long and Short Lines. Provide children with rulers and have them draw long and short lines using crayons, chalk, or markers. Vary the activity by using large sheets of paper and letting the children use yardsticks for long lines and rulers for short lines.

Fine Motor Center. Provide a variety of green and yellow items for making collages. Make yellow and green play dough with the children and set it out with a rolling pin and cookie cutters which represent the March themes. Provide St. Patrick's Day shapes, transportation and medical object pictures, and shapes for lacing. Provide predrawn shapes for children to cut, as well as paper for snipping and tearing. Allow children to fold, bend, and freely manipulate pipe cleaners. Provide yarn to glue around predrawn shapes. Set out green and yellow beads and shells for stringing. Allow plenty of time for children to experiment freely with and manipulate the materials provided at the fine motor center each day. It is important not to overwhelm them by providing too many materials at one time. Set out only the materials for one or two of the suggested fine motor center activities each day.

2. PREWRITING

Path Tracing. The transportation unit lends itself to path tracing. Use the chalkboard or paper and pencil. A sampling of ideas include: take the car to the garage, the airplane to the hangar, the school bus to the school, the boat to the dock, or the train to the station.

Road Trip. Prepare a road or highway on the chalkboard or on paper. Have children follow the road with small cars, their fingers, or with a pencil, marker, or chalk. The road can be a simple oval or rectangle shape, or it can contain turns, bumps, and sharp corners.

Mazes. Prepare simple mazes for children to drive small matchbox-type cars through. To make the mazes more interesting, add stop signs, traffic lights, and train crossings.

Car Tracks. Dip small cars into tempera paint and follow paths as described in Path Tracing. Through this activity, children's eye and hand movements will practice going from left to right. Draw a road and ask children to keep their cars within the boundaries of the two lines, a prerequisite for printing in the lines.

Copy the Design. Provide each child with a blank piece of paper divided into four *square* sections. Sit with the children and tell them to copy the design you produce in the same square. Designs will be determined by the children's ability levels. Allow children the opportunity to play teacher and have the others copy their design.

Thermometers. Give each child a tongue depressor. Have them write numerals one through eight on it and use it as a thermometer.

Prewriting Center. Provide stencils of March shapes for children to trace, color, and cut. Also provide prepared dot-to-dot pictures and starter pictures of March shapes for children to complete, color, and cut. Include four leaf clovers, shamrocks, and an assortment of simple vehicle shapes (e.g., sailboats, airplanes, and simple cars.). Provide plenty of green and yellow crayons, markers, paints, colored pencils, and chalk.

PERCEPTION

Air, Land, or Water Vehicle?. After completing the language activity which includes sorting air, land, and water vehicles, have children independently sort pictures of vehicles that travel in the air, on land, or in the water. Provide the children with varied pictures of the three types of vehicles and pictorially labeled boxes. Children sort the pictures into the appropriate box.

Vehicle Match. Prepare laminated cutouts of vehicles that differ in various characteristics such as color or design. Each cutout should have a match. Children make pairs out of the matching vehicles.

Drive On. This is a card game played like Go Fish using the laminated cutouts from the vehicle match game. Deal out four to six cards to two or three children and place the remainder of the cards in the middle. One child asks another for a match to his/her card, e.g., "Do you have a green car with red stripes?" Game continues until all matches have been played.

Transportation Lotto. A simple way to prepare a lotto game is by using stickers purchased at a store. Buy two identical sticker books which contain stickers depicting various forms of transportation. Use one of the sticker books to make the lotto cards and the other sticker book to make the matching cue card. Each child tries to match the cue card to a picture on his/her lotto card. Vary the number of pictures on the lotto game depending on the age and developmental level of the children.

Guess the Picture. Cover vehicle pictures with construction paper. Cut four flaps in the construction paper so that each flap opens individually. Expose one flap at a time while the children attempt to guess what is under the paper.

What's Missing?. Draw pictures or silhouettes of different vehicles that have a part missing. Children must identify and name the missing part.

Simple Classification. Provide pictures of common objects. Have children classify pictures into transportation and not transportation pictures. To make the activity more difficult, sort pictures into groups of vehicles, pets, foods, furniture, etc.

I'm Going on a Trip (auditory memory game). Begin this game by saying "I'm going on an airplane trip (or car, train, or boat trip) and I'm taking a (*fill in an item*)." Each child in turn repeats the full sentence and adds his/her own item. At the end of the game there will be a list of items. The game can be simplified by giving visual cues. For developmentally younger children, have them repeat the sentence stating only one item. If children have difficulty thinking of items, allow them to choose from teacher-provided pictures, or items pulled from a suitcase.

Attribute Block Designs 1. Make patterns of sailboats and cars using attribute blocks for children to copy. A sailboat can be made using a triangle and a rectangle, cars and trucks can be produced with rectangles, squares, and circles. Ask children to copy the teacher-made model.

Attribute Block Designs 2. Trace attribute block designs on paper. Have children match attribute blocks to the shapes drawn on the paper. Shapes might include cars, trucks, and sailboats.

Visual Memory Game. Use three to five medical objects at a time, depending on the level of the children. Display the objects on a tray, label and talk about each object. Cover the tray with a cloth. Have children try to remember which objects were on the tray.

What's Missing?. This game is similar to the visual memory game. Again, display three to five medical objects on a tray. Label and talk about the objects. Have children cover their eyes, and then remove one or two objects, depending on the level of the children. The children guess which object is missing.

Matching Objects to Outlines. On a large piece of tagboard, draw the outline of the medical objects which have been part of the doctor and nurse unit. Have children match the objects to the outline.

Tell the Order. Display three medical objects on a tray. Have the children look at the objects and tell what is first, last, and in the middle. Then cover the tray and ask children to remember what was first, last, and in the middle. Mix up the items and repeat the activity. Replace one item at a time and repeat the activity.

Leprechaun Lotto. Prepare a lotto game using St. Patrick's Day shapes. Use green and yellow shamrocks, four leaf clovers, and leprechaun hats and pipes. Vary the color and design of the pictures.

Shape/Object Sort. Provide various shapes/objects for children to sort (e.g., squares, St. Patrick's Day, vehicle, and medical themes.) Organize the activity by dividing and pictorially labeling a large sheet of tagboard with examples of the shapes/objects. Children can sort shapes/objects into the designated area of the tagboard.

Feely Bag. Place objects that children are familiar with from previous activities completed during the month in a feely bag. Have children identify the objects using their sense of touch. Objects might include an assortment of vehicles, medical objects, and St. Patrick's Day shapes

March Patterns. Provide cutout shapes for children to sequence, following a pattern. Children can glue their patterns to paper, use the flannel board with March shapes, or simply do it as a table activity. Shape examples include shamrocks, four leaf clovers, leprechaun hats, or a varied assortment of vehicles.

Peg Designs. Create pegboard patterns for children to copy, including squares, triangles, circles, and rectangles. Combine the shapes to make pictures of cars, trucks, and boats, or other shapes of interest to the children.

Pattern Cards. Prepare pairs of cards which contain the same color and design. Display one of each card on the table or floor. Give a child the matching cards and have him/her match his/her cards to the display card that is the *same.*

Block Designs. Create designs and patterns using blocks. Ask children to use their blocks to make the same design or pattern with the same colored blocks.

Bead Patterns. Create a bead design using a specific color sequence, such as green, yellow, orange, blue, green, yellow, orange, blue. Ask children to make one that is the same. Vary the activity by making necklaces or belts out of colored macaroni.

Perception Center. This month at the perception center, focus on sequencing patterns and the concept of same. Have children sequence patterns using St. Patrick's Day shapes, vehicles, and medical tools. Use the terms *first, middle,* and *last* and encourage children to do the same. Provide opportunities for sorting yellow from nonyellow objects. Create block and peg designs for children to copy using yellow and green. Provide attribute blocks for children to invent their own patterns and shapes or copy teacher-made patterns. Provide puzzles which represent the March themes. Many of the activities presented in this perception section lend themselves to being independent center-based activities, in addition to teacher-directed small-group activities.

GROSS MOTOR

Riding Toys. If the weather permits, allow children to ride tricycles and big wheels, and pull wagons outside. Stress that children's riding toys are vehicles or a form of transportation. In inclement weather, use the riding toys in the gymnasium, if possible.

Road Course. Set up a road course indoors or outdoors depending on the weather. Include right and left turns, stopping for stop signs and red lights, yield signs, stopping at crosswalks, and railroad crossings. Traffic signs and lights can be teacher-made. Children can ride big wheels, tricycles, or other play vehicles through the course.

Stop and Go Game. Use a teacher-made traffic light to play this game. Children can play on riding toys or simply by running. When you show green, the children go. When you show yellow, they slow down and prepare to stop. When red is shown, children stop.

Red Light, Green Light. In this organized game, the goal is to get from the starting line to the finish line. When you call "green light," the children run or walk (depending on your directions) toward the finish line. When you call "red light," the children stop.

Traffic Light Game. Draw a traffic light on a large sheet of paper and tape it on the floor. Prepare a set of cards which contain either a red, yellow, or green circle. To play the game, children choose a card and toss their bean bag to the *same* color on the traffic light.

People Train. Children form a people train by holding onto the waist of the person in front of them. Each child can decide what kind of car she/he wants to be. Set up a chalk track for the train to follow. Have the train move fast and slow. Vary the activity by making a long and a short train. As the trains pass each other they can toot their whistles.

The Conductor Says. This game is played the same way Simon Says is played. The conductor tells the other children to perform an action. If the conductor doesn't say "Conductor says" before giving the direction, the children do not perform the action.

Movin' Through. Have children pretend they are different kinds of vehicles moving through different weather or road conditions: snowstorm, dust storm, rain, ice, bumpy road, etc.

Heartbeat. Beat a drum and pretend it's the sound of a heart. Have children put their hands over their hearts and feel the differences after moving fast or slow to the sound of the drum.

Man from Mars. Play this version of tag which reinforces color concepts. One person is "It." The others call "Man from Mars, Man from Mars, may we take a trip to the stars?". "It" replies, e.g., "Only if you are wearing yellow." Those children wearing yellow run to a goal line trying not to be tagged by "It."

Musical Shamrocks. Play this game like musical chairs. Cut shamrocks from paper, arrange them in a circle on the floor. Children march around the shamrocks while music plays. When the music stops, they must find a shamrock to stand on.

Doctor May I?. The "doctor" gives directions to the children, such as "Jump up and down" or "Touch the ground." The children respond by saying "Doctor May I?" If the doctor responds by saying yes, the children follow the doctor's order. If the doctor says no, the children wait for the next order.

Bean Bag Toss 1. Prepare a bean bag floor game by drawing eight shamrocks on a large sheet of paper. Number the shamrocks one to eight. Have children try to throw a bean bag on each of the shamrocks in numerical sequence from one to eight.

Bean Bag Toss 2. Place three baskets in a line on the floor. Tell the children to throw their bean bag in the first basket, then in the middle basket, and finally in the last basket.

Listen for the Color. In this movement game, give a direction using color concepts. Say, e.g., "If you are wearing yellow, stand up and jump on two feet" or "If you are wearing stripes, hop on one foot."

Twister. Make a twister game by drawing different colored vehicles on a large sheet of paper to put on the floor. Make a spinner with colored vehicles which correspond to those on the floor. Next to each vehicle on the spinner, draw a small hand or foot. Each child in turn spins the spinner and puts either his/her hand or foot on the vehicle which matches the spinner. Make the activity more difficult by spinning the spinner while the children maintain their positions on the playing sheet until their next turn. On the next turn, they continue to maintain the previous position and move their other hand or foot to the new position.

SENSORY EXPERIENCES

Listening Walk. Go for a walk and listen for sounds. Begin by identifying some sounds for the children. Ask questions such as, "Do you hear the bird singing, the car honking?" Follow by asking the children to identify the sounds they hear. Find an outside place to sit down, then have the children close their eyes to listen for and identify sounds.

Familiar Sounds. Make a tape recording of sounds identified on the listening walk. Upon returning from the walk or at a later time, play the tape and ask the children to identify the sounds.

Environmental Sounds. Make a tape of sounds which occur in the children's daily environment. Examples include the toilet flushing, a car horn, teacher's voice, etc. Play the tape for the children and have them identify the sounds.

Background Music. Play background music while the children play and work. Vary the types of music played. Include music with different tempos and beats. Include children's music, classical music, popular songs, etc. Allow children to take turns choosing the music they want to hear.

Children's Voices. Tape record the children's voices. Play the tape to the class and ask the children to identify their own and their classmates' voices.

Ears are for Hearing. Stress to the children that their ears are what they hear with. Have them experiment by covering their ears with their hands and listen. Have them listen to music and stories through headphones. Have them speak and sing loudly and softly to experiment with sounds and their sense of hearing.

The Sound of Yellow. Fill glasses or baby food jars with varying amounts of water containing yellow food coloring. Have children tap the jars with a spoon and listen to the different sounds. You can also use this activity to discuss the concepts of empty/full and more/less.

Changing Sounds. Fill empty coffee cans with various substances, such as beads, dry beans and peas, styrofoam, sand, feathers, water, macaroni, etc. Have the children strike the coffee cans with a spoon and listen for the sounds the different substances make. Use the various substances at the exploration table and allow children to fill the coffee cans with differing amounts of the substances. Provide opportunities for filling and emptying the containers and experimenting with and feeling the substances.

Exploration Table. The transportation unit provides children with a fun theme at the exploration table. Provide a variety of vehicles for children to experiment with. Include cars, trucks, dump trucks, bulldozers, cranes, cement mixers, tractors, boats, trains, and an assortment of other vehicles. Alternate water, sand, sawdust, cornmeal, rice, and other substances in the exploration table throughout the month.

Reinforce the color concepts by using colored water. Allow children to add the food coloring to experiment with varying shades of yellow.

When talking about doctors, provide children with syringes for squirting water and empty medicine bottles and measuring spoons to pour and measure medicine. Be sure to stress that it is only pretend. Review the rules regarding medicine, i.e., (1) only take it when a doctor prescribes it for you, (2) never take medicine unless a mother, father, or other caretaker gives it to you, (3) only take medicine if your name is on the bottle.

PREMATH

Train Count. Bring in a toy train with at least eight cars. Have the children count the cars.

Park the Cars. Draw a parking lot on a large sheet of paper. Number the parking spaces from one to eight. Using small match box type cars, put a numeral from one to eight on them or draw a set containing from one to eight dots on each car and park the car in the appropriate parking place.

Numeral Matching. Set up classroom chairs in rows, as on an airplane. Number the seats from one to eight. Give children a ticket with a numeral written on it. Have them find their seats by matching the numerals.

Vehicle Hunt. Take a walk around the school neighborhood. Have children count the number of different vehicles they see.

Sorting. Set out eight shoeboxes, each containing a numeral from one to eight and a corresponding set of dots. Provide children with sets of small plastic cars, airplanes, trucks, etc., or cutouts of the same. Children will put the number of vehicles which corresponds to the numeral into each box.

Pack the Suitcase. Make flannel board cutouts of eight suitcases. Label each with a numeral from one to eight. Also provide articles of clothing cut from flannel pieces. Have children take turns choosing a suitcase to put on the flannel board, and then place the correct number of clothing items which correspond to the numeral on the suitcase. Vary the activity by using real objects.

Calendar. Use cutouts of vehicles and/or shamrock shapes on the calendar this month. Reinforce one-to-one correspondence, numeral recognition, patterning, and counting skills. Count how many days until the weekend, St. Patrick's Day, or someone's birthday. Clap the days of the week, guess what day of the week or month comes next.

Long/Short Sort. Vertically divide a table into two sections. Make one section longer and the other shorter. Provide a variety of pairs of long and short items. Have children put the long items on the long section of table and the short items on the short section of the table. Sample items to sort include long and short strips of paper, long and short pipe cleaners, a yardstick and a ruler, long and short strings, pictures of long and short trains, trucks, buses, and airplanes, long and short socks, etc.

Flannel Board Train. Cut eight train cars out of felt and on each one write a numeral from one to eight. Have children assemble the train on the felt board, properly sequencing the numerals. This activity can also be done with concrete objects i.e., a milk carton train or a model train.

Long and Short Trains. Provide toy model train cars. Ask the children to make long or short trains. This activity could also be done with flannel train car cutouts on the flannel board, or with laminated paper train car cutouts.

Block Trains. Make long and short trains out of building blocks. Numerical sequencing can be reinforced simultaneously by labeling blocks with a numeral from one to eight. Long trains can have eight cars while shorter trains might have only three or four cars. Have children assemble their long and short trains in correct numerical sequence.

Doctor's Office. Set eight envelopes on the table—each containing a numeral from one to eight. Provide at least thirty-six tongue depressors. Children put the appropriate number of tongue depressors in each envelope.

Doctor's Instruments. Using a play medical kit, label each item with a numeral from one to eight. Have the children put the instruments away in numerical order, first number one, then number two, etc.

Eye Chart. Prepare an eye chart similar to those used at the doctor's office. Instead of letters or animal pictures, use numerals for children to identify and sets for them to count. Put the eye chart on the wall. Children can pretend they are at the doctor's office.

How Big Am I?. If your school has a nurse's office, take the children on a mini-field trip to the office. Weigh and measure each child. Make a chart for each child telling his/her height and weight. Graph the heights and weights of the class. If a nurse's office and/or scale are not available, bring a scale and a yardstick into the classroom.

What Do I Hear?. Use the sense of hearing to reinforce counting skills. Set out a variety of items which can be used to produce sounds. Examples include a drum, a tambourine, a baby food jar with water, a bell, etc. Strike the objects and have children count the number of times the sound is made. Vary the activity by using a screen to hide the objects and have children guess the object as well as count. Allow one child to make the noises while the other children count.

Making Sets. Using concrete objects or the flannel board, ask children to make sets. Utilize the monthly themes. Examples might include make a set of things that fly, things that go in the water, things with four wheels, things the doctor uses, etc. Ask children to find a specific number of items for their sets or let them count the number of items they find.

Shamrock Math. Cut shamrocks out of felt to use on the flannel board. Use them to reinforce various math concepts, e.g., counting, one-to-one correspondence, making sets, simple addition and subtraction concepts, and simple story problems.

Guessing Game. Children can practice estimating skills by guessing how many treats are in the jar. Use treats that are easy to count, such as raisins, goldfish crackers, or jelly beans. Have the children guess how many are in the jar. Use counting skills when passing out the treat.

Card Match. Make a deck of playing cards by combining two or three decks of cards. Use only the cards with numerals two through eight. Deal three to five cards to each child and put the remaining cards in the center. Children must match numerals. If they don't have the card in their hand, they draw until they can play.

Counting Collage. Give each child a piece of construction paper with a large numeral written on the center of it. Have the children glue the correct number of items on the paper. Provide special items for gluing or use materials from the collage table. Give each child a different numeral and numerically sequence the collages when they are finished.

SONGS AND FINGERPLAYS

Sing favorite songs relating to the transportation theme.

"Wheels on the Bus" (Substitute words for train, car, airplane, boat, etc.)
"I've Been Working on the Railroad"
"Row, Row, Row Your Boat"

The Wiper (fingerplay).

I'm a window wiper,
This is how I go (Bend arm back and forth.)
Back and Forth
In the rain and snow.

The Train (fingerplay).

Here is the engine on the track (Hold up thumb.)
Here is the tank car just in back (Hold up pointer finger.)
Here is the box car to carry freight. (Hold up middle finger.)
Here is the mail car, don't be late. (Hold up ring finger.)
Way back here at the end of the train rides the caboose through
The sun and the rain. (Hold up little finger.)

My Friend Mary (tune: "Old McDonald").

My friend Mary had a garage, eei, eei, o
and in her garage she had a car, eei, eei, o
with a vroom-vroom here,
and a vroom-vroom there,
Here a vroom, there a vroom,
Every where a vroom-vroom.
My friend Mary had a garage eei, eei, o.

My friend Mary had a garage eei, eei, o
And in her garage she had a bike, eei, eei, o
With a zoom-zoom here, and a zoom-zoom there,
Here a zoom, there a zoom,
Everywhere a zoom-zoom.
My friend Mary had a garage eei, eei, o.

(Repeat verses substituting airplane, train, boat, etc.)

Down at the Station (traditional song).

Down at the station early in the morning
See the little puffer bellys all in a row.
See the engine driver pull the little throttle.
Chug, chug, poof poof off we go!

Nurse (tune: "Mary Had a Little Lamb").

1. The doctor's nurse helps us; helps us; helps us.
   the doctor's nurse helps us when we're sick.

2. She takes our temperature, temperature, temperature.
   She takes our temperature when we're sick.
3. She gives us shots, shots, shots.
   She gives us shots to make us well.
4. She weighs us on the scale, scale, scale.
   She weighs us on the scale and measures our height.

The Doctor (tune: "Have You Ever Seen a Lassie?").

My doctor has a stethoscope, a stethescope, a stethescope.
My doctor has a stethoscope to listen to my heart.
My doctor has an otoscope, an otoscope, an otoscope,
My doctor has an otoscope to look in my ears.
My doctor has a thermometer, a thermometer, a thermometer,
My doctor has a thermometer to take my temperature.
My doctor has a blood pressure cuff, blood pressure cuff, blood pressure cuff,
My doctor has a blood pressure cuff to take my blood pressure.

(Make up additional verses to go with the doctor tools you discuss.)

St. Patrick's Day (tune: "She'll Be Coming Round the Mountain").

March 17th is St. Patrick's Day.
The Leprechauns will all come out and play,
We will all wear green and have some fun.
We'll dance a jig and jump and run.
March 17th is St. Patrick's Day.

RECIPES

Pretzels.

　　1 pkg. yeast dissolved in 1 1/2 cup warm water
　　1 teaspoon salt
　　1 tablespoon sugar
　　4 cups flour
　　1 egg

Mix and knead dough. Roll into letters or shapes. Place on a greased cookie sheet. Brush with beaten egg and sprinkle with salt. Bake at 425 degrees until golden brown. (To reinforce March concepts, make long and short pretzels squares and shamrock shapes.)

Dilled Nibbles.

　　1/2 cup butter
　　1 6-ounce pkg. Rice Chex™
　　1/2 teaspoon salt
　　2 teaspoons dill weed
　　1 1/2 ounces parmesan cheese

Melt butter in a large pan on low heat. Stir in cereal, turn often with a fork until lightly browned. Mix in salt, dill weed, and cheese. Remove from heat, sprinkle with cheese mixture, and stir.

Applesauce Raisin Bread.

1 1/2 cups flour	1 cup raisins
1 teaspoon baking powder	1 cup uncooked oatmeal
1 teaspoon baking soda	2 eggs
1 1/2 teaspoons cinnamon	1/3 cup vegetable oil
1/2 cup brown sugar	1 cup applesauce

Stir until wet. Pour into greased loaf pan. Bake 1 hour at 350 degrees. Remove to cool.

Vegetable Pizza.

Roll out one package of refrigerator crescent rolls. Bake according to package directions. Spread with a mixture of 8 ounces cream cheese, 2/3 cup mayonaise, and 2 tablespoons dill. Top with vegetables of choice, such as broccoli, tomato, carrots, mushrooms, green onions, etc.

Cheese Cookies.

1/4 lb. butter
1 lb. cheddar cheese Spread
2 cups flour
1 package Lipton Onion Soup™

Cream butter and cheese together. Add remaining ingredients. Form into four rolls. Wrap each roll in wax paper. Refrigerate 3–4 hours (or overnight). Slice into very thin rounds. Bake at 325 degrees for 12–15 minutes or until golden brown.

Banana Muffins.

1 egg
2 cups Bisquick™
1 cup mashed bananas (2 medium)
1/4 cup sugar
2 tablespoons milk
2 tablespoons vegetable oil

Line muffin tins with paper baking cups or grease bottoms of tins. Beat egg slightly. Stir in remaining ingredients, till moistened. Pour batter into muffin tins. Bake 15–17 minutes or until golden brown.

MARCH SNACKS

Long and Short Snacks. Many snack foods can be cut into *long* and *short* servings: Try some of the folowing:

carrot sticks

celery sticks—plain or topped with spreads such as cream cheese,
processed cheese spreads, or peanut butter

cucumber sticks

zucchini sticks

toast or bread served with favorite spreads and cut into long and short strips

long and short pretzels (see March recipes for homemade pretzel recipe)

french toast cut into long and short strips

long and short pieces of banana

long and short servings of hot dog

long and short tootsie rolls

long and short bread sticks

St. Patricks Day Theme.

shamrock-shaped pretzels (see March recipes for homemade pretzel recipe)

green milkshakes

shamrock-shaped cookies

rainbow Jello™

shamrock-shaped pancakes

pistachio pudding

cream cheese with green food coloring spread on crackers, toast, or celery

Yellow Snacks.

bananas

egg salad served on crackers

yellow cupcakes or muffins

yellow apples

vanilla pudding with yellow food coloring added

corn

toast with butter

lemonade

yellow candies (e.g., Gummie Bears)

yellow popcorn

yellow jello

CREATIVE DRAMATICS

Doctor's Office. Create a doctor's office in the dramatic play area. Provide a reception area with a phone, appointment book, and pencil and paper for the "receptionist" to take messages. Set up an examining room with a table or chair for "patients" to sit or lie on, and a desk and a chair for the doctor. Doctor supplies will include doctor tools, e.g., stethoscope, thermometer, syringe, otoscope, Band-Aids,™ blood pressure cuff, etc. Provide doctor and nurse uniforms (throw-away surgical robes can be obtained from a local hospital). Nurse hats can be made from construction paper. If possible, provide a real scale and tape measure for weighing and measuring. Provide dolls and stuffed animals to act as patients. Also provide doctor books to read to children to create the mood for the dramatic play theme.

Transportation Play. Various transportation modes can be set up in the dramatic play area depending on class interest. An airplane can be created by making rows of chairs. Number each chair so that children can match their ticket seat assignment to the correct seat. If possible, furnish real seat belts or make your own. Children can alternate playing pilot, flight attendant, and passengers. Set up a cockpit with a control panel (children can draw one) and a steering wheel.

Similarly, trains, cars, buses, and boats can be created using chairs, large cartons, tables, blocks, or other building supplies.

You can set up a specific transportation theme for a structured lesson. Many concepts can be reinforced during play. Examples include matching and identifying numerals and colors; positional concepts such as first, middle, and last, beginning and end; and premath concepts, such as counting and one-to-one correspondence.

Give children the opportunity to create their own dramatic play using the transportation theme. Inspire them by reading stories, providing motivating activities, or by going on field trips which reinforce the transportation theme.

The Gingerbread Man. Read a version of *The Gingerbread Man* to the children or tell the story using pieces on the flannel board. Encourage children to chime in with the repetitive verse as you tell the story. As children prepare to dramatize the story, be sure to provide play dough, raisins, buttons, etc., for children to make their own version of the lively gingerbread man. They will enjoy finding and making simple props for use in telling the story. Include an apron and rolling pin for the little old woman and a "beard" and hat for the little old man. Children can make simple paper plate masks for story characters: cow, bear, fox, etc. Allow children to include other animals who may have tried to catch the gingerbread man. Encourage all to participate in some way. If children have difficulty remembering what to say, encourage all children to imitate or make up their own lines.

Children might enjoy pantomiming the story and having others guess who they are playing or what they are doing. An exciting culminating activity is having children make, decorate, and bake their own gingerbread men for snack.

Gingerbread Man (ginger dough).

1/2 cup sugar	2 1/2 cups flour
1/2 cup butter	2 teaspoons baking soda
1/2 cup molasses	1/2 teaspoon ginger
1/2 tablespoon vinegar	1 teaspoon cinnamon
1 small egg, beaten	1/4 teaspoon clove
raisins	1/2 teaspoon salt

1. Cream sugar and butter together.
2. Pour molasses over sugar mixture. Add vinegar. Stir until well blended. Cool.
3. Add egg to molasses mixture.
4. Sift dry ingredients together. Gradually add to molasses mixture. Mix well. Cover and chill dough.

5. Heat oven to 375 degrees. Grease cookie sheets lightly.
6. Flour surface. Roll dough 1/4" thick and cut gingerbread men with a floured cutter.
7. Transfer to sheets with a broad spatula. Decorate with raisins.
8. Bake 8–10 minutes. Yeild: 18 3"-men.

CHILDREN'S LITERATURE

Alexander, Anne. *ABC of Cars and Trucks*

Allen, Pamela. *Who Sank the Boat?*

Asch, Frank. *Yellow, Yellow*

Bank Street College of Education. *Green Light Go*

Barton, Byron. *Airport*

———. *Boats*

———. *Trains*

———. *Trucks*

Berenstain, Stan. *The Berenstain Bears Go to the Doctor*

Breinburg, Petronella. *Doctor Shawn*

Brown, Margaret Wise. *Whistle for the Train*

———. *Red Light Green Light*

Bruna, Dick. *Miffy in the Hospital*

Brustlein, Janice. *Little Bear Marches in the St. Patrick's Day Parade*

Burton, Virginia Lee. *Choo Choo, the Story of a Little Engine Who Ran Away*

———. *Maybelle, the Cable Car*

Calhoun, Mary. *The Hungry Leprechaun*

Charlip, Remy, and Supree, Burton. *Mother, Mother, I Feel Sick*

Chlad, Dorothy. *When I Ride in a Car*

Crews, Donald. *Freight Train*

Donahue, P. *Germs Make Me Sick*

Ehrlich, Amy. *The Everyday Train*

Emberly, Edward Randolf. *Green Says Go*

Florian, Douglas, *Airplane Ride*

Gilbert, Helen Earle. *Dr. Trotter and His Big Gold Watch*

Greene, Carla. *Doctors and Nurses: What Do They Do?*

———. *Railroad Engineers and Airplane Pilots: What Do They Do?*

———. *Truck Drivers: What Do They Do?*

Highsmith, Robert. *Wheels*

Hoban, Tana. *Is It Red? Is It Yellow? Is It Blue?*

Holl, Adelaide. *The ABC of Cars, Trucks, and Machines*

Jubelier, R. *Jill's Check Up*

Kraus, Robert. *Rebecca Hatpin*

———. *Tony the Tow Truck*

Krementz, Jill. *Jamie Goes on an Airplane*

Lenski, Lois L. *The Little Train*

Lerner, Marguerite Rush. *Doctor's Tools*

Lionni, Leo. *Little Blue and Little Yellow*

Marino, Barbara Pavis. *Eric Needs Stitches*

McCrady, Lady. *The Perfect Ride*

McNaught. *Trucks*

Moore, Lilian. *Papa Albert*

Piper, Waty. *The Little Engine That Could*

Pomerantz, C. *How Many Trucks Can a Tow Truck Tow?*

Pope, B. *Let's Go to the Doctor's Office*

Rey, Hans Augusto. *How Do You Get There?*

Rey, Margaret and H. A. *Curious George Takes a Job*
Rey, Margaret Elisabeth Waldstein. *Curious George Goes to the Hospital*
Rockwell, Anne. *Cars*
Rockwell, Harlow. *My Doctor*
Ross, Jessica. *Ms. Klondike*
Sattler, Helen Roney. *Train Whistles: A Language in Code*
Scarry, Richard McClure. *The Great Big Car and Truck Book*
_____ . *Cars and Trucks and Things That Go*
_____ . *Nicky Goes to the Doctor*
Shay, Arthur. *What Happens When You Go to a Hospital*
Shortail, Leonard W. *One Way; a Trip with Traffic Signs*

Stone, Bernard. *Emergency Mouse*
Thompson, Frances B. *Doctor John*
Weber, Alfons. *Elizabeth Gets Well*
Whitney, Alma Marshak. *Just Awful*
Witty M. *A Day in the Life of an Emergency Room Nurse*
Wolde, Gunilla. *Betsy and the Doctor*
Wooley, Catherine. *Andy and the Runaway Horse*
Young, Miriam Burt. *If I Drove a Train*
Zaffo, George J. *The Giant Nursery Book of Things That Go*
Zimelman, Nathan. *To Sing a Song As Big As Ireland*

Evaluating March Concepts

Throughout the month, continue to update and record significant progress and/or changes made by the children. Use the checklists found in the Appendix for the language concepts, gross motor, perception areas, etc. Children's vocabulary related to the transportation and community helper themes should be assessed and individually logged. You should observe children's ability to sequence simple story events or picture cards during structured lessons, or more informally at story or sharing time.

In addition, you can observe each child's ability to follow age appropriate, one-to-three-step directions in the classroom. You can note if repetition of directions is necessary, or if picture cues are needed. Inability to follow directions can be due to hearing difficulties, cognitive delays, processing or behavioral problems. The child can be more successful in the classroom when she/he can respond and participate fully to the directions you give.

CONCEPTS FOR MARCH (parent copy)

LANGUAGE AND VOCABULARY

- Transportation—naming, describing, sorting, and classifying things that move
- Doctor and nurse—how they help us, staying healthy
- St. Patrick's Day theme—real and make-believe
- Sequencing Stories, Pictures, and Events So That They make Sense
- Cooking Experiences
- Color—yellow
- Directional and Positional Concepts—first, middle, and last

FINE MOTOR

Lacing, painting, coloring, gluing, play dough manipulation, cutting, block tower building, bead stringing, path tracing, design copying (square)

PERCEPTION

Same and different, draw a person, puzzles, copying block, peg, and bead designs, patterning and sorting

GROSS MOTOR

Organized games, movement, and bean bag activities

PREMATH

One-to-one correspondence, calendar activities, sorting, number and numeral 8, long and short, shamrock shape

CREATIVE DRAMATICS

SENSORY EXPERIENCES

MARCH
Parent-child activities

SUN	MON	TUE	WED	THU	FRI	SAT
BEND, TWIST, TAP, OPEN, AND CLOSE AS MANY BODY PARTS AS YOU CAN THINK OF.	GO TO THE LIBRARY AND SELECT SOME BOOKS ABOUT TRANSPORTATION, DOCTORS, AND NURSES.	FOLD SQUARE WASHCLOTHS.	GO TO THE TRAIN STATION WATCH AND COUNT THE TRAINS THAT GO BY.	TRACE AROUND A SQUARE BOX. COLOR THE SQUARE AND CUT IT OUT.	MAKE A TRAIN USING KITCHEN CHAIRS. CUT SCRAP PAPER AND SELL "TICKETS."	PREPARE LEMON YELLOW PUDDING OR JELLO SEQUENCE EVENTS ALOUD.
LOOK FOR CARS, TRUCKS, BUSES, PLANES, ETC. COUNT THEM.	MAKE A VEHICLE COLLAGE, CUT PICTURES FROM MAGAZINES AND GLUE ON PAPER.	PRACTICE MARCH SONGS AND FINGERPLAYS.	FIND SOMETHING YELLOW IN EVERY ROOM OF THE HOUSE.	PRACTICE PATTERNS. CLAP, CLAP, TAP OR CLAP, TAP, SNAP, ETC. REPEAT THE PATTERN.	DRAW AN INCOMPLETE PERSON. ASK WHAT PART IS MISSING.	SNIP OR CUT YELLOW PAPER. GLUE PIECES ON A PAPER PLATE TO MAKE A SUN.
PRACTICE ROTE ACTIVITIES— COUNTING, DAYS OF THE WEEK, ABC'S.	FIND AND COMPARE OBJECTS THAT ARE LONG OR SHORT, E.G.: TOOTHPICK VS. STRAW.	HAPPY SAINT PATRICK'S DAY! EAT SOMETHING GREEN.	FIND ALL THE 8'S IN A DECK OF CARDS.	PLAY A GAME WITH FAMILY MEMBERS.	PREPARE A HEALTHY SNACK TOGETHER.	PRETEND PLAY— DOCTOR AND NURSE—PROVIDE PURSE, SHIRT, EAR SWABS, COTTON BALLS, BANDAIDS, ETC.
PLAY WAR WITH CARDS 1–8. WHICH IS MORE, WHICH IS LESS.	TALK ABOUT THE IMPORTANCE OF USING TISSUES, HAND WASHING AFTER USING THE BATHROOM, ETC.	PRACTICE EXERCISES TO STAY HEALTHY.	TALK ABOUT HOW DOCTORS/NURSES HELP US. DRIVE PAST A HOSPITAL.	FLOAT A BOAT IN THE TUB.	HELP MAKE THE BED, TALK ABOUT WHAT YOU DO FIRST, NEXT, AND LAST.	COUNT THE PLANTS IN YOUR HOUSE.
TALK ABOUT WHAT HAPPENED AT THE BEGINNING OF THE DAY AND THE END OF THE DAY.	PLAY COPY CAT TOGETHER . . . WAVE, MAKE FACES, DO SIMPLE ACTIONS, ETC.	READ A STORY. WHAT HAPPENED FIRST, IN THE MIDDLE, AND LAST IN THE STORY?				

APRIL

CONCEPTS FOR APRIL

LANGUAGE AND VOCABULARY

1. Spring—weather and nature's changes, clothing, activities, and vocabulary
2. Farm Theme—mother and baby animals, sounds they make, products, farmer's jobs, equipment, planting
3. Nursery Rhymes and Rhyming—listening activities and Mother Goose rhymes
4. Color—purple
5. Directional and Positional Concepts—in front, behind, beside, and between

Suggested field trips/classroom visitors: Visit a forest preserve or park to see nature's changes. Visit a farm, dairy, or plant nursery. Have a forest ranger or farmer visit the class.

FINE MOTOR: 1. MANIPULATION, AND 2. PREWRITING

Lacing, painting, coloring, gluing, play dough manipulation, cutting, block tower building, bead stringing, centers, path tracing, design copying (triangle)

PERCEPTION

Same and different, draw a person, center activities: puzzles, copying block, peg and bead designs, patterning and sorting

GROSS MOTOR

Organized games, movement activities, galloping, outside climbing activities, review any previous activities

PREMATH

One-to-one correspondence, calendar activities, sorting, number and numeral 9, more and less, diamond shape

SENSORY EXPERIENCES

Exploration table, sense of sight

CREATIVE DRAMATICS

- Farmer's Market
- Nursery Rhymes
- *The Three Billy Goats Gruff*

RECIPES

Farm theme

SNACK

Food related to monthly concepts and themes

SELF-HELP

Provide activities at children's developmental levels

REVIEW

Any previous concepts

ACTIVITIES FOR APRIL

LANGUAGE AND VOCABULARY

1. SPRING

Spring Brings. Introduce the spring season using pictures which depict spring. Find pictures of spring scenes in books or magazines or use pictures specifically intended for classroom use. Discuss what spring brings, including nature's changes, warmer air, green grass, buds and leaves on trees, birds, insects, and rain. Also discuss spring clothing and outdoor activities.

Brainstorming. Expand on the *Spring Brings* activity by displaying winter and spring scenes. Compare the two seasons by having children brainstorm the differences between the two seasons. On large chart paper, label one column "spring" and one column "winter." List the children's observations under the appropriate heading.

Dress for Spring. Use a real doll or a flannel board figure dressed for winter, including a hat, boots, mittens, sweater, etc. Ask the children which clothes can be put away until next winter. Redress the doll or figure in spring clothes. Label the clothes and body parts as part of the activity. Spring clothes might include a light-weight jacket or sweatshirt, a raincoat, an umbrella, sneakers, a short-sleeved shirt, light-weight pants, etc.

Pack for Spring. Bring in two suitcases, one for spring clothes and one for not spring clothes. Include clothing items appropriate for winter, spring, and summer. Pack one suitcase for a springtime trip and the other for a not springtime trip.

Spring Walks. Take advantage of the spring weather by going for short walks outside. The children can use their different senses when you provide a different theme for each walk. On one walk, *look* for nature's changes such as grass and leaves. On another walk, *listen* for birds. Bring bags to collect spring items such as a leaf or blade of grass on a *touching* walk. *Smell* the flowers on another walk.

Spring Scavengers. Prepare picture lists of spring items for children to find on a scavenger hunt. Give each child his/her own bag to use on the scavenger hunt Include indoor and outdoor items such as umbrellas, raincoats, flowers, leaves, grass, seeds, feathers, etc.

2. THE FARM

Farm Play. If possible, introduce the farm unit using a play farm with parts that can be manipulated. Name the various parts and inhabitants of the farm, e.g., the barn, silo, tractor, wagon, farm animals, and farmer. Encourage the children to name the different animals and to make the animal sounds. As the children play with the farm, encourage conversation. Many commercially made farm sets are available in toy stores. If a farm set is not available, introduce the unit using farm pictures

Farm Animals. Label and describe farm animals in the farm set or from pictures. Discuss the noises they make and the products we get from them. Include the many animals found on a farm. Sing "Old Mac Donald Had a Farm" and have the children supply the names of the animals and the animal noises. Use farm animal toys or pictures as visual cues. Encourage sequencing skills by having the children repeat the animals and noises in sequence with each verse.

What We Get From the Farm. On the flannel board, table, or floor, display pictures of various farm animals. Include a cow, pig, chicken, and a sheep. Show the children pictures of products we get from the various animals. Label and discuss each picture and let the children decide which farm animal the product comes from. Pictures might include milk, cheese, ice cream, yogurt, meat, bacon, ham, sausage, eggs, wool clothing and blankets.

Farm Animals and their Young. Using figures or pictures of farm animals, show the children only the adult animals. Then show the figures or pictures of the baby farm animals. Have the children pair the babies with the adults. Label the baby animals. Sing "Old MacDonald" using the names of the baby animals. Use the baby animal figures or pictures as visual cues.

Animal Noises. Play the game, "What animal am I thinking of?" Give the clue, "I'm thinking of an animal that says moo, what animal am I thinking of?" Children may need additional clues, e.g., "You get milk from me." Continue with all the farm animals previously discussed. Visual cues may be necessary.

The Farmer's Jobs. Begin learning about the jobs of the farmer by reviewing what each child's mother and father's jobs are. Discuss jobs at home and at "work." Lead the children into a discussion of the farmer's jobs by asking leading questions such as "Who feeds the animals? Who drives the tractor? Who plants the corn, beans, etc.? Who harvests the foods?" If possible, show pictures of the farmer doing the various jobs. Role-play the farmer's jobs while singing "The Farmer in the Dell," but substitute the verses.

1. The farmer plants the corn.
2. The farmer drives the tractor.
3. The farmer feeds the animals.
4. The farmer milks the cow.
5. The farmer collects the eggs.

Allow the children to make up their own verses.

The Farmer's Tools. Display pictures of tools and machines used by the farmer on the flannel board, table, or floor. Label and discuss each picture. Play a guessing game, "I'm thinking of a machine the farmer uses to plow the field. What is it?" Play a visual memory game by removing one picture at a time and asking the children to guess what's missing.

What the Farmer Grows. Display pictures, plastic, or real vegetables and flowers grown on the farm. Label each one. Discuss what plants need to grow, i.e., seeds, soil, sun, and water. Use the flannel board to display the various parts of a plant—the roots, stem, flowers, etc. Show how the roots grow under the soil. Ask the children to point to the various parts of the plants.

Root Experiment. Help the children to understand how plants drink water through their roots. Fill a jar half full of water and add a few drops of red food coloring. Cut the bottom off of a stalk of celery with leaves. Put the celery in the water, and have the children watch throughout the day and the next as the celery turns red.

Spring Planting 1. Have each child create his/her own terrarium. Fill a wide-mouthed jar with a layer of gravel, covered by 2 to 3 inches of soil. Plant a few small plants in the soil and water them. Pound a nail to create a few air holes in the lid, and cover the terrarium. Keep in indirect sunlight. Terrariums require little watering.

Spring Planting 2. Have the children get a head start on gardening by starting a few plants indoors. Ideas for plants might include tomatoes, beans, peas, or sunflowers. Review the parts of plants: Talk about roots, stems, and blossoms. Also review what plants need to live: soil, sun and water. The children can water their plants daily and watch them grow.

3. NURSERY RHYMES

Rhyme Fill-Ins. Read nursery rhymes during snack, story time, and free moments of the day. Recite them when lining up and when on walks. When the children are familiar with a particular rhyme, have them fill in missing words, e.g., Humpty Dumpty sat on a wall. Humpty Dumpty had a great _____ .

Rhyme Review. Play a game to demonstrate to the children what rhyming words are. Recite silly lists of words like *car, star, jar.* Encourage the children to add words to the silly list. As you go around a circle of children, each child adds a rhyming word. Nonsense words are acceptable if they rhyme.

Rhyming Riddles. Give riddles to the children which require a rhyming word for an answer, e.g., "It rhymes with bed, it's a color—what is it?" "It's something you drive and it rhymes with star—what is it?"

Rhyming Pictues. Prepare a game of rhyming pairs by drawing or pasting a picture on a small piece of paper. Each picture should have a pair that rhymes with it, e.g., a picture of a car and a picture of a star, a dog and a log, etc. Put one picture from each pair on the table. Hold up the other picture pair and ask the children to find the picture that rhymes with it.

Rhyming Story. Make up a rhyming story by having the children supply rhyming words to complete the sentences. Write the story on chart paper so the children can reread their rhymes. Allow the children to illustrate the story. A copy of the story might be produced for each child. A sample follows:

> There was a dog who sat on a _____ .
> The dog saw a cat who wasn't skinny but _____ .
> The cat liked to eat fish out of a _____ .
> The fish he would bake, came from a _____ .

4. COLOR—PURPLE

Purple Shaving Cream. Introduce the color purple by creating purple shaving cream finger paint. Give each child a mound of shaving cream. Review the color white. Sprinkle red powdered tempera into the paint, let the children mix it in and play with the *red* paint. Next, add blue powdered tempera and ask the children to mix it in with the red shaving cream. Ask the children if they know what color they made by mixing red and blue. If necessary, tell them the color name. Allow the children to experiment and play with the purple finger paint.

Purple Riddles. Display a number of purple items on the floor or table. Label and discuss each item with the children. Follow by giving a riddle about each item, one at a time. The children will try and identify the correct item.

Purple Play Dough. Display a picture recipe for making play dough. Allow each child to "read" the recipe, add an ingredient, and help mix the dough. Color the dough purple by adding red and blue food coloring. Use it for fine motor activities.

Purple Play Day. On this special day, the children can wear purple clothing and bring purple toys to school. Purple activities and snacks should be stressed on purple play day.

Purple Mask Glass. Make the world look purple by cutting out the center of a large paper plate. Staple purple cellophane to the rim of the plate, covering the center. Staple a tongue depressor to the bottom of the rim. The children can hold the mask in front of their faces to make the world look purple. Go on a walk and talk about how things look different. The children will enjoy talking about the purple world.

5. DIRECTIONAL AND POSITIONAL CONCEPTS—IN FRONT, BEHIND, BESIDE, BETWEEN

Chair Play. Set up two chairs in the classroom and give the children directions to follow, such as "Stand in front of the chair, sit behind the chair, put the book between the chairs, stand beside the chair."

Musical Directions. Set up a row of chairs for this version of musical chairs. Before the music begins give a direction, "When the music stops everyone should be standing in front of a chair." Play music for a short time, then stop it. The children will then remember and follow the directions given. Repeat with the remaining words, *behind, beside,* and *between.*

Animal Directions. Using a play farm, have the children follow directions with animal figures, e.g., "Put the cow behind the barn, put the pig between the chicken and horse, put the duck beside the goat, and put the cow in front of the horse." Make up additional directions with the barn and animal figures. Vary this activity by using vegetables or spring objects.

Direction Talk. During the course of the month, use the terms *in front of, behind, beside,* and *between* when the children line up, when sitting on the rug or at the table, and when looking at pictures in books. Allow the children to practice hearing and using these words in the everyday environment.

FINE MOTOR

1. MANIPULATION

Paper Dolls. Cut paper dolls from tagboard. Provide children with spring clothing patterns to cut out and put on their dolls. Clothes can be either traced or dittoed on colored construction paper. If cutting the clothes is too difficult for the children, have the clothes precut and have the children simply dress the dolls. Remember to put tabs on the clothes so they can easily be put on and taken off the dolls. Vary the activity by having the children dress real dolls in spring clothes.

Spring Color Kite Collage. Provide the children with stencils of different shapes and pastel-colored tissue paper. Have them trace the stencils, cut out the shapes, and glue them on paper. Have them glue yarn around the shapes. The collage will give the illusion of unusually shaped kites.

Purple Umbrellas. Provide each child with umbrella-shaped paper and a large-sized cotton ball. Have them dip the cotton ball into purple paint and then onto their paper umbrellas. Vary the activity by using red and blue paint. As the children "print" red and blue cotton balls on paper, some of the color will mix to create purple.

Bubble Pictures. Add food coloring to bubbles. Using the easel or paper taped to an inside or outside wall, have children blow colored bubbles onto the paper.

Laced Butterflies. Cut butterfly shapes from various colors of construction paper and laminate them. Punch holes around the shapes and have the children lace the butterflies. Hang them from the ceiling.

Butterfly Print. Provide each child with a light-colored piece of construction paper, which might be cut into the shape of a butterfly. Have the children fold their paper in half, and paint a design on one half of the paper. While the paint is still wet, have them fold the paper. Both halves will contain the same design.

Laundry Day. Hang a clothesline in the classroom. Children can practice the pincer grip and develop muscles in the hand by pinching open clothespins to hang spring clothes on the line. The children will enjoy washing the clothes at the water table before hanging them on the line. For easy handling use doll clothes.

Kite Time. Reinforce the diamond shape by making kites. Have the children cut kites out of construction paper containing a predrawn diamond shape, then cut a piece of string or yarn and staple it to the kite for a tail. Children can practice tying, by tying a few pieces of yarn down the length of the tail. The children can fly their kites outside or hang them in the classroom.

Class Bulletin Board. Have the children create a cooperative class bulletin board over the course of the spring unit. Ideas to include are: snipping green paper to create grass for the bottom border, painting in the outline of a large tree, sponge painting birds and blossoms on the tree, gluing on balls of cotton to create clouds, and cutting strips of yellow paper and gluing them on a large yellow sun. Allow the children to brainstorm other ideas to include.

Easel Painting. Have the children mix blue and red paint at the easel to create purple, or supply purple paint for use at the easel. During the course of the month, provide various shapes drawn on the easel paper, including diamond shapes, animal shapes, umbrellas, raindrops, etc. Try cutting the shapes out of the easel paper for negative space painting.

Tube Collages. Provide each child with a toilet tissue or paper towel tube. Children make a collage by decorating their 3D collages with paper, fabric, "junk," crepe paper, etc. Hang from the ceiling.

Cupcake Flowers. The children can create spring flowers by gluing a cupcake liner on paper, cutting a strip of paper for a stem, and two ovals for petals.

Coffee Filter Flowers. Provide containers of different colors of food coloring mixed with a small amount of water. Have the children use eyedroppers to drop the different colors onto wet, round coffee filters. The colors will spread to create beautifully colored flowers.

Egg Shell Collage. Prepare hard-boiled eggs for snack time. Have the children remove the egg shells. Dip the shell pieces into egg dye, dry them, and glue them on paper to create a colored egg shell collage.

Seed Pictures. Create seed collages using different kinds of seeds. Have children strengthen their hand muscles by squeezing glue onto a paper. Follow by sprinkling seeds onto the glue. Shake off excess seeds.

Tractors. Have the children trace rectangles and circles from stencil shapes. Have them cut the shapes and assemble them into a tractor. The tractors can be decorated with crayons or markers. If the activity is too difficult for the children, provide predrawn or precut shapes.

Pet Chickens. Provide children with an outline of a chicken and a large sheet of yellow tissue paper. Have them tear the tissue paper into small pieces, spread glue on the outline of the chick, and cover the glue with the torn paper. The children can review the sound the chicken makes.

Purple Potato Shapes. Carve diamond and triangle shapes in a potato which has been cut in half. Dip the potato in purple tempera paint and print the shapes on construction paper. The shapes can be decorated by gluing colored pieces of yarn on them.

Farm Animal Booklet. Have each child trace farm animal stencils, one each day. Save the pictures to create a coloring book, which the children can color. The activity can be extended by having the children dictate a sentence about each animal for you to write. The children will enjoy reading their own books.

Furry Friends. Use potatoes shaped like various animals. Scoop out a hole in the "animal's" back. Fill the hole with soil, plant quick-growing seeds such as cress, mustard, or grass seeds, and keep it moist. Decorate the animals by using toothpicks or matchsticks for legs. Cut ears, eyes, and mouth out of paper. Use yarn or pipecleaners for a tail.

Group Barn. For a group cooperative project, have the children paint a large box red, cut out a door and windows, and use it as a barn.

Clay Animals. Make farm animals from clay. Roll a ball for the body, add another ball for the head. Add legs by rolling the clay into leg shapes. The animals can live in the red barn created by the class.

Farmer Hats. Provide the children with paper cut into the shape of farm hats. Have them snip the hats to make the fringe. Vary the activity by having the children cut the hats from a predrawn pattern. Snip the fringe on them.

Cereal Designs. Let the children create their own designs on paper plates, from various types of breakfast cereal which was grown from wheat, corn, oats, or rice. Use low-sugar cereals that can be eaten after the designs are created.

Pussy Willows. Have the children draw a vertical line for the pussy willow stem. Mix white and black paint to create gray. Put the paint into a styrofoam meat tray. Have the children dip their thumb into the paint and then print along the stem to make pussy willows.

Colorful Caterpillars. Caterpillars can be made by tracing and cutting out circles. Glue the circles side by side in a "wiggly" line. Try using different colored circles for colorful caterpillars.

Finger Painting Fun. Provide finger paint paper which has been cut into shapes representing April themes. Examples might include butterfly, caterpillar, animal, barn, or tractor shapes. Supply various colors of finger paint for the children to use for painting on the shapes.

Feed the Birds. Have the children tear up pieces of stale bread. Go for a spring walk and feed the birds or ducks.

Spring Glasses. Make sunglasses for those sunny spring days. Have the children cut yellow cellophane circles and glue them to a small paper plate with the middle circle cut out. Attach pipecleaners to complete the sunglass frame.

Muddy Fun. Mix mud with liquid dish soap. The children can paint on paper, the playground, or on windows. Designs are simply washed away with a hose.

Humpty Dumpty. Make Humpty Dumpty dolls by having the children cut out ovals and fold paper strips accordian style to make arms and legs. Use scraps to make facial features.

Fine Motor Center. The April fine motor center offers a variey of collage themes. Provide paper cut into spring or farm shapes, including eggs, butterflies, farm animals, etc. Provide paper cut into diamond or triangle shapes. The children can glue a variety of spring objects, paper or fabric, on the shapes. For a varied texture, glue on Easter basket grass or egg shells.

The center should also include farm animal stencils for tracing and animal-shaped cookie cutters for use with play dough. Add various sized boxes or other containers for nesting and stacking activities. Spring-shaped, animal-shaped, and triangle- and diamond-shaped paper with holes punched around the edges can be provided for lacing activities. Continue to provide materials for play dough manipulation, bead stringing, and cutting.

2. PREWRITING

Flower Stems. Give each child a garden full of flowers without stems. Have them draw vertical lines to create flower stems.

Caterpillar Designs. Draw caterpillar outlines on the chalkboard or on construction paper. Have the children complete the caterpillars by drawing verticle lines inside the outline.

Spring Dot-to-Dot Pictures. Children will enjoy creating spring objects by connecting the dots. Dot-to-dot pictures might include kites, umbrellas, raincoats and boots, or pretty trees and flowers.

Maze. Create a farm maze either on paper or on the chalkboard. Ideas for the maze might include getting an animal to the barn or a tractor to the field. Ponds and fences can act as barriers to go around.

Stencils. Provide stencils of triangle shapes of varying sizes. Encourage the children to trace the triangles with fingers, crayons, markers, pencils, and chalk. Next, encourage the children to copy triangles by simply looking at the stencils. They may want to decorate their creations.

People Shapes. Spread large sheets of kraft paper on the floor. Have three children lie on the paper to form a triangle. Other children can walk around the "triangle," or trace the triangle with large crayons or chunks of chalk.

Prewriting Center. The April prewriting center will again focus on practice holding and writing with control, using various utensils. Add purple pencils and markers. Provide stencils of triangles, farm and spring theme shapes. Provide predrawn models of simple designs which were previously taught. Chalkboards might contain dot-to-dot and path-tracing activities. Allow for free exploration of materials provided at the center as well as specific activities to try. Allow children to create dot pictures for their friends to complete.

PERCEPTION

Picture Sort. Provide various pictures which specifically depict spring or not spring scenes or objects. Have the children sort the pictures into two groups—one group for spring pictures, the other group for not spring pictures.

Spring Puzzles. Find pictures which depict spring scenes, mount them on cardboard, and laminate them. Cut them into puzzle pieces for children to assemble.

Kite Match-Ups. Prepare ten kites, making each one a different color or design. Laminate them and cut them in half lengthwise either with a straight or zig-zag line. Have children match the kite halves.

Umbrella Pairs. Prepare ten pairs of matching umbrellas. Cut them out and laminate them. Spread them out on the floor or table and have the children pair the matching umbrellas.

Flower Patterns. Prepare a flower with petals that follow a specific color pattern, e.g., pink, purple, yellow, pink, purple, etc. Provide children with the center of the flower and appropriate colored petals. Have them assemble the flower according to the prepared pattern.

How I Look in April. Have the children draw self-portraits to be included in their booklets. Ask them to add spring clothing or a spring background. Review body parts on the flannel board before beginning this activity.

Flower Lotto. Prepare a lotto game using flower stickers. Children can match cue cards to playing cards for an individual game, or play a traditional lotto game with small groups of children.

Jelly Bean Sort. Have children sort jelly beans by color into sections of an egg carton.

Egg Puzzles. Make decorated paper eggs which differ in size, color, and design patterns. Laminate and cut the eggs in half using different zig-zag patterns Children assemble the egg puzzles.

Card Games. Prepare a deck of playing cards with four suits: circles, triangles, diamonds, and squares. Each suit can be prepared in different colors including purple, yellow, red, blue, green, etc. Use the deck of cards for the following games:

1. Have the children find all purple colors, red colors, blue colors, etc.
2. Have the children find all the diamonds, triangles, circles, etc.
3. Have the children find a specific card such as the purple triangle, red diamond, etc.
4. Play "Go Fish." Cards can be matched by color or shape.

Size Sequencing. Prepare a set of kites, eggs, or flowers in different sizes. Have the children sequence the objects from smallest to largest and largest to smallest.

Animal or Vegetable. Divide the flannel board into two sections, one section containing the cutout of a barn, the other section containing a garden. Provide pictures of plants and animals. Have the children put the animal pictures on the barn section and the vegetable pictures on the garden section. This activity can also be done on the floor or at a table.

Missing Animals. Show either animal figures or pictures to the children. While the children close their eyes, remove one or two animals. The children try and guess which animal is missing. The game can be simplified by using fewer animals and removing only one. Make it more difficult by increasing the number of animals and removing more than one at a time.

Who's in the Barn?. Prepare a piece of red construction paper to look like a barn. Cut out windows and a door. Hide a picture of an animal behind the barn. Open one window or door at a time. The children can try and guess which animal is in the barn by seeing only part of the picture.

Farm or Zoo?. After completing language activities about farm animals, have the children sort farm animals from zoo animals. Use either pictures or figures. The children can put farm animals in a barn and zoo animals in a cage.

Animal Parade. Practice visual sequential memory skills by having children recreate a parade of animals. Show the children a sequence of farm animals, e.g., horse, cow, pig, chicken. Mix up the animals and ask one child at a time to put them in their original order. The activity is easier with fewer animals or more difficult with more animals. Vary the activity by using farm tools.

Farm Lotto. Prepare a farm lotto game. Use pictures of objects, animals, or plants found on a farm. The children can match the cue cards to the picture on their lotto cards.

Feely Bag. Make an animal or vegetable feely bag. Use plastic or real vegetables or animal figures. Show the items to the children before placing them in the bag. Let each child feel the objects and guess what they are. Vary the activity by asking each child to find a particular item, using only his/her sense of touch.

Animal-Product Match-Up. Display pictures of farm animals. Put products we get from the animals into the feely bag. Examples might include an egg, a small carton of milk, a piece of wool, etc. Ask each child to find an object, e.g., "Find what comes from a chicken." The child can then match his/her object to the appropriate picture.

Silly Pictures. Prepare laminated pictures of farm animals with missing parts. The children must guess what part of the animal is missing. If possible, have children fill in the missing part. The picture will be reusable if laminated.

Perception Center. This month at the perception center stress the color purple, the triangle and diamond shapes, and the farm and spring themes. Have the children sort and classify triangles, diamonds, and purple items. Have them match pictures of flowers, birds, butterflies, kites, umbrellas, farm animals, and vegetables. Have them follow patterns using colors and shapes. Provide block and peg designs to copy, in the shapes of triangles and diamonds. Provide farm puzzles either commercial or teacher-prepared by laminating and cutting apart pictures. Provide patterns for picture assembly. Ideas might include flowers, butterflies, umbrellas, and farm animals.

GROSS MOTOR

Puddle Jumps. Draw a chalk puddle on the floor. Have the children jump or hop over the puddle.

Bunny Hop. Draw a starting line and a bunny's burrow as the finish line. Have the children pretend they are bunnies and jump or hop to their burrows.

Shapely Moves. Draw large triangle and diamond shapes on the floor. Have the children move around the shapes to music. They can hop, jump, gallop, skip, or walk around depending on the tempo of the music.

Farm Tag. "It" tries to catch the other children as they move across the room from the start to the finish line. If the child being "tagged" can think of something that lives, grows, or can be found on a farm, he/she shouts out the item and can then keep running to the finish line. The children take turns being "it."

Farmer in the Dell. The children will enjoy playing this favorite game. The game can be extended by adding animals, vegetables, and tools to the verses. Each child can think of a different item to add, e.g., The farmer takes a cow, the cow takes a chicken, etc.

Musical Farm Animals. Spread pictures of farm animals on the floor in a large circle. Play music. When the music stops, each child must be standing on a animal and try to identify what it is. Vary the activity by using vegetable shapes or color pictures.

Ring Around the Rosie. Play this game the traditional way or vary by changing the action from "fall down." Change the end each time. Examples might include jump up, touch our heads, hop on one foot, touch the floor, etc.

Kite Flying. Fly the kite made in the fine motor section on a nice spring day. Have the children run, walk, gallop, and skip with their kites.

Ball Play. Practice favorite spring ball games with the children. Try baseball with an oversized bat and ball. The children might enjoy hitting the ball off a batting tee. Reinforce eye-foot coordination by having the children kick a soccer ball from one goal line to another. Large rubber balls can be used to play kick the ball.

Growing Seeds. Have the children pretend they are growing seeds. They start by curling themselves into little balls on the floor. Slowly they uncurl and begin to stretch and grow until they are standing up with their hands stretched high above their heads. Play music with a slow tempo to encourage the children to move slowly.

Farm Animal Move. Encourage the children to pretend they are various farm animals and move like the animals move. Cows and pigs will move on four legs. Ducks might waddle, chicks will flap their wings, horses will gallop. Allow the children to use their imaginations as they move.

Caterpillar Obstacle Course. Let the children pretend they are caterpillars and slide around on their stomachs. An obstacle course might be set up for them to follow. Vary the activity by having them move like a caterpillar using a scooter board.

Playground Fun. If your school has a playground, allow the children to enjoy the warm spring air by freely exploring the playground equipment. Encourage the children to pump their feet to make their swing move, and alternate feet while climbing the rungs of the ladder. Be sure to stress playground safety rules that might have been forgotten over the long winter months.

Obstacle Course. Set up an obstacle course with large boxes, tunnels, hoops, balance beams, etc. Encourage the children to use the vocabulary words *in front behind, beside, between* when going through the course.

Flying Birds. Have the children stand on their tiptoes and wave their arms slowly up and down. As the wings move faster the children can run, as the wings slow down the children walk. Play music with a varying tempo.

SENSORY EXPERIENCES

Encourage children to use their sense of sight when going for walks, outside at play, and inside when in the classroom. Look for signs of spring, colors, and shapes. The children can observe colors change by making different shaded glasses as suggested in the fine motor and purple language activities. Ask children to make comparisons of objects and people by looking closely at them. Children use their sense of sight in almost everything they do. Help them become more aware of what they are looking at and seeing with their eyes through many of the activities presented during the month.

Exploration Table. This month the exploration table can reinforce the spring and farm themes. Fill the table with Easter basket grass or shredded paper. Hide eggs, small farm animals, and other small manipulatives in the grass. The children can use their sense of touch and sight to uncover the treasures.

Reinforce the farm theme by filling the exploration table with rice, barley, seeds, dried corn, or sand. Supply small toy tractors, plows, or other farm machinery. Provide small toy shovels, rakes, hoes, and buckets.

PREMATH

Treasure Count. Have each child count the items she/he collected on one of the nature walks. Have him/her display the items. Each child can either write or find the numeral which tells how many treasures she/he found. Children can also count each other's treasures and label them with the correct numeral.

Scavenger Hunt Graph. Graph the number of each item found on the spring scavenger hunt.

Rainy Day Graph. On a rainy day, make a class graph depicting the number of different colored raincoats worn by class members.

Umbrella Count. On a rainy day, count the number of umbrellas brought to school. Count how many red, blue, polkadot, etc., umbrellas.

Calendar Count. Use kite cutouts on the April calendar. Count them each day. Count how many days until Easter or spring break. On rainy days, use an umbrella cutout instead of a kite. At the end of the month, count how many rainy days there were in April.

Jelly Bean Math. Label sections of an egg carton with the numerals one through twelve. An additional picture cue of one to twelve dots may also be used. Supply enough jelly beans to fill each section of the egg carton with the correct number of jelly beans, and put them in the appropriate section.

If You Were the Bunny. Introduce the concept of more and less using jelly beans. With the children watching, pour a large number of jelly beans into one pile and a small amount into another pile. Show the children a toy bunny rabbit and ask "Which pile of jelly beans would you want if you were the bunny?" Most children will choose the pile with more jelly beans. Ask "Why?" trying to elicit the words *more* and *less*. Continue the activity by pouring piles of jelly beans for the children. Let them choose between more or less and have them tell if they chose more or less and why.

More and Less Guess. Use the spring items collected on spring nature walks or scavenger hunts. Divide objects into groups containing more or less items. Have children estimate or guess which group has more or less items. Count to check the correctness of their answer.

What Weighs More?. Use a two-sided balance scale to weigh classroom objects. Choose a variety of objects that are distinctly heavy and light. Have the children weigh the objects and decide which one weighs more or less. Classify the objects into two groups, one group of objects which weighs more and one group which weighs less.

Expand on the activity by weighing children. Let them guess who will weigh more or less. Graph the weights of the children. Who weighs the most? Least?

Kite Time. Have children make kites for a fine motor activity. Allow each child to measure and cut his/her own kite string. When the kites are complete, children compare lengths of kite string with a friend. Have children determine who has more or less string.

Bunny Math. Provide each child with a simple cutout of a bunny. Write the numeral 9 on each bunny and have the children glue on nine cotton balls for decorations. Vary the activity by writing a different numeral, one through nine, on each bunny. Each child glues the corresponding number of cotton balls on his/her bunny. Have the children sequence the bunnies in numerical order from one to nine.

Flower Power. Have children trace and cut circles or provide them with precut circles which will be the center of the flower. Provide each child with nine purple petals to glue onto the circle. Encourage the children to print the numeral 9 in the middle of the flowers. Have the children add a stem and leaves to their flowers.

Chicken Little. Provide each child with a cutout of "Chicken Little" and chicken feathers. Have them count out nine feathers and glue them onto "Chicken Little."

Diamond Shape. Show the children a large cutout of a diamond shape. Describe it calling attention to its four sides and four angles. Make a diamond shape using four children lying on the floor. Review other "body-made" shapes through experimentation.

Diamond Hunt. Prepare a large picture which contains many shapes. Have the children find and count all of the diamond shapes.

Diamond Sort. Prepare cutouts of shapes including circles, squares, triangles, rectangles, and diamonds. Laminate the shapes. Ask the children to sort the shapes putting all of the same shapes together.

War. Older children will enjoy playing the card game "War." Evenly deal the entire deck of cards to the children. All of the children turn one card over. The person with the highest card (more diamonds, hearts, clubs, or spades) gets to keep the cards which were played. If two or more children play the same card, a war is played. Three cards down, one up. Whoever plays the highest card up wins the cards played in the war.

Graphing. When learning about the farm, vote on the children's favorite farm animal and graph the responses. When learning nursery rhymes, graph the children's favorite nursery rhymes. Compare votes and discuss results using the words *more* and *less.*

Seriating. Cut paper towel rolls or straws into graduated sizes. Have the children arrange the pieces in order from smallest to largest or largest to smallest.

Find a Set. Prepare a set of cards, each one containing a numeral from one to nine. One at a time, have the children choose a card and find that number of different objects, e.g., nine crayons, blocks, books, etc.

Egg Guess. Put differing numbers of eggs in a basket. Have the children guess (estimate) how many eggs are in the basket. Count them to see whose guess was the closest.

SONGS AND FINGERPLAYS

Where Is Farmer? (tune: "Where Is Thumbkin?").

Where is Farmer? (hands behind back)
Where is Farmer? (hands behind back)
Here I am, (Hold up left thumb.)
Here I am. (Hold up left thumb.)
How are you today sir? (Hold up right thumb.)
Very well I thank you. (Hold up left thumb.)
Run away, (left hand behind back)
Run away. (right hand behind back)

Repeat with:

Where is Chicken? (Use pointer fingers.)
Where is Mr. Cow? (Use middle fingers.)
Where is Ms. Pig? (Use ring fingers.)
Where is Mr. Horse? (Use little finger.)

I've Been Working on the Farm (tune: "I've Been Working on the Railroad").

I've been working on the farm, all the live long day.
I've been working on the farm,
Just to pass the time away.
Can't you hear the cows mooing?
Watch the tractor mow the hay.
Look at all the vegetables growing
On this nice spring day.

Have You Ever Seen a Farmer? (tune: "Have You Ever Seen a Lassie?").

Have you ever seen a farmer, a farmer, a farmer,
Have you ever seen a farmer go this way and that?
Go this way and that way, Go this way and that way,
Have you ever seen a farmer go this way and that?
(Actions might include digging a hole, planting a seed, feeding an animal, etc.)

A Trip to the Farm (tune: "Twinkle Twinkle Little Star").

See the eggs the chickens lay.
Listen to the horses nay.
Taste the milk we get from the cow.
Watch the way the farmer can plow.
A trip to the farm is lots of fun.
Let's go now everyone.

Birds (fingerplay).

Up, up in the sky, the little birds fly, (Fingers fly like birds.)
Down, down in the nest, little birds rest. (Hands form a nest.)
With a wing on the left, and a wing on the right, (Hands on each hip.)
Let the little birds rest all night. (Head to one side, like tucking under the wing.)

This Little Cow (fingerplay).

(Hold up one hand, fingers erect, bend one finger each line.)

This little cow eats grass,
This little cow eats hay,
This little cow drinks water,
And this little cow runs away.
This little cow does nothing,
But lie and sleep all day!

Here Is the Bunny (fingerplay).

Here is the Bunny with ears so funny (Fingers form ears, hands form head.)
And here is the hole in the ground (Hand on hip forms hole in the ground.)
When a slight noise he hears,
He pricks up his ears, and jumps in the hole in the ground.

My Garden (fingerplay).

This is my garden, (Hold right hand out, palm up.)
I'll rake it with care. (Rake palm with left hand.)
And then some flower seeds (Plant seed with left thumb and index finger.)
I'll plant in there.
The sun will shine, (Make circle with two hands.)
And the rain will fall. (Fingers flutter down.)
And my garden will blossom, (Make flowers out of cupped hands.)
And grow straight and tall.

Well-Known Songs to Sing in April.

Old MacDonald
B–I–N–G–O
Mary Had a Little Lamb
Eensy Weensy Spider
The Farmer in the Dell
Baa Baa Black Sheep

RECIPES

Oatmeal Cookies.

1 1/4 cups butter	1 1/2 cups whole wheat flour
3/4 cup brown sugar	1 teaspoon baking soda
1/2 cup granulated sugar	3 cups oatmeal
1 egg	1/2 teaspoon cinnamon
1 teaspoon vanilla	

Beat butter and sugars until fluffy. Add egg and vanilla. In another bowl combine flour, baking soda, and cinnamon. Add to butter mixture. Mix well. Stir in oatmeal. Form into cookies on ungreased cookie sheet. Bake for 10 minutes in preheated 375-degree oven. Raisins or chopped nuts can be added to the recipe.

Peanut Butter Crisps.

3 cups quick oats	1/2 cup margarine
3/4 cup brown sugar firmly packed	Peanut butter
1/2 teaspoon salt	

Combine oats, sugar, and salt. Add margarine and blend well. Firmly pack half of mixture into 11″ × 7″ pan. Melt peanut butter, spread over oat mixture, packing lightly. Bake 25–30 minutes at 350 degrees. Let cool and refrigerate before cutting.

Pigs in a Blanket.

1 package refrigerator crescent roll dough (8)
1 package hot dogs
2 slices american cheese

Divide crescent rolls into 8 triangles. Cut each slice of cheese into 4 strips. Cut the hot dogs down the center, not all the way through, and place a piece of cheese into each slit. Put the hot dog on the wide end of the triangle dough and roll up. Put on cookie sheet, seam side down. Preheat oven to 375 degrees. Bake 10–15 minutes until dough is lightly browned and the meat is warmed through.

Bunny Salad.

    6 carrots
    1/4 cup raisins
    3 tablespoons mayonaise

Wash and scrape carrots. Trim off ends and grate into a mixing bowl. Add raisins and mayonaise. Toss well. Line plate with lettuce and serve salad.

Kid's Dip.

    2 cups cottage cheese   2 diced radishes
    1/4 cup grated carrot   1/4 teaspoon dried dill
    2 tablespoons chopped green onion   Dash pepper
    2 tablespoons chopped green   1/2 teaspoon salt
    pepper

Blend cottage cheese in a blender. Place in bowl. Stir in vegetables and seasonings. Cover and chill. Serve on crackers.

Oatmeal Play Dough.

    1 part flour
    2 parts oatmeal
    1 part water

Add water gradually to bind mixture.

Oatmeal Crackers.

    1/4 cup oil   1 cup flour
    1/3 cup water   1/4 cup apple juice concentrate
    1 cup rolled oats   1/4 to 1/2 teaspoon salt

Mix all ingredients together and place on a cookie sheet. Roll with a rolling pin thinly and evenly. Cut dough into squares and prick with fork. Bake 15 minutes at 375 degrees. Remove the brown ones from around the edges, and bake the rest until done. Serve with cheese, peanut butter, egg or ham salad.

Graham Crackers.

    1 cup graham flour   1/4 cup vegetable oil
    1 cup whole wheat flour   1 banana sliced
    1/2 teaspoon baking soda   1 teaspoon vanilla
    1/2 teaspoon salt   1 teaspoon cinnamon
    1/4 cup apple juice concentrate

Blend apple juice, vegetable oil, banana, vanilla, and cinnamon in a blender. Combine graham flour, whole wheat flour, baking soda, and salt ingredients in a bowl and stir well. Stir in blender contents, mixing well. On a floured surface, roll half the dough as thin as possible. Poke dough with fork, cut into pieces, and transfer to a cookie sheet. Bake at 350 degrees for 6 to 8 minutes. Repeat with rest of dough. Yield: 3 dozen 2″ crackers.

Sunflower Salad.

1 cup shredded carrots
1 cup thinly sliced celery
2 firm bananas sliced
1/2 cup sunflower seeds, hulled and
roasted without salt
3 tablespoons oil

1 tablespoon frozen orange juice
concentrate
2 teaspoons lemon juice
1/8 teaspoon salt
Dash pepper
Crisp lettuce leaves

Combine carrots, celery, bananas, sunflower seeds. In a separate bowl combine oil, orange juice, lemon juice, salt, and pepper. Pour over first mixture. Toss lightly. Serve on lettuce leaves.

APRIL SNACKS

Snacks from the Farm.

Cheese
Yogurt
Ice Cream
Macaroni and cheese
Eggs

Egg salad on crackers
Deviled eggs
Hot dogs
Pigs in a blanket
Chicken salad
Lunch meats (cut in triangles)
Cut up vegetables and dip:
   cucumbers
   zucchini
   carrots
   celery
   tomatoes
   corn
   popcorn
   beans
   peas

Oat products such as oatmeal cookies, muffins, bread, and cereal.
Wheat products such as whole wheat bread, crackers, cookies, and cereals.
Corn products such as bread, corn muffins, corn dogs.
Carrot cake
Zucchini bread and muffins

Things that Are Purple.

Grapes
Grape jam on toast
Grape jello
Grape juice
Grape popsicles (made from grape juice)

Purple Cow. Add frozen grape juice to a glass of milk. Stir and enjoy.

Things that Are Triangle Shaped.

Pieces of pizza
Breads and spreads cut into a triangle shape
Sandwiches cut in half diagonally
French toast cut in half diagonally
Homemade pretzels shaped like triangles

Things that Are Diamond Shaped.

Breads and spreads cut into diamond shapes
Pancakes formed into diamond shapes
Cheese slices cut into diamond shapes
Lunch meat pieces cut into diamond shapes
Homemade pretzels shaped like diamonds

CREATIVE DRAMATICS

Farmer's Market. The creative dramatics area might house a farmer's market for the month of April. All of the young farmers can come and sell their produce and wares. Use real or plastic vegetables. The children can also sell plants, flowers, farm tools, hats, eggs, seeds, etc. Set up tables to display the farmers' products and wares. Umbrellas may be set up in case of rain. The farmers will need cash registers and play money for making transactions. Read the book *Let's Grow a Garden* by Gyo Fujikawa to prompt ideas for play. Play might also be prompted by visiting a nursery or farm supply store which sells plants, seeds, and farm tools. The farmers can wear farm hats and aprons when working at the farmers' market.

Nursery Rhymes. After children have learned some of the familiar Mother Goose Rhymes, they will enjoy dramatizing the rhymes using simple props found in the classroom. Allow them to think of other actions or words the Mother Goose characters could say or do. Some children may want to make up new verses or versions for you to write down so they can "illustrate." Prompt and encourage thinking by asking a variety of questions: Where else could Jack and Jill climb? What else could Little Jack Horner eat? What else could Jack Be Nimble jump over?

Three Billy Goats Gruff. Read the story of the *Three Billy Goats Gruff* several times throughout the month until children become familiar with it. Encourage children to tell their own version as they look at the pictures in the story. Allow them to suggest possible props they might like to use to help them retell the story, e.g., blue kraft paper to represent water under the bridge, a classroom slide to be the bridge, green kraft paper to be the grassy meadow, etc. Children will enjoy changing the tone and quality of their voices as they take on the different roles of the billy goats. Remind children that there can be more than one mean troll, large billy goat, etc. Continue acting out the story and creating new versions while interest is high. Remind children that there is no right or wrong way to dramatize the story. Encourage their creativity.

CHILDREN'S LITERATURE

Alexandra, Martha. *No Ducks in Our Bathtub*

Asbjornser, P. C. *The Three Billy Goats Gruff* (Illus. by Paul Galdone)

Ayer, Jacqueline B. *The Paper Flower Tree*

Barrett, Judith. *Old MacDonald Had an Apartment House*

Battles, Edith. *What Does the Rooster Say, Yoshio?*

Baum, Arline and Joseph. *One Bright Monday Morning*

Beer, Kathleen. *What Happens in the Spring?*

Brand, Millen. *This Little Pig Named Curly*

Bright, Robert. *My Red Umbrella*

Brook, Judy. *Tim Mouse Visits the Farm*

Brooke, Leonard. *Johnny Crow's Garden*

Brooks, Ron. *This Little Pig Went to Market*

Brown, Margaret Wise. *The Golden Egg Book*

———. *The Runaway Bunny*

Carle, Eric. *The Rooster Who Set Out to See the World*

———. *The Tiny Seed*

———. *The Very Hungry Caterpillar*

Carrick, Carol. *Swamp Spring*

Chandoha, Walter. *A Baby Goat for You*

Clifton, Lucille. *The Boy Who Didn't Believe in Spring*

Cohen, Carol. *Wake Up Groundhog*

Collier, Ethel. *I Know a Farm*

Craig, Jean. *Spring Is Like the Morning*

Delton, Judy. *Three Friends Find Spring*

DePaola, Tomie. *Four Stories for Four Seasons*

Dunn, Judy. *The Little Lamb*

Ellentuck, Shan. *A Sunflower As Big As the Sun*

Ets, Marie Hall. *The Cow's Party*

Fisher, R. M. *A Day in the Woods*

Flora, James. *The Day the Cow Sneezed*

Freeman, Don. *A Rainbow of My Own*

Fruedberg, Judy. *Some, More, Most*

Friskey, Margaret. *Chicken Little Count to Ten*

Fujikawa, Gyo. *Let's Grow a Garden*

Galdone, Paul (Illus.). *The Little Red Hen*

Ginsburg, Myra. *Mushroom in the Rain*

Graham, John. *A Crowd of Cows*

Hayward, Linda. *Sesame Seasons*

Hogrogian, Nonny. *Billy Goat and His Well Fed Friends*

Holl, A. *The Rain Puddle*

Hurd, Edith Thaatcher. *The Day the Sun Danced*

Ipcar, D. Z. *Bright Barnyard*

———. *Brown Cow Farm*

———. *Ten Big Farms*

Israel, Marion. *The Tractor on the Farm*

Jeffers, Susan. *All the Pretty Horses*

Johnson, Crockett. *A Picture for Harold's Room: A Purple Crayon Adventure*

Kasza, Keiko. *The Pig's Picnic*

Keats, Ezra Jack. *A Letter to Amy*

_____ . *Over in the Meadow*

Keller, Holly. *Will It Rain?*

Kellogg, Steven. *Can I Keep Him?*

Kennel, Moritz. *Old McDonald Had a Farm*

Koch, Dorothy. *When the Cows Got Out*

Krauss, Ruth. *The Carrot Seed*

Krahn, F. *April Fools*

Kumin, Maxine W. *Spring Things*

Kuskin. *James and the Rain*

Lexau, Joan. *Who Took the Farmer's Hat?*

Lionni, Leo. *Little Blue and Little Yellow*

Lobel, Arnold. *Frog and Toad All Year*

Maestro, Giulio, *One More, One Less*

Maril, Lee. *Mr. Bunny Paints the Eggs*

Martin, Bill. *Brown Bear, Brown Bear, What Do You See?*

Meeks, Ester K. *Curious Cow*

_____ . *Friendly Farm Animals*

Miller, Albert. *The Hungry Goat*

Mother Goose. *Brian Wildsmith's Mother Goose*

_____ . *Nursery Rhymes from Mother Goose in Signed English*

_____ . *To Market to Market*

Otto, Margaret J. *The Little Brown Horse*

Palazzo, Tony. *Animal Babies*

Potter, Beatrix. *Appley Dapply's Nursery Rhymes*

Provensen, Alice and Martin. *Our Animal Friends at Maple Hill Farm*

_____ . *The Year at Maple Hill Farm*

Quackenbush, Robert (Illus.). *Old MacDonald Had a Farm*

Richards, Jane. *A Horse Grows Up*

Robinson, William W. *On the Farm*

Rockwell, Harlow. *The Compost Heap*

Rojankovsky, F. S. *Animals on the Farm*

Scarry, Richard. *Best Mother Goose Ever*

Seignbose, Francoise. *Jeanne-Marie Counts Her Sheep*

Sipherd, Ray. *Down on the Farm with Grover*

Skaar, Grace. *What Do the Animals Say?*

Skelsey, Alice. *Growing Up Green*

Smith, Donald. *Farm Numbers One Two Three*

Stereus, Carla. *Hooray for Pig*

Tresselt, Alvin. *Hi Mr. Robin*

Welber, Robert. *Songs of the Seasons*

Weygant, Noemi. *It's Spring*

Williams, Garth. *Baby Farm Animals*

Williams, G. M. *The Chicken Book*

Wolf, Robert J. *Hello Yellow*

Wright, Dare. *Look at a Calf*

_____ . *Look at a Colt*

Yolen, Jane. *An Invitation to the Butterfly Ball: A Counting Rhyme*

Zion, Gene. *Really Spring*

Evaluating April Concepts

Throughout the month, continue to update and record significant progress and/or changes made by the children. Use the checklists and individual student logs. During April, assessment of vocabulary should include spring-related vocabulary, names of farm animals, and spring words stressed throughout the month. Memory and rhyming can be checked as individual children recite Mother Goose nursery rhymes.

Throughout the month, observe how children respond to challenging tasks. Do they demonstrate persistence, respond with encouragement, or refuse to try? Are tasks completed very quickly or very slowly? Objective observations should be recorded with a brief description of the activity or task. Look for response patterns exhibited by the children in regard to task, time of day, group size, etc. This information will be helpful when preparing appropriate lessons for the children.

CONCEPTS FOR APRIL (parent copy)

LANGUAGE AND VOCABULARY

Spring—weather and nature's changes, clothing, activities, and vocabulary

Farm Theme—mother and baby animals, their sounds and products, farmer's job and equipment

Nursery Rhymes and Rhyming

Cooking Experiences

Color—purple

Directional and Positional Concepts—in front, behind, beside, and between

FINE MOTOR

Lacing, painting, coloring, gluing, play dough manipulation, cutting, block tower building, bead stringing, path tracing, design copying (triangle)

PERCEPTION

Same and different, draw a person, puzzles, copying block, peg and bead designs, patterning and sorting

GROSS MOTOR

Organized games, movement activities, galloping, outside climbing activities

PREMATH

One-to-one correspondence, calendar activities, sorting, number and numeral 9, more and less, diamond shape

CREATIVE DRAMATICS

SENSORY EXPERIENCES

SONGS AND FINGERPLAYS

APRIL

Parent-child activities

SUN	MON	TUE	WED	THU	FRI	SAT
TAKE A WALK. ENJOY AND TALK ABOUT SIGNS OF SPRING YOU SEE.	BLOW BUBBLES OUTSIDE.	CUT PICTURES FROM A MAGAZINE TO MAKE A PURPLE COLLAGE.	PRACTICE RECITING SOME MOTHER GOOSE RHYMES.	VISIT THE LIBRARY. SELECT MOTHER GOOSE RHYMING BOOKS, STORIES ABOUT SPRING, FARMS, ANIMALS, ETC.	EAT PURPLE GRAPES OR PLUMS.	PRACTICE SILLY RHYMING HAIR, DARE, FAIR; FEET, TREAT, MEAT, ETC.
DO SOME "SPRING CLEANING." TALK ABOUT CLEANING SUPPLIES.	FLY A KITE OUTSIDE.	PRACTICE RHYMING USING FAMILY MEMBERS' NAMES.	ARRANGE 3 TO 5 OBJECTS ON A TABLE. TELL WHAT'S BETWEEN TWO OF THEM.	CLEAN YOUR CLOSET. NAME SOME CLOTHING WORN IN SPRING.	"READ" THE PICTURES IN A BOOK TO TELL THE STORY.	WHAT'S "BEHIND" AND "IN FRONT" OF YOUR HOUSE?
REVIEW NAMES OF FRUITS AND VEGETABLES SEEN AT THE GROCERY STORE.	FEEL SPRING! JUMP OVER TWIGS, CLIMB A TREE, ROLL IN THE GRASS.	PLAY A FARM GAME: TOSS A BALL INTO A BUCKET. KEEP COUNT.	DRAW A PERSON. REMEMBER ALL THE PARTS.	HELP YOUR CHILD TO TRACE TRIANGLES.	SORT SOME OBJECTS INTO EGG CARTONS, THEN COUNT AND COMPARE.	USE A SEED CATALOG TO MAKE A FLOWER OR VEGETABLE COLLAGE.
PLANT SOME VEGETABLE OR FLOWER SEEDS.	CUT PAPER, ARRANGE, AND GLUE TO MAKE FLOWERS.	MAKE SETS OF NINE WITH BEAN SEEDS.	PRETEND YOU ARE A FARM ANIMAL. MAKE THE SOUND AND MOVE LIKE IT.	EAT BACON, CHEESE, EGGS, AND DRINK MILK. TALK ABOUT WHERE THEY CAME FROM.	FIND SOME THINGS MADE OF WOOL AND LEATHER IN YOUR HOUSE.	PRACTICE SONGS AND FINGERPLAYS.
SET THE TABLE. COUNT EACH SET OF OBJECTS.	HELP MAKE A SPECIAL DESSERT.					

MAY

CONCEPTS FOR MAY

LANGUAGE AND VOCABULARY

1. Zoo—animals and their characteristics, zookeeper's jobs
2. Machines—naming and describing, how they make jobs easier, sorting, and classifying
3. Police Officer and Safety—Officer's jobs, how to stay safe from harm
4. Summer—weather and nature's changes, clothing and activities, safety in play
5. Color—Blue
6. Directional and Positional Concepts—above and below

Suggested field trips/classroom visitors: Visit a zoo, factory, or police station. Have a police officer visit.

FINE MOTOR: 1. MANIPULATION, AND 2. PREWRITING

Lacing, painting, coloring, gluing, play dough manipulation, cutting, block tower building, bead stringing, centers, path tracing, design copying (rectangle)

PERCEPTION

Same and different, draw a person, center activities: puzzles, copying block, peg and bead designs, patterning and sorting

GROSS MOTOR

Movement activities, organized games, skipping, outside riding/pulling activities, review any previous activities

PREMATH

One-to-one correspondence, calendar activities, sorting, number and numeral 10, ordering numbers 1–10, oval shape

SENSORY EXPERIENCES

Exploration table, sense of smell

CREATIVE DRAMATICS

- Police Station
- *The Little Red Hen*

RECIPES

Foods to keep us cool and foods that smell good

SNACK

Food related to monthly concepts and themes

SELF-HELP

Provide activities at children's developmental levels

REVIEW

Any previous concepts

ACTIVITIES FOR MAY

LANGUAGE AND VOCABULARY

1. ZOO

Who's at the Zoo? Introduce several zoo animals over a period of days. Talk about why and how these "wild" animals are different from farm animals and pets. Show a picture of each animal as it is introduced. Name each animal. Talk about its color and important physical characteristics. Animals to begin teaching about could include bear, camel, elephant, hippopotamus, kangaroo, lion, monkey rhinoceros, seal, snake, giraffe, tiger, turtle, and zebra.

Spots, Stripes, and Solids. Talk about which animals have fur, feathers, hide, or scales. Have children sort animal pictures into categories according to designs covering their bodies: spots, stripes, and solids. Tell children that the animals' color and design help it to hide, keep safe, and find food.

Moving. Name all the animals with legs and those without. Count the number of legs. Talk about how each animal can move: fast or slow, swim, fly, slither, climb, run, hop, gallop, etc. Encourage children to move like the animals.

Size. Children can sort the wild animals by size: big and little, or large, medium, and small.

Zoo or Barn. Make a large cage with bars, and a barn out of kraft paper. Children name a variety of farm and zoo animal pictures. Tape them to the correct home.

Zoo Match-Up. Draw or cut out pictures of mother and baby zoo animals from magazines or old workbooks. Glue pictures on heavy paper and laminate. Children match the mother and baby animal cards.

Riddles. Give children a riddle about each zoo animal. They guess the animal after hearing as few clues as possible.

EXAMPLE:

> I am a zoo animal.
>
> I am big.
>
> I have long legs.
>
> I have a long neck.
>
> What am I?

Animal Escape. Play a memory game with children. Place three or four zoo animal pictures under an upside-down laundry basket. Remove one picture. Children name the animal that escaped.

Zookeeper. Help children understand the important jobs of zookeepers—feeding the animals, cleaning them and their cages or homes. Children might be interested to learn which animals eat meat, fruit, vegetables, hay, leaves, or grass, etc.

Make it Right. Make an incorrect statement about an animal. Children must correct it.

EXAMPLE:

> A lion has a trunk.
>
> A zebra has spots.
>
> An elephant roars.
>
> A monkey growls.

Animal Sounds. Talk about the sounds animals make. Which are loud, which are quiet? Have children practice familiar zoo animal sounds like roar, growl, and chatter.

2. MACHINES

What's a Machine?. Ask children to tell about jobs each family member has at home and how they do that job. Have children tell what "tool" family members use while they do the job. Ask if they know what a machine is. Acknowledge their answers and point out the attributes of a machine: It has different parts that move, it makes work easier, and it is not something alive.

From Box to Machine. Fill a large box with heavy books, toys, etc. Have children push the box to the classroom library or play area. Ask children if they can think of an easier way to get the heavy box from one place to another. Try out any ideas. Put the box on a large truck, scooter board, etc., and have children try moving the box again. Ask them what made it easier this time. This simple experience may help them understand that wheels are a kind of machine.

Is It a Machine?. Have a variety of familiar objects available, include a toy car, a plant, a balloon, a pencil sharpener, a wind-up toy, an apple, etc. Name each object; sort objects into machine/not machine categories by comparing each to the three attributes of a machine.

Brainstorming. Have children brainstorm a list of all the machines they can think of that have wheels.

Machines Around the House. Show children a variety of objects found in and around the house. Include pictures of a toaster, typewriter, mixer, dryer, vacuum cleaner, chair, plate, napkin, pillow, carrot, pet, etc. Children name each object and tell why each object is or is not a machine.

Quiet or Noisy. Have simple machines or pictures of machines available. Children can try using the machines or rely on past experiences and sort the quiet machines from the noisy machines.

Machine Riddle. Tell a riddle about a machine. Children name the machine.

EXAMPLE:

I am a machine with wheels.

You put things in me.

I have a handle you can pull.

What am I? (wagon)

If I Were a Machine. Have children dictate individual or class stories about their favorite machine, what they could do if they were a machine, etc.

3. POLICE OFFICER—SAFETY

Busy Police Officer. Have a police officer visit the classroom, or show a picture of a police officer. Encourage children to share any experiences they have had with police officers or tell anything they know about this community helper. Stress the jobs of an officer: make sure that rules are followed, direct traffic on busy street corners, help find Mom or Dad if you get lost, help people in trouble or who are hurt, and help keep our town safe to play outside.

About Our Friend. Through pictures, experiences, or storytelling, have children talk about and name the clothing an officer wears, the tools she/he uses, what she/he drives, and where she/he works. Vocabulary to include: uniform, badge, walkie talkie, gun, police car, motorcycle, siren, traffic light, stop sign, police station, park, neighborhood, highway, etc.

Role-Playing. Have children take turns dramatizing and role-playing the different jobs of the police officer. Other classmates pretend to be driving on a busy street, pretend to be lost, hurt, or in need of help. These experiences help children to understand that police officers are our friends and helpers.

I'm Lost. Have children share any experiences they have had getting lost at shopping malls, in stores, and other busy places. Elicit ideas from children about what to do. Encourage them to look for police officers, moms with children, or people who work at stores, when they are lost and need help. Help each child review and practice telling their name, address, parents' names, etc., to the best of their ability.

Stranger Danger. Through pictures and flannel board stories, present possible "what if" situations. Encourage children to begin talking about staying safe. Stress: Never take candy/toys from strangers, never go with a stranger, never play alone or wander away from parents or playmates.

Police Officer Sorting. Cut out pictures of objects, tools, uniforms, vehicles, etc., used by familiar community helpers. Mount on tagboard and laminate. Children name objects and sort those used by an officer.

Who Wears the Hat. Draw or cut out a picture of the hat worn by familiar community helpers. Name a job responsibility, tool, etc., used by a specific community helper, the children can take turns telling who wears the hat represented by that job, tool, etc.

4. SUMMER

Summer Walk. Take a walk outdoors to observe changes seen in nature and felt by people during the summer. Ask questions and expand children's knowledge. Ideas to develop: The weather feels very warm, the daylight hours are longer (children can play outside after dinner), trees, flowers, and gardens grow and may need to be watered, sand and sidewalks get hot from the sun, people go barefoot, get tanned skin from the sun, and try to stay cool in many ways.

Summer Vacation. Talk about what and why people wear different kinds of clothing in the summer. Have children share any family vacation experiences they have had. Children name and sort through pictures of clothing or articles of clothing in a laundry basket and place only the summer clothing in a suitcase as they pretend to pack for a summer vacation.

Summer Sorting. Cut pictures from magazines or old workbooks that show a wide range of seasonal activities. Mount pictures and laminate. Children tell what is happening in each picture and sort activities by season or into summer and not summer categories. Encourage children to tell why the activity can happen during the season.

Brainstorm. Children brainstorm a list of activities to do in summer. Write down their responses on a piece of typing paper, on which a simple sketch depicting summer has been drawn. Xerox the paper and have children color the picture Expand the activity by encouraging families to choose some activities to do as they plan for summer vacation.

Finish the Story. Tell the beginning of stories and have children finish them using their knowledge of summer. *Examples:* "It was so hot, we wanted to stay cool, so we . . ." (went swimming, ate a Popsicle™, put on a fan, etc.) "We went to the park and saw children . . ." (playing ball, sliding, riding skateboards, etc.) "I helped Mom in the garden, we . . ." (pulled weeds, watered, picked vegetables, etc.)

Summer Safety. Talk about the importance of staying safe while enjoying summer activities. Role-play situations that help children understand some simple safety rules: Sit, rather than stand on playground equipment and bikes, never walk or stand in front of swings or slides, play where a grown-up can see you, stay away from hot grills or campfires, etc.

5. COLOR–BLUE

Mystery Box. Introduce the color blue by naming blue objects and pictures found in the mystery box. Children answer "wh" (who, what, where, when, why) questions about each object named. Children can put the objects back into the box by answering riddles or using classification skills. *Example:* "I am blue. I keep the sun from shining in your eyes. What am I?" (Child puts sunglasses back in the box.) or "Put all the blue things used in the kitchen in the mystery box." (napkin, plate, dishcloth, etc.)

Memory Game. Place several blue objects on a tray and have children name each object. Cover the tray and chant, "Blue, blue, *child's name* remember a few." That child names the blue objects she/he remembers. The game continues as you add and change blue objects when other children take their turn.

Concentration. Cut picture pairs of blue objects from magazines and catalogs. Mount each on small pieces of tagboard and laminate. Arrange four to eight cards, blue-picture-side down, on the table. Children take turns picking up two cards at a time trying to name the objects and make a match. If a match is not made, the cards are put back down in the same place. If a child makes a match, she/he keeps the cards. Add cards as play continues and matches are made.

6. DIRECTIONAL AND POSITIONAL CONCEPTS—ABOVE AND BELOW

Follow Me Above and Below. Move your hands above and below various body parts. The children copy your movements and tell where their hands are, for example, "Above head, below knees."

Directional and Positional Cards. Mount three pictures of familiar objects vertically on tagboard cards. Prepare about twelve to sixteen cards using pictures cut from catalogs or old workbooks. The children take turns choosing a card, naming all the pictures, and answering questions, e.g., "Where is the hat?" and "Where is the sun?" Encourage the children to use the words *above* and *below*.

Traffic Light. Each child begins with four precut shapes: one black rectangle, one green, one red, and one yellow circle. Give directions that children follow to make a traffic light. "Place the yellow circle in the middle of the long rectangle. Place the red circle above the yellow circle. Place the green circle below the yellow circle." Children glue the lights on the traffic signal.

FINE MOTOR

1. MANIPULATION

Brown Bear. Provide children with an outline shape of a bear cut from heavy paper. Children spread glue on the picture or use a brush to paint on a glue-water mixture. They sprinkle on dried coffee grounds to get a three-dimensional, textured effect.

Elephant Ears. Children cut out a pair of big, floppy elephant ears from large brown paper bags. Staple them to a headband made from a strip of construction paper cut to fit around the child's head.

Paper Plate Lion. Children color a small paper plate brown. They cut long strips of brown paper to glue around the plate for a mane. Paper scraps can be glued on the paper plate to make a face. Add ears and whiskers.

Animal Spots. Provide children with the outline of zoo animals that have spots, e.g., giraffes, leopards, etc. Children make thumbprint spots or sponge paint spots on the animals.

Mural Art. Provide shades of blue, green, and yellow for the children to use in painting a tropical jungle on mural paper. Children could glue on any of the zoo animals they have created.

Make-Believe Machine. Supply children with construction paper circles of different sizes and colors, styrofoam meat trays, fabric and wallpaper scraps, and other collage materials. Children glue "wheels" and "gears" and other machine parts onto the construction paper to design their own machine. Have children dictate a story sentence about what the machine can do.

Class Robot. Provide children with boxes of various shapes and sizes, juice cans, buttons, yarn, fabric scraps, and pie plates. Supply glue and tempera paint. Children glue together their robot creation and paint.

Machines. Allow children practice in safely manipulating simple machines, e.g., old typewriter, adding machine, record player, stapler, egg beater, mixer, etc.

Wheel Collage. Children cut pictures of different kinds and sizes of wheels from magazines. Glue on paper to make a collage.

Animal Cages. Use a hole punch to punch holes evenly across the top and bottom of a foam meat tray. Prepare a tray for each child. Cut pictures of zoo animals from magazines for children to glue in their meat tray. Tape one end of long lengths of black yarn for children to use as they sew through the holes, going around the front and back to form the bars of a cage.

Zebra Stripes. Give each child a zebra shape cut from white construction paper Children draw stripes on the zebra using thick white crayons. Children paint over the entire picture using a black watercolor wash.

Summer Skies. Children tear free-form shapes from white construction paper and glue on light blue paper to make a summer sky.

Here We Go!. Children make a "good-bye banner" toward the end of the school year by taking turns walking across mural paper with painted feet. Pour paint in a 9- by 13-inch cake pan and have children step into the pan with both feet. Guide each child across the paper (it can be very slippery), leading them toward a bucket of warm, soapy water for clean-up. Do this activity outside on a warm day.

Outside Painting. Attach a large piece of paper to a wall or a fence using clothespins. Children make a mural in a variety of ways: Use brushes to paint or splatter on paint or use spray bottles filled with slightly thinned tempera paint.

Sidewalk Art. Children paint with water on sidewalks using a variety of brushes. Provide thick pieces of chalk for children to draw with on the sidewalk.

Dandelion Prints. Children practice pincer grip while picking dandelions, leaving a long stem on each. Dip the dandelion in paint and print on paper.

Summer Tree. Use sponges or cotton balls to paint lush green trees.

Picnic Collage. Children cut pictures of favorite foods they would like to eat on a picnic. Glue pictures on a large paper plate.

Pastel Bubbles. Mix liquid detergent, water, and food coloring in a small plastic margarine tub. Make at least three different colors. Children blow air out through a straw creating a mound of bubbles in the mixture. Gently place a piece of white paper over the popping bubbles. Continue until bubbles from all the colors have been printed onto the paper. (Make certain children know how to blow air out of the straw rather than suck in!)

Butterflies. Draw around the right and left foot of each child so that the big toes are touching. You or the children cut out the shape. Children decorate the butterfly with tissue paper.

Caterpillars. Cut an egg carton in half the long way. Children paint and decorate the caterpillar with buttons and pipecleaners.

Sand Pictures. Add food coloring to white school glue. Children brush or squeeze colored glue onto heavy paper. Sprinkle sand on the glued areas. Shake off excess.

Smelly Art. Add cinnamon, nutmeg, lemon extract, etc., to tempera paint. Mix well. Children will enjoy painting pictures that smell!

Daisy Plates. Children snip around the edge of a small paper plate, cut and glue a yellow circle for the center of the flower. Glue on a pipecleaner for a stem.

Signs. Get wooden paint stirs from a paint or hardware store. Staple on large road sign shapes cut from heavy tagboard. (*Example:* pentagon, octagon, rectangle, etc.) Provide paint, crayons, markers, and collage materials for children to decorate their signs. Children can dictate sentence stories that tell about their sign. You can write each child's story on the back of the sign.

Scribble Designs. Using a black crayon, make a scribble design on a white piece of construction paper. Color sections with different colors.

Rolling Colors. Place drops of several colors of tempera paint on a sheet of white paper. Place another paper on top of it. Roll the top of the second paper with a rolling pin or smooth jar. Lift and see the colors.

Torn Paper Flowers. Provide a variety of paper scraps including tissue, wrapping paper, construction, foils, etc. Children tear paper and glue to create summer flowers.

Button Necklaces. Twist the ends of two pipe cleaners together for each child. Children push the pipe cleaner through the holes on buttons to make a necklace.

Going on Vacation. Have children practice folding clothing, such as shirts and shorts that they might take on a vacation. Children can practice packing an old suitcase.

Record Player Art. Cut pieces of construction paper into circles the size of records. Poke a hole in the middle of the paper and fit it over the spindle of a record player. Turn the record player on while a child holds a colored marker on the paper. Circles will be formed while the record player goes around. Change markers to make different colored circles.

Take it Apart. Ask parents to send safe, but broken, machines to school (typewriters, telephones, etc.). Provide children with a variety of screwdrivers and other tools to use as they take the machines apart.

Fine Motor Center. Provide blue paper, pictures, string, and other blue items for children to use for making blue collages. Shape collages can be created by providing items which are rectangular or oval shaped. Provide oval- and rectangular-shaped paper for children to use as the base for their collages. Machine collages can be made. Provide items such as springs, small wheels, screws, nuts, and bolts. Have the children make blue play dough and provide cookie cutters shaped like zoo animals, machines, rectangles, ovals, etc. Have children trace and cut star shapes to use as police badges in creative play. Precut zoo animal shapes with holes punched around the edges can be used for lacing. Provide beads for stringing, and paper and scissors for cutting. Encourage the children to create paper machines by tracing, and cutting any combination of shapes and gluing them on paper to create their own machines.

2. PREWRITING

Tracing. Draw a picture of a house that includes many rectangular doors and windows. Xerox a copy for each child. Children trace on top of each rectangle.

Dot to Dot. Give each child a paper with several sets of four predrawn dots. Children connect the dots to form a rectangle.

Construction. Children use straws, Popsicle™ sticks, and toothpicks to manipulate and make different rectangles of many sizes.

Stencils. Children trace around prepared rectangular-shaped stencils and familiar objects (e.g., books, games, boxes, and playing cards, etc.).

Roads. Draw a large rectangular road on kraft/mural paper. Draw stop signs at three of the four corners and a green light at the fourth corner where children start. Children take turns driving small cars and trucks around the road, stopping to make sharp corners at the turns.

Prewriting Center. Provide blue pens, pencils, markers, chalk, and other writing materials. Stencils for May might include animal shapes, ovals, and rectangles. Provide summer items to trace around such as sand box shovels, rakes, and hoes. Zoo mazes can be drawn and Xeroxed for the children. Provide paper cut into cage shapes and have children draw vertical lines to create bars. Provide zebra and tiger shapes and have the children draw vertical lines on them to create stripes. Provide shapes and designs for children to copy either on paper or on chalkboards.

PERCEPTION

What's Missing?. Show pictures of various zoo animals. Cover one part on each animal. Children name the missing part. Include the elephant's trunk, the giraffe's neck, the lion's mane, the monkey's tail, the kangaroo's pouch, etc.

Zoo Puzzles. Mount pictures of zoo animals on tagboard. Laminate the pictures and cut into pieces. Children assemble the puzzles.

Zoo Silhouette. Draw or trace the outline of each zoo animal's body Children try to identify the animal.

Part-Whole. Draw or cut out pictures of zoo animals. Cut the pictures in half and laminate. Children practice matching halves to make a whole.

Noisy Machines. Make a tape of the noisy sounds made by familiar machines found in school, at home, and in the neighborhood. Children listen to the tape and name the machine. Have pictures of the machines heard on the tape available if visual cues are needed by the children.

Match-Up. Cut out pictures of machines from magazines or catalogs. Mount pictures on tagboard. Cut them in half and laminate the pieces. Children find the two pieces that make a whole machine.

Peek-a-Boo Pictures. Laminate a half sheet of construction paper. Use a razor blade to cut several lines across the paper so that flaps are made, or cut three or four half circles in the paper so that flaps are made. Place a picture of a zoo animal or machine under the construction paper cover and turn open flaps until the children can name the animal or machine.

Feely Bag. Place some small machines in a feely bag or box. Children reach inside, feel the object, and name the machine. Include toy cars and trucks with wheels, an egg beater, or a pencil sharpener, a stapler, wind-up toy, etc.

What Fits Inside?. Provide a variety of different sized boxes, some large, some small, some square or rectangular shaped. Have an equal number of familiar objects available that fit inside the boxes. Children guess what object fits best in each box. Children can assess the correctness of their guesses by making sure every object fits in a box.

Feel the Shape. Put circle and oval plastic attribute blocks or teacher-prepared shapes in the mystery box. Children can feel the shapes, search for only the circles, only the ovals, find two that are the same, two that are different, etc.

Cracked Eggs. Cut twelve to fourteen oval robins' eggs from light blue construction paper. Cut each egg apart in two pieces, varying the location and formation of the crack. Laminate pieces. Children match the two halves that form the robin's egg.

Animal Match. Cut out twelve to fourteen pairs of one or two kinds of zoo animals (e.g., six pairs of leopards, six pairs of zebras, etc.). Use markers to add stripes, spots, and designs on the animal pairs. Children match the two animals that are exactly the same.

Seashell Sorting. Place a variety of seashells on the floor or table. Children sort the shells into categories rough, smooth, bumpy, etc.

Underwater Search. Put one seashell in the water-filled sensory table or in a small tub of water. Place a wide assortment of seashells on the table. Children take turns finding a shell on the table that feels the same as the one felt underwater. Encourage the child to tell what the shells feel like. Other children should be given the opportunity to feel the shells and agree or disagree on what they feel like. Lead children to understand that two shells that look the same may not feel the same, and vice versa.

Summer Sounds. Make a tape of sounds typical of the summer season (water splashing, balls bouncing, carnival music, etc.). Children try to identify the sound and tell where it could be heard.

What's Inside, Heavy or Light?. Place an object inside a box and close the lid. Children try to identify the object by its weight and through your clues. Children should be encouraged to rule out objects because they would be too light or too heavy.

Feet Feelings. On a warm day, provide opportunities for children to remove shoes and socks and walk on the warm sidewalk, in the grass, in sand, in mud, and finally in warm water. Help them describe how it felt.

Fishing. Using laminated fish prepared for all the colors and shapes, children can fish for and catch only blue fish or fish with the oval shape using the pole and magnet bait.

Vacation Smells. Collect the small-sized soaps from motels. Unwrap the soap. Children compare the soap smells, finding two that are the same and one that smells different.

Perception Center. At the perception center, alternate design-copying activities using blocks, pegs, and beads. Children can create patterns by manipulating various shaped and colored blocks. Patterns can be created using beads and pegs. Provide teacher-made and commercial puzzles which depict the zoo, police officer, machine, and summer themes. Have the children create their own puzzles by cutting apart pictures and reassembling them. Children can sort animal pictures, separating zoo from farm animals. Provide cards or attribute blocks for sorting by shape and color. Zoo lotto games can be used as an independent center activity by having the children find and match the animal pictures that are the same.

GROSS MOTOR

Shape Moves. Draw large shapes in a spacious playground area, using chalk. Include circle, square, rectangle, triangle, oval, heart. Children follow individual directions from you, or the group follows the same direction.

EXAMPLE:
"Walk around the rectangle."

"Skip around the oval."

"Hop inside the heart."

Body Shapes. Show and name a shape cut from construction paper. Children form groups and make the shape by standing and joining hands or stretching out on a grassy outdoor area. Talk about how many children are needed to make the shape, could they do it another way, could they use more or less children, etc.

Animal Moves. Children move like zoo animals, jump like kangaroos, leap like leopards, sway like lumbering elephants, etc.

Machines. Name a machine and talk about how its parts move. Children try to imitate the movements of simple machines, e.g., wind-up toys, pencil sharpener, dump truck, mixer, typewriter, etc. Change the "machine" speeds from fast to slow.

Foot Fun. Children pretend to be barefoot and walk through the sand, walk across pebbles, walk on a hot sidewalk, jump through puddles, walk through mud, walk across slippery grass, etc.

Monkey Climb. Visit a park or well-equipped playground. Encourage children to climb ladders, climb across horizontal ropes and other equipment. Be sure children are aware of safety rules.

Above and Below. Draw a chalk line or place a line of masking tape on an outside school wall or fence. Each child has a ball and stands facing the wall/fence. Give the children directions to follow, e.g., "Throw the ball above the line, throw the ball below the line."

Partners. Set up a net outside or in the gym. Divide the class in half, some children on each side of the net. Assign each child a partner on the opposite side. Give directions for children to follow such as roll or throw the ball above or below the net to their partner.

Tug-O-War. Play a tug-o-war game outside on a grassy area. Children are divided into two groups facing each other. Provide a smooth plastic rope for teams to use while trying to pull the other side.

Read the Light. Select half the children to be traffic police while the other half are the drivers. Traffic police hold up red, green, or yellow teacher-prepared signs on the playground or sidewalks around school. Drivers on bikes and other riding toys must follow the stop, go, and slow rules.

Obstacle Course. Set up an obstacle course on the playground. Children on riding toys, pulling wagons, or on scooter boards maneuver through the course.

Stop, Go, or Slow. Children must read the sign and listen to you to play this game. Children stand in a long row, facing you, standing 6 to 10 feet away. Hold up a sign (red, green, or yellow) and tell children how to move (walk, run, skip, gallop, jump, hop, etc.). Children follow the visual clue and move according to the verbal clue. Remind children not to move any way when you hold up the red sign.

Animal Tunnel. Use a commercial plastic tunnel or cut openings at both ends of a large appliance box for children to crawl through. Children pretend to crawl like snakes, bears, or other zoo animals. If two tunnels are available, teams of "zoo animals" can repeat the activity as an animal relay race.

Organized Games. Teach children familiar organized games like "London Bridge," "Bluebird, Bluebird Go through the Window," and "Ring around the Rosie." Play versions of "Duck, Duck, Goose" including "Stop-Sign, Stop-Sign, Go" or "Lion, Lion, Roar," etc.

Skipping. Demonstrate how to skip, saying "step-hop, step-hop" as you skip. Have children practice skipping slowly with long steps and short steps.

SENSORY EXPERIENCES

Outside Smells. Provide experiences outside for children to become aware of different smells:

> Walk outside during or after a rain,
> Smell freshly cut grass,
> Smell different flowers,
> Dig in and smell freshly turned-over dirt.

Water Play. Put several drops of cooking extract in the water in which the children play. Include peppermint, lemon, orange, etc. Invite children to think of words to describe the smell.

Bring in Summer. Put freshly cut grass, flower petals, and dandelions in the exploration table.

At the Beach. Provide seashells, sand, and sand toys in the exploration table.

Make Mud. Let children make mud in large tubs, using sterilized potting soil and water. Provide baking toys, spoons, etc., so children can make pies and cakes. Do this activity outside and provide lots of soapy water for clean-up.

PREMATH

Bear Caves. Cut the tops off of eleven half-pint milk cartons. Cover the cartons with brown construction or self-stick vinyl. Number the bear caves zero to ten with a black marker. Cut out fifty-five small bear shapes from construction paper. Use fifty-five candy gum bears or commercial plastic bears. Children take turns selecting a cave, reading the numeral, and placing the correct number of bears in the cave. Children may order the caves from zero to ten.

Balancing Balls. Cut eleven large black seals from construction paper and number from zero to ten with a white crayon and laminate. Cut out fifty-five multicolored circles and laminate. Children take turns choosing a seal, reading the numeral, and stacking the correct number of multicolored balls on the seals nose. Children may order the seals from zero to ten.

Feed the Monkeys. Cut eleven monkeys from brown construction paper, number them from zero to ten, and laminate. Cut out fifty-five yellow bananas and laminate. Children take turns choosing a monkey, reading the numeral, and feeding the correct number of bananas to the monkey. Children may order the monkeys from zero to ten.

Spots and Stripes. Children touch and count the spots or stripes on pictures of zoo animals cut from magazines or prepared by you. Include turtles, leopards, tigers, giraffes, zebras, etc.

Wheelin' Machines. Children collect all the machines in the play area that have wheels. They sort cars from trucks, jeeps, motorcycles, etc. Children touch and count all the wheels on each set of machines.

Summer Sets. Children touch and count seashells, flowers, balloons, etc., and group into sets of ten.

Flying High. Give each child a small handful of balloons and lengths of string or yarn. Children practice one-to-one correspondence by matching a string to each balloon.

Number March. Spread numeral/dot cards zero to ten in a large circle formation on the floor. Children march around the numbers while lively music is playing. When the music stops, children stop on the numeral they are on and name it. If children have difficulty naming the numeral, they can touch and count the number of dots on the laminated cards.

Number Path. Place large numeral cards zero to ten in different areas around the room. Leave a different supply of objects, enough for each child to take one at every location (balloons, cotton balls, paper clips, etc.). Each child receives a small brown paper bag at the number one starting area. Children take turns following the number path in order. Children pick up one object at each location and place it in their bag. When children finish, they can dump out the contents of the bag checking to make sure that they have ten different objects.

Shape Patterns. Give each child twelve precut pieces of two different shapes (twelve circles and twelve ovals or twelve ovals and twelve squares, etc.). Children make a pattern using the two different shapes. They glue the shape pattern on construction paper.

Shape Riddles. Give clues about shapes. Children listen and name the shape, e.g., "I'm thinking of the shape of an egg. It has no corners or sides. What shape is it?"

Think Shapes. Divide a large piece of paper into sections, drawing a shape at the top of each section. The children brainstorm the names of objects in their environment that are that shape. Write down or sketch children's responses. This experience fosters creative thinking, perception, and language.

Eggs in a Nest. Cut the tops off of eleven half-pint milk cartons. Cover the cartons with brown construction or self-stick vinyl. Number the bird nests zero to ten with a black marker. Put some grass, twigs, thread, etc., in the bottom of each nest. Children take turns selecting a nest, reading the numeral, and placing the correct number of small oval plastic eggs or teacher-prepared cut paper oval eggs in the nest. Children may order the nests from zero to ten.

Crack the Egg. Save the blue plastic eggs pantyhose come in. Fill ten to twelve eggs with small objects ranging from zero to ten. Place the eggs in a large basket. Children take turns selecting an egg, shaking it, guessing what and how many objects are inside, then finally cracking open their oval egg to touch and count what's inside. This activity keeps all students interested.

What Doesn't Belong?. Place various shaped objects or pictures of various shaped objects on a table, e.g., a gameboard, a book, a box, and a record. Children name the objects, tell what doesn't belong, and why.

Picnic Plates. Cut out ten pictures of hamburgers from magazines or grocery ads and glue each one on a large paper plate. Write a number from one to ten on each plate. Cut out fifty-five green pickle shapes, laminate them, and puts them in an empty jar. Place the plates and pickle jar in a picnic basket. Children take turns choosing a hamburger plate, reading the numeral, and taking the correct number of pickles from the jar to put on the plate.

Caterpillar Crawl. Give each child eleven multicolored oval shapes cut from construction paper. Leave one oval empty and write each number from one to ten on the other shapes. Tell children to make a caterpillar by ordering and gluing the ovals together from one to ten. They can draw a face on the empty oval and add legs.

Shape Rummy. Cut thirty-five 4- by 6-inch cards from tagboard or construction paper. Draw or glue a shape on each card (circle, square, triangle, rectangle diamond, oval, heart). Make five cards for each shape and laminate. Shuffle the cards. Two, three, or four children may play. Deal five or six cards to each child Spread the rest of the cards, shape-side down, on the table. Before the game begins, each player puts down all the shape pairs she/he has (two circles, two ovals, etc.). Children take turns asking others for a card to make a pair, "Jose, do you have a square?" If Jose has a square, he gives it and that person puts down this pair. When a player doesn't have the shape asked for, she/he chooses one card from the table. If she/he can make a pair, she/he does so, if not, the card is his/hers. The play then continues on to the next person. The game ends when a child runs out of cards. The winner is the child with the most pairs.

Dandelion Math. Two children work together cooperatively to practice one-to-one correspondence. Each pair of children receives an egg carton. They pick dandelions in the school yard and put one dandelion in each section.

Petal Power. Cut ten circle shapes from construction paper. Put a number one to ten in the center of each circle. This forms the center of a flower. Cut fifty-five multicolored shapes to be used as petals. Laminate all the pieces. Children take turns picking a circle center, reading the numeral, and arranging the correct number of petals around.

Calendar. Select two May theme objects (flowers, machines, stop signs, sun, etc.) to be patterned on the calendar. Children should continue to practice anticipating what object or symbol comes next for tomorrow. Challenge them to think about what will go on the calendar in two or three days, etc. Touch and count the days forwards and backwards, developing a rhythm with clapping, tapping, snapping, etc. Chant the names of the days of the week. Talk about the name of yesterday's day, tomorrow's day, etc.

SONGS AND FINGERPLAYS

Five Little Monkeys (children pantomine motions).

Five little monkeys jumping on the bed.
One fell off and bumped his head.
Called for the doctor and the doctor said,
"No more monkeys jumping on the bed."

(Continue with four little monkeys, etc.)

Lion's Cage (tune: "Did You Ever See a Lassie?").

Did you ever see a lion's cage, a lion's cage, a lion's cage?
Did you ever see a lion's cage, where some lions live?
Watch me draw a lion's cage, a lion's cage, a lion's cage.
Watch me draw a lion's cage. Then you have a turn.

(Draw the lion's cage on a small chalkboard, then children take turns.)

A Trip to the Zoo (tune: "Frère Jacques").

See the lion, see the lion.
In his cage, in his cage.
Listen to loud roaring, listen to loud roaring.
I can roar, too. I can roar, too. (Roar!)

See the Kangaroo, see the kangaroo.
In his cage, in his cage.
Watch him as he jumps, watch him as he jumps.
I can jump, too. I can jump, too. (Jump!)

See the polar bear, see the polar bear.
In the water, in the water.
He can swim in water, watch him as he splashes.
I can swim, too. I can splash, too. (Swim and splash!)

See the striped snake, see the striped snake.
Curled up small. Curled up small.
He can crawl so quickly, he can crawl so quickly.
I can crawl, too. I can crawl, too! (Crawl!)

The Policeman (tune: "Mary Had a Little Lamb").

The policeman is our friend, is our friend, is our friend,
The policeman is our friend, he helps us many ways.
The policeman helps us if we're lost, if we're lost, if we're lost.
The policeman helps us if we're lost, to find our way back home.
The policeman stops the busy traffic, busy traffic, busy traffic.
The policeman stops the busy traffic and then tells it when to go.

Weather Song (tune: "Farmer in the Dell").

The sun shines bright,
The sun shines bright,
Way up high in the summer sky,
The sun shines bright.

Verses:

The moon shines at night.
The stars twinkle light.
The clouds float by.
The raindrops fall.

Summer Vacation (tune: "She'll Be Coming Round the Mountain").

We're going on vacation in the summer.
We're going on vacation in the summer.
We'll be packing all our clothes, we'll be packing all our clothes,
We'll be packing all our clothes for vacation.

We'll be driving to the beach in the summer.
We'll be driving to the beach in the summer.
We'll be putting on our suits, we'll be putting on our suits,
We'll be putting on our suits in the summer.

We'll build castles in the sand at the beach.
We'll build castles in the sand at the beach.
We'll be swimming, we'll be splashing, we'll be swimming, we'll be splashing.
We'll be having summer fun at the beach.

Summer Fun (tune: "You Are My Sunshine").

It is the summer,
It is the summer.
We'll take vacations
When skies are blue.
We'll go camping, swimming, and fishing.
In the summer,
When skies are blue.

RECIPES

Caramel Fruit Dip.

> 1/4 cup granulated sugar
> 3/4 cup packed light brown sugar
> 1 teaspoon vanilla
> 1 8-oz. package softened cream cheese
> Fresh fruit for dipping, such as apple slices, strawberries, nectarine slices, and bananas.

Put sugars, vanilla, and cream cheese in a blender or mixer and blend or mix until smooth. Serve with seasonal fruit. Have children help wash and cut.

Berry-Yogurt Sauce.

> 1 package (10 oz.) frozen strawberries or raspberries, thawed
> 2 cups plain yogurt
> 1/2 teaspoon almond extract

Blend berries in a blender until smooth. Combine with yogurt, add extract. Chill. Serve with seasonal fruit.

Strawberry Blueberry Delight.

> 1 6-oz. strawberry Jello™   2 cups sour cream
> 2 cups hot water   1 can blueberry pie filling

Dissolve Jello™ in the hot water. Add sour cream and pie filling. Stir well. Refrigerate until firm.

Blueberry Muffins.

> 1 3/4 cups of flour   1 egg beaten
> 1/4 cup sugar   3/4 cup milk
> 3 teaspoons baking powder   1/2 cup fresh blueberries
> 1/2 teaspoon salt   1/3 cup sugar
> 1/2 cup margarine   1 teaspoon cinnamon

Combine flour, 1/4 cup sugar, baking powder, and salt in a mixing bowl. Cut in margarine until mixture resembles cornmeal. Combine egg and milk; mix well. Add to flour mixture, stirring just enough to moisten. Gently stir in blueberries. Spoon batter into twelve paper-lined muffin cups, filling two-thirds full. Combine 1/3 cup sugar and cinnamon. Sprinkle mixture over each muffin. Bake at 400 degrees for 20 minutes, or until a wooden pick inserted into muffin comes out clean.

Blueberry Turnovers.

1 8-oz. can of refrigerated crescent rolls
Filling:

1/2 cup of honey	1 tablespoon raisins
1 tablespoon chopped nuts	1/4 cup fresh blueberries

Combine all ingredients listed for the filling. Unroll the crescent rolls and put a spoonful of filling mixture in the middle of each triangle of dough. Moisten the edges of dough, fold over, and press edges together, sealing firmly. Bake on a greased cookie sheet at 375 degrees for 10–12 minutes.

MAY SNACKS

Monkey Shakes. Blend bananas and milk. Sprinkle with chopped nuts.

Frozen Bananas. Cut bananas in half, spread with peanut butter, roll in graham cracker crumbs or cereal. Wrap and freeze.

Pudding Cones. Prepare pudding according to package directions. Spoon into flat-bottomed ice cream cones.

Cool Sandwiches. Spread cream cheese on wheat bread, top with sliced cucumbers.

Cheese Rolls. Roll baloney, ham, or turkey with cottage cheese or cream cheese.

Freezies. Freeze juice in ice cube trays or paper cups.

Fruit Mix. Combine drained fruit cocktail, miniature marshmallows, and yogurt.

Banana Dips. Cut bananas into small pieces, put toothpicks through fruit, dip in melted chocolate chips. Dip in chopped peanuts.

Blueberry Yogurt.

Camp Mix. Combine and mix equal parts of raisins, nuts, coconut, tiny crackers, pretzels, and unsweetened cereal.

Egg-citing Ovals.

Peel and eat hard-boiled eggs.

Slice hard-boiled eggs in slicer and serve on crackers.

Deviled eggs—add raisins to make a face.

Eat egg salad on oval crackers or bread.

Cream Pops. Mix 1 cup of fruit juice (grape, orange, apricot, etc.), 2 cartons of plain yogurt, and 1/2 teaspoon vanilla until well blended. Pour into ice cube trays or paper cups.

Animal Crackers.

Zoo Animals. Cut wheat bread with zoo animal-shaped cookie cutters. Add spreads.

CREATIVE DRAMATICS

The Little Red Hen. Read the story *The Little Red Hen* to the children. You may exaggerate the conversation of the red hen and her friends so the voices of the characters are different and more easily remembered. Ask children to retell the story in their own language. With the younger children, you could narrate the story and have children pantomine the roles of the animals. When the children become more familiar with the story and its repetitive lines, they should choose their roles for story dramatization. More than one child may want to be the red hen, the dog, the cat, etc. This allows children to help one another and encourages greater participation. Allow children to suggest simple props that can be used to help tell the story. Leave the story and props on a table where children will want to look at the story and act it out on their own.

Police Station. Set up a police station in the dramatic play center. Walls can be built out of blocks. Provide police uniforms (blue shirts), badges which can be made by tracing stars at the fine motor center, hats, flashlights, small notebooks for writing tickets, traffic signs, police cars made out of blocks, a telephone, key rings, and any other additional materials the children can think of. Many children will be interested in police guns. Use the opportunity to talk about how police officers only use guns on rare and extreme occasions and only for self-defense. If the children want to carry guns, they can cut gun shapes out of cardboard. Holsters can be made by stapling two rectangular-shaped pieces of paper together. Remind the "police officers" to keep the guns in the holsters. Children might also be interested in creating a jail. Blocks or large sheets of paper with bars cut out can be used. Interest in the police station can be fostered by reading books about police officers and by visiting a real police station.

CHILDREN'S LITERATURE

Adams, Pam. *If I Weren't Me . . . Who Would I Be?*
Bahr, Robert. *Blizzard at the Zoo*
Barner, Bob. *Mr. Elephant's Park*
Berenstain, Janice and Stan. *The Berenstain Bears Learn about Strangers*
Berry, Joy. *Teach Me about Danger*
Booth, Eugene. *At the Zoo*
Bruna, Dick. *Miffy at the Playground*
_____ . *Miffy at the Seaside*
_____ . *Miffy at the Zoo*

Calmenson, Stephanie. *Where Will the Animals Stay?*
Chlad, Dorothy. *When I Ride in a Car*
Crary, Elizabeth. *I'm Lost*
Downs, Kathy. *My ABC Zoo Book*
Ets, M. *Elephant in a Well*
Eugenie. *Jenny's Surprise Summer*
Fisher, A. *Once We Went on a Picnic*
Hale, Irina. *Brown Bear in a Brown Chair*
Hoban, Tana. *A Children's Zoo*

_____ . *Dig, Drill, Dump, Fill*
Kent, Jack. *The Biggest Shadow in the Zoo*
Krementz, Jill. *Zachary Goes to the Zoo*
Kunhardt, Edith. *Summer Vacation*
Lewellen, John. *The True Book of Toys at Work*
Label, Arnold. *Zoo for Mister Muster*
McClaskey, Robert. *Blueberries for Sal*
McNaughton. *At the Park*
Momcure, Jane B. *What Do the Animals Do in the Zoo?*
Osborne, Judy. *My Teacher Said Good-bye Today*
Palmer, Jan. *Who Lives in the Zoo?*
Pine, Tillie S. *Simple Machines and How We Use Them*

Ray, Deborah. *Sunday Morning We Went to the Zoo*
Relf, Patricia. *Follow the Zookeeper*
Rice, Eve. *New Blue Shoes*
Rockwell, Anne. *At the Playground*
_____ . *Machines*
Schaub, Peter. *Colors*
Schumacher, Clair. *King of the Zoo*
Taylor, M. *Henry Explores the Jungle*
Thaler, Mike. *The Rainbow*
Tison, Annette, and Talus, Taylor *Adventures of Three Colors*
Udry, Janice. *A Tree Is Nice*
Webb, Joan. *Play It Safe: A Book about Safety All Year Round*
Zolotow, Charlotte. *A Tiger Named Thomas*

Year-End Evaluation

As the end of the school year approaches, you must be prepared to consolidate information and observations for each child. IEP objectives must be reviewed and year-end progress recorded. The checklists found in the Appendix will be helpful in determining exactly where each child is functioning in the developmental scheme. The anecdotal records that were kept on each child will also be a useful tool when recording each child's progress. When reviewing checklists and anecdotal records, look for patterns of learning style:

Does the child perform better on auditory, visual, or tactile activities?

Does the child need to be involved motorically?

Where has the most/least growth occurred?

What areas are consistently strong/weak?

If students will be continuing in the early childhood special education program, projected goals may need to be written for the following year.

CONCEPTS FOR MAY (parent copy)

LANGUAGE AND VOCABULARY

Zoo—animals and their characteristics, zookeeper's jobs
Machines—how they make jobs easier, naming, describing
Police officer—jobs and staying safe
Summer—weather and nature's changes, clothing, activities, and vocabulary
Cooking Experiences
Color—blue
Directional and Positional Concepts—above and below

FINE MOTOR

Lacing, painting, coloring, gluing, play dough manipulation, cutting, block tower building, bead stringing, path tracing, design copying (rectangle)

PERCEPTION

Same and different, draw a person, puzzles, copying block, peg and bead designs, patterning, sorting

GROSS MOTOR

Organized games, movement activities, skipping, outside riding/pulling activities

PREMATH

One-to-one correspondence, calendar activities, sorting, number and numeral 10, ordering numbers, oval shape

CREATIVE DRAMATICS

SENSORY EXPERIENCES

MAY
Parent-child activities

SUN	MON	TUE	WED	THU	FRI	SAT
PRACTICE BALL HANDLING SKILLS: ROLL, THROW, BOUNCE, CATCH, AND DROP-CATCH.	FIND BLUE OBJECTS IN A MAGAZINE. CUT AND GLUE ON PAPER TO MAKE A COLLAGE.	PROBE TO FIND OUT WHAT YOUR CHILD KNOWS ABOUT A POLICE OFFICER.	TALK ABOUT STRANGER DANGER WITH YOUR CHILD.	PRACTICE FULL NAME, ADDRESS, AND PHONE NUMBER WITH YOUR CHILD.	CONSIDER VISITING A POLICE STATION AND HAVE YOUR CHILD FINGERPRINTED.	TAKE A WALK. COUNT EVERYTHING . . . STOP SIGNS, HOUSES, CARS, BIRDS, ETC.
FOLD NAPKINS INTO RECTANGLES, SQUARES, AND TRIANGLES.	COUNT ALL YOUR TOYS THAT HAVE WHEELS.	FIND AND TALK ABOUT MACHINES FOUND IN THE KITCHEN THAT MOVE.	PLAY WITH YOUR RIDING TOYS, BIKE, WAGON, ETC.	LISTEN TO SOUNDS MACHINES MAKE INSIDE.	FIND AND TALK ABOUT MACHINES FOUND IN THE GARAGE/BASEMENT.	FIND SOMETHING BLUE IN EVERY ROOM OF THE HOUSE.
LISTEN TO SOUNDS MACHINES MAKE OUTSIDE.	PLAY "WAR" WITH A DECK OF CARDS.	PRACTICE MAY SONGS AND FINGERPLAYS.	MAKE A CIRCLE, TRIANGLE, SQUARE, AND RECTANGLE. COLOR SHAPES AND CUT THEM OUT.	SMELL DIFFERENT KINDS OF FLOWERS IN THE YARD OR PARK.	HELP WASH THE CAR.	HELP MAKE BREAKFAST. CRACK OVAL EGGS.
GO TO THE LIBRARY. SELECT SOME STORIES ABOUT WILD ANIMALS.	LOOK AT A CATALOG. FIND AND NAME THE SUMMER CLOTHES . . . SANDLES, SHORTS, SWIMSUITS, ETC.	MAKE THE SOUNDS OF ZOO ANIMALS—MONKEY, LION, ETC.	GO OUTSIDE. PICK 10 DANDELIONS, THEN PUT THEM IN A VASE.	MOVE LIKE SOME ZOO ANIMALS—SNAKE, ELEPHANT, ETC.	EAT LUNCH OUTSIDE. COUNT THE ANTS.	PLAY IN THE PARK. CLIMB, SWING, AND SLIDE.
MAKE POPSICLES: 2 CUPS HOT WATER, 2 CUPS LEMONADE, 1 PKG. STRAWBERRY JELLO—FREEZE.	MEMORIAL DAY. HAVE A PICNIC!	TALK ABOUT WHAT THE FAMILY DID YESTERDAY.				

SUMMER

READING

Activities for Summer

Summer provides the opportunity for less structured time and with it many opportunities for less structured learning experiences. Children learn while playing alone, while interacting with other children and with adults. They learn when being read to, while watching television, while riding in the car, when going on walks, or taking trips to the grocery store. Children learn from the moment they awaken until they go to sleep at night. This learning can be enhanced and enriched, however, by providing opportunities for thinking and talking about what they see, smell, hear, taste, and touch.

In this chapter, ideas for summer activities for parent and child are presented. In addition, it can be stressed to parents that virtually anything done with their children can be a learning experience. When children are included in daily routine activities, concepts will be reinforced and skills strengthened. Imagination and creativity can be encouraged and fostered by talking, questioning, and pretending with children. The ideas for summer activities presented in this chapter were included because they take little extra time, money, or materials, just some thought when planning the summer day.

The information in this chapter can be reproduced and shared with parents. The activities will give children the opportunity for learning and growing while enjoying a carefree summer with their parents.

Summer Activities for Families

TAKE FIELD TRIPS

Places Near Your Home:

Parks, playgrounds, and sandbox areas
Pools, lakes, beaches
Walks to stores to let your child help purchase small items
Sound and color walks
   Listening for various sounds for identification and awareness
   Color walks—e.g., red walks, find all red things possible
   Identifying simple objects
Picnics, forest preserves, nature centers
Visits to the fire station, police station, post office, hospital

High-interest Learning Places:

Zoos
Farms and pet shops
Museums

Sports and Transportation Activities:

Swimming
Miniature golf
Bowling
Boating (row, canoe, speed, or paddle)
Fishing
Pony rides
Baseball games
Train rides
Bus rides
Boat trips
Airport
Skyscrapers

Miscellaneous Activities:

Visits to restaurants
Shopping centers
Toy stores
Community free concerts

Children's theater productions

Movies

Circus

Parades

County fairs

Local carnivals

DEVELOP READINESS SKILLS

Take your child/children to the library often.

Set aside time each day for reading to your children.

Have children tell back familiar stories.

Have children act out or pantomime familiar stories.

Discuss the day's events with your child at bedtime.

Watch TV with your child and talk about the show.

Ask children to "draw pictures" to tell about stories and experiences.

Cook with your child.

Record summer fun with photographs, children's drawings and sentence stories, tape and video recordings, etc.

Subscribe to children's magazines or newspapers.

Encourage children's collections, e.g., shells, rocks, postage stamps, etc.

Encourage children to begin "reading": people's faces, road signs, advertisements, logos, etc.

Talk, talk, talk with your child!

HELP YOUR CHILD FEEL GOOD ABOUT HIMSELF/HERSELF

Give your child opportunities to make decisions and choices (choose a family trip, choose an outfit to wear).

Allow children to solve problems and try to work problems out themselves Don't be too quick to jump in and resolve conflicts.

Allow children to make mistakes when attempting and learning new tasks Provide encouragement for good effort.

Teach children rules and limits. Let them be aware of consequences of behavior by consistent follow-through.

Listen to your child and give focused attention.

PLAN, SHOP, AND COOK TOGETHER

Children are fascinated with what goes on in the kitchen. It takes much more effort to keep children out of the kitchen sometimes than it does to include them Try inviting them into the kitchen, where they can enjoy the company of parents doing "adult" activities. Children will also learn many social skills that go with food: manners, conversation, setting the table, sharing, etc. Because a certain amount of mess goes along with the cooking-learning process, schedule cooking with children when the kitchen needs to be cleaned anyway. You'll have a clean kitchen, a yummy treat, and a very happy child when you're all done!

Bubble Pie.

1 package 3-oz. lemon Jello™	1 cup sugar
1 1/2 cups hot water	Juice and rind from 1 lemon

Mix the ingredients together, let set to congeal. Whip 1 can of Milnut™ and combine with the jello mixture. Pour into a graham cracker shell. Sprinkle graham cracker crumbs on top. Refrigerate pie.

Hot Dog Surprise.

Hot dogs
Pickles
Cheddar cheese

Children chop hot dogs and pickles into small pieces. Grate cheese and add to hot dog and pickle mixture. Add enough Miracle Whip™ salad dressing to moisten ingredients. Spread on lightly toasted English muffin halves. Bake at 350 degrees until cheese begins to melt and brown.

Dad's Day Coffee Ring.

1 package Pillsbury™ biscuits
3 tablespoons melted margarine
1/3 cup cinnamon sugar (mix white sugar with 1 teaspoon cinnamon)

Melt margarine in a small saucepan. Put sugar in a small bowl. Separate biscuits, dip into melted margarine and then into cinnamon sugar, coating both sides. Arrange in a ring mold with biscuits slightly overlapping. Bake about 10 minutes in a 375-degree preheated oven. Invert on plate and serve warm.

Hamburger By-the-Yard.

2 lb. ground beef	2 teaspoons salt
1/2 cup chopped onion	1/4 teaspoon pepper
1 can (12 oz.) corn, drained	1 long loaf of French bread
2 eggs, slightly beaten	8–12 slices of American cheese
2 tablespoons prepared mustard	

Mix hamburger, onions, corn, eggs, and seasonings in a bowl. Split French bread in half crosswise, then in half lengthwise. Mound beef mixture on bread and arrange in a shallow baking pan. Bake at 350 degrees for about 40 minutes or until heated through and browned. Top with cheese slices in a zig-zag pattern. Bake 5 minutes more. Cut and serve.

Fourth of July Cake.

1 can cherry pie filling	1/4 cup fresh blueberries
1 package Jiffy™ yellow cake mix	Cool Whip™
1 stick of melted margarine	

Put pie filling in a greased 8″ or 9″ pan. Sprinkle cake mix on top. Drizzle margarine on mixture. Bake 45 minutes in a 350-degree oven. Top with Cool Whip and fresh blueberries.

Strawberry-Banana Shake.

2 cups fresh strawberries	1 small ripe banana, sliced (1/2 cup)
2 cups nonfat buttermilk	3 tablespoons honey

Wash and cap strawberries, drain well. Place a single layer of strawberries in a shallow pan; freeze. Combine remaining ingredients in a blender. Process until smooth. Slowly add frozen strawberries, process until smooth.

Orange-Pineapple Drink.

1 (8 oz.) carton pineapple lowfat yogurt
1/2 cup unsweetened orange juice, chilled
Ice cubes

Combine yogurt and orange juice in a blender, process until smooth. Slowly add enough ice cubes to bring mixture to the 2-cup line. Process until smooth.

REINFORCE CONCEPTS TAUGHT DURING THE SCHOOL YEAR

June Parent-Child Activities
July Parent-Child Activities
August Parent-Child Activities

SUN	MON	TUE	WED	THU	FRI	SAT
THINK OF A NEW WAY TO PLAY WITH AN OLD TOY.	LOOK IN A MIRROR. NAME AND MOVE 10 DIFFERENT BODY PARTS.	PLAY A RUNNING GAME. MOVE NEAR AND FAR.	FOLD THE BREAKFAST NAPKINS INTO TRIANGLES.	FINGER PAINT WITH PUDDING! YUM!	CATCH FIREFLIES. COUNT THEM.	LEARN A FINGERPLAY. PRACTICE SOME FAMILIAR SONGS.
HELP SORT THE LAUNDRY. PICK OUT EVERYTHING THAT IS BLUE.	VISIT THE LIBRARY. SELECT SOME BOOKS AND RECORDS.	GO FOR A RIDE. USE THE WORDS STOP AND GO AND FAST AND SLOW.	MAKE THE SOUNDS OF PETS, ZOO, AND FARM ANIMALS.	MAKE A KITE BY CUTTING OUT A DIAMOND SHAPE. DECORATE.	FIND AND COUNT ANYTHING RED THAT MOVES.	TRY A COOKING ACTIVITY. TALK ABOUT WHAT YOU DO FIRST, NEXT, AND LAST.
BATHE ALL THE DOLLS LIVING AT YOUR HOUSE. WASH THEIR CLOTHES, TOO.	SAY SOME NURSERY RHYMES.	MAKE AND WRAP SANDWICHES FOR A FAMILY PICNIC.	CLOSE YOUR EYES. LISTEN FOR SOUNDS INSIDE AND OUTSIDE. IDENTIFY THE SOUNDS.	HELP PULL WEEDS OUT OF THE GARDEN.	MAKE A TRIANGLE, SQUARE, RECTANGLE, AND DIAMOND USING STRAWS OR TOOTHPICKS.	THINK OF 3 THINGS NEEDED AT THE STORE. HAVE YOUR CHILD REMEMBER THEM.
PRACTICE SAYING YOUR NAME, ADDRESS, AND PHONE NUMBER.	MAKE A TENT WITH CHAIRS AND BLANKETS. GIVE DIRECTIONS. MOVE IN, OUT, AROUND, UNDER, BESIDE, ETC.	WATCH A BASEBALL GAME AT A LOCAL PARK.	COUNT ALL THE DOORS IN YOUR HOUSE.	NAME FRUITS AND VEGETABLES SEEN AT THE GROCERY STORE OR FARMER'S MARKET.	TRY A COOKING ACTIVITY. WHEN MEASURING, TALK ABOUT MORE AND LESS.	PACK A LUNCH AND TAKE A HIKE INSIDE, E.G., BASEMENT—DARK CAVE—HALLWAY—TUNNEL.
PRACTICE BUTTONING, SNAPPING, AND ZIPPING.	HELP WASH THE CAR.					

JUNE

Parent-child activities

SUN	MON	TUE	WED	THU	FRI	SAT
FIND SOMETHING ROUGH AND SMOOTH, HARD AND SOFT, WET AND DRY.	NAME TWO THINGS THAT ARE HOT AND TWO THINGS THAT ARE COLD.	REVIEW FIRE SAFETY RULES, INCLUDE STOP, DROP, AND ROLL.	HAPPY FOURTH OF JULY!	TALK ABOUT WHAT SPECIAL THINGS YOU DID YESTERDAY.	MAKE POPCORN. EAT IT AND MAKE A POPCORN PICTURE.	MAKE A COLLAGE WITH CEREAL AND MACARONI. GLUE ON A PAPER PLATE.
WATER THE FLOWERS. PLAY IN THE SPRINKLER.	FIND THINGS THAT ARE TALL AND SHORT, INSIDE AND OUTSIDE.	VISIT THE LIBRARY. SELECT SOME RECORDS AND BOOKS.	HELP SET THE TABLE. FOLD 5 NAPKINS INTO RECTANGLES.	PRACTICE SOME FAMILIAR SONGS AND FINGERPLAYS.	PICK UP SMALL OBJECTS WITH TWEEZERS, TONGS, OR CLOTHESPINS.	GO OUTSIDE. NAME THINGS YOU FIND UP HIGH AND DOWN LOW.
TAKE A WALK. LOOK FOR EVERYTHING THAT IS YELLOW.	PLAY SIMON SAYS. REVIEW BODY PARTS BY TOUCHING.	HAVE YOUR CHILD TELL YOU A STORY BY "READING" THE PICTURES.	MAKE GREEN JELLO TOGETHER.	MAKE A SANDWICH. CUT IT INTO 4 SMALL SQUARES.	HAVE A TRICYCLE AND RIDING TOY CAR WASH.	MAKE PINK LEMONADE. STIR IT AND POUR IT.
TASTE SOMETHING SWEET, SOUR, AND SALTY.	TAKE A ROPE, MOVE OVER IT, UNDER IT, NEXT TO IT, ETC.	DRAW A PICTURE OF YOURSELF. NAME ALL THE PARTS.	CUT LONG AND SHORT STRING TO GLUE ON A ROUND PAPER PLATE.	PLAY A GUESSING GAME. PUT OUT 6 OBJECTS, REMOVE ONE, TELL WHAT'S MISSING.	MATCH SOCKS, COUNT THE PAIRS.	SORT NAILS, BUTTONS, SCREWS, ETC., INTO A MUFFIN TIN.
TALK ABOUT WHAT YOU WILL DO TOMORROW.	GO ON A FAMILY PICNIC. LOOK FOR ANIMALS AND INSECTS.	EAT A FEW COOKIES. EAT MANY GRAPES.				

JULY
Parent-child activities

AUGUST
Parent-child activities

SUN	MON	TUE	WED	THU	FRI	SAT
PRACTICE COPYING DESIGNS LIKE CIRCLE, I, MINUS AND PLUS SIGN, /, \, X AND SQUARE, AND RECTANGLE.	GO ON A NUMBER HUNT. LOOK FOR ANYTHING THAT HAS NUMBERS.	PLAY HIDE AND SEEK IN DIFFERENT ROOMS OF THE HOUSE.	FIND SOMETHING SQUARE. TRACE AROUND IT, COLOR IT BLACK, AND CUT IT OUT.	FINGER PAINT WITH DAD'S SHAVING CREAM.	PLAY A GAME OF CATCHING, THROWING, BOUNCING, KICKING, AND ROLLING A BALL.	STRING MACARONI TO MAKE A NECKLACE.
WHEN TAKING A BATH, NAME AS MANY BODY PARTS AS YOU CAN.	GO ON A SCAVENGER HUNT. FIND THINGS THAT ARE BIG AND LITTLE.	TRY A COOKING ACTIVITY. USE THE WORDS *EMPTY* and *FULL*.	TAKE A DECK OF CARDS. MATCH COLORS, NUMBERS, AND SHAPES.	PLAY RECORDS AND DANCE TO MUSIC.	CLIMB ON AND OFF PLAYGROUND EQUIPMENT.	VISIT THE LIBRARY. SELECT SOME RECORDS AND BOOKS.
DRAW PICTURES OF THINGS THAT CAN BE PURPLE AND TELL ABOUT EACH.	PRETEND TO BE AN ANIMAL: RABBIT, SNAKE, HORSE, THEN HOP, CRAWL, GALLOP, ETC.	GO TO A PARK. USE THE SLIDE. TALK ABOUT UP AND DOWN AND TOP AND BOTTOM.	PRACTICE SOME SONGS AND FINGERPLAYS.	STRETCH ROPE BETWEEN 2 CHAIRS. HANG UP CLOTHES USING CLOTHESPINS.	TALK ABOUT WHAT YOU DID AT THE BEGINNING AND END OF THE DAY.	FIND SOMETHING WHITE TO WEAR.
DRAW A CHALK LINE ON THE SIDEWALK. BALANCE AND WALK ON IT.	"PAINT" SIDEWALK PICTURES WITH WATER, WATCH THEM DISAPPEAR.	FIND FOUR BROWN PICTURES, CUT THEM OUT AND GLUE ON PAPER.	PLAY DRESS-UP. NAME THE BODY PARTS THE CLOTHING COVERS.	HAVE AN ICE CUBE RACE. WILL IT MELT FASTER IN THE SHADE OR SUN?	BACKYARD WATERPLAY: USE OLD SPOONS, CUPS, FUNNELS, BASTERS, ETC.	PUT HOUSEHOLD OBJECTS IN A BAG, REACH IN TO FEEL, THEN GUESS WHAT'S INSIDE.
SHOP FOR SCHOOL SUPPLIES. PUT NAME ON EVERYTHING.	PRACTICE PUTTING CLOTHING ON A HANGER.	PRACTICE ROTE COUNTING.				

APPENDIX

- Norm-Referenced Tests
- Criterion-Referenced Tests
- Classroom Materials
- Checklists for Evaluation

  Evaluation—Language
     Body Parts
     Colors and Shapes
     Directional/Positional Concepts

  Evaluation—Fine Motor
     Play Dough Manipulation
     Bead Stringing
     Cutting
     Prewriting

  Evaluation—Perception
     Block Building
     Puzzles
     Pegs and Pegboards

  Evaluation—Gross Motor
     Object and Body Movement

  Evaluation—Math
     Quantitative Concepts
     Numbers, Numerals, Counting
- Blank Calendar

Norm-Referenced Tests

Detroit Tests of Learning Aptitude (Cognitive Development)
Bobbs-Merrill Company, Inc.

Gesell Preschool Test (Cognitive Development)
Programs for Education Book Service

McCarthy Scales of Children's Abilities (Cognitive Development)
The Psychological Corporation

Stanford-Binet Intelligence Scale—Form L–M (Cognitive Development)
Houghton-Mifflin Company

Test of Learning Aptitude (Hiskey-Nebraska; Cognitive Development)
Marshall S. Hiskey

Wechsler Preschool and Primary Scale of Intelligence (Cognitive Development)
The Psychological Corporation

Carrow Elicited Language Inventory (Communication)
Learning Concepts
Austin, Texas

Goldman-Fristoe Test of Articulation (Communication)
American Guidance Service

Peabody Picture Vocabulary Test—Revised (Communication)
American Guidance Service

Test for Auditory Comprehension of Language (Communication)
Teaching Resources Corporation

Test of Early Language Development (Communication)
Western Psychological Corporation

Bruinenks Oseretsky Test of Motor Proficiency (Visual Perception, Fine and Gross Motor)
American Guidance Service

Developmental Test of Visual-Motor Integration (Visual Perception, Fine and Gross Motor)

Illinois Test of Psycholinguistic Abilities (Visual Perception, Fine and Gross Motor)
Western Psychological Services

California Preschool Social Competency Scale (Social, Emotional)
Consulting Psychologist Press, Inc.

Child Behavior Rating Scale (Social, Emotional)
Western Psychological Services

Preschool Attainment Record (Adaptive Behavior/Self-Help)
American Guidance Service

Vineland Social Maturity Scale (Adaptive Behavior)
American Guidance Service

Criterion-Referenced Tests

Boehm Test of Basic Concepts
The Psychological Corporation

Brigance Inventory of Early Development
Curriculum Associates

Carolina Development Profile
Science Research Associates

Functional Profile
Peoria Outreach Project
Peoria, Illinois 61603

Learning Accomplishment Profile Revised–1981
Kaplan Press

Marshalltown Behavioral Developmental Profile
Marshalltown Project
Marshalltown, Iowa

Portage Checklist Revised 1976
Portage Preschool Project
Portage, Wisconsin 53901

Uulpe Assessment Battery Revised
Publications
Downsview (Toronto, Ontario)

Classroom Materials

LANGUAGE

* Library books
* Picture file
* Child-made books
* Flannel board and cutouts
* Poems, story starters
* Toys and manipulatives for language prompting and enhancement: zoo animals, farm animals, community helper figures, family member figures, furniture, vehicles (cars, trucks, airplanes, boats, police, and fire vehicles, etc.)
* Tape recorder, tapes
* Magazines, catalogs, old workbooks
* Puppets
* Blank booklets, story chart paper
* Large box for mystery box
* Materials and equipment for cooking experiences: Pots, pans, bowls; measuring cups, spoons, spatulas, whisk, can opener, sifter, egg beater, paper goods recipes (picture recipes and cookbooks)

FINE MOTOR/ART

* Scissors
  left- and right-handed, dual loop
  training scissors, loop scissors
* Dressing frames
* Strings and beads
* Stacking toys
* Stencils
* Play dough
* Cookie cutters
* Pegs and pegboards
* Cooking utensils
* Lacing boards
* Nuts and bolts
* Woodworking center
* Easel
* Magazines and catalogs
* Orange juice cans
* Finger paint
* Paintbrushes
* Paste, glue
* Sponges
* Styrofoam pieces
* Ribbons
* Yarn
* Cardboard rolls (toilet paper,
  paper towels, tin foil)
* Markers
* Pipe cleaners
* Pencil grips
* Snap blocks
* Theraplast
* Shape-sorting box
* Nesting cups
* Bristle blocks™
* Rulers
* Clay
* Blocks—varied in sizes, shapes
* Paper punch
* Legos™
* Hammer and nails
* Smocks
* Collage materials
* Wallpaper samples
* Tempera paint
* Watercolors
* Papers: finger paint,
  construction, tissue paper, easel
  paper
* Fabrics
* Plastic meat trays
* Aluminum foil
* Chalk—white and colored
* Crayons
* Lead and colored pencils, jumbo
  and regular sized

PERCEPTION

* Puzzles with knobs
* Sequential puzzles
* Form boards
* Attribute blocks
* Pegs, peg boards, and pattern
  cards
* Lotto games (commercial or
  homemade)
* Pictures and objects for
  classification activities
* Geoboards and pattern cards
* Wooden puzzles of varying degree
  of difficulty
* Shape-sorting box
* Cubes and pattern cards
* Bead, string and bead design
  cards
* Color and Shape Bingo™
* Sequence cards
* Feely box or bag
* Parquetry and design cards

GROSS MOTOR

* Jump ropes
* Hoops
* Bikes, tricycles
* Scooter boards
* Horizontal ladders
* Wooden stairs
* Shovels, rakes
* Rocking boat

* Balls (varied sizes)
* Bean bags
* Wagons, wheelbarrows
* Low balance beams
* Large boxes
* Old tires
* Tunnel
* Movement records

SCIENCE/SENSORY

* Magnifying glasses
* Eyedroppers, basters
* Graduated cups
* Planting materials, plants, terrarium
* Objects to float/not float
* Simple machines to take apart, reassemble
* Sand and water table

* Cages, fishbowls, fish, small pets aquarium
* Funnels
* Thermometers
* Magnets
* Objects to see, touch, taste, hear smell
* Shells, rocks

PREMATH

* Counters (e.g., sticks, buttons, beads, blocks, etc.)
* Felt numerals and cutouts
* Balance
* Counting frame
* Measuring tools (yardstick, ruler, spoons, cups, etc.)
* Egg cartons
* Magnetic board, numerals and objects to count

* Geoboards
* Attribute blocks
* Scale
* Items to weigh
* Cash register, play money
* Cuisenaire™ rods
* Calendar and cutouts
* Small dishes, boxes, or other containers
* Clocks

MUSIC

* Tape recorder/tapes
* Record player/records
* Headphones
* Scarves for movement activities
* Homemade instruments
* Drums

* Rhythm Instruments: rhythm sticks, tambourines, cymbals, bells, triangles, tone blocks, maracas
* Song and fingerplay books

DRAMATIC PLAY

* Dishes, pots, pans
* Broom, mop, dust-pan
* Play foods
* Props for community helpers
* Dolls and doll clothes
* Pillows
* Cash register
* Stove, sink, table refrigerator
* Mirror
* Puppet theater
* Dresser
* Utensils
* Tablecloth
* Telephones
* Dress-up clothes and accessories (donated)
* Blankets
* Doll bed
* Ironing board and iron
* Buggy
* Puppets
* Clothes rack
* High chair

BODY PARTS

Name _____

	Receptive	Expressive	Notes
1. mouth			
2. eyes			
3. nose			
4. feet			
5. hair			
6. tongue			
7. teeth			
8. hand			
9. ears			
10. head			
11. legs			
12. arms			
13. fingers			
14. thumb			
15. toes			
16. neck			
17. stomach			
18. chest			
19. back			
20. knee			
21. chin			
22. heel			
23. elbow			
24. ankle			
25. shoulder			
26. jaw			
27. hips			
28. wrist			
29. waist			

COLORS AND SHAPES

Name _____

	Match	Receptive	Expressive	Notes
1. Orange				
2. Black				
3. Brown				
4. Green				
5. White				
6. Red				
7. Pink				
8. Yellow				
9. Purple				
10. Blue				
1. Circle				
2. Triangle				
3. Square				
4. Rectangle				
5. Diamond				
6. Oval				

DIRECTIONAL/POSITIONAL CONCEPTS

Name _____

	Receptive	Expressive	Notes
1. In			
2. Out			
3. Up			
4. Down			
5. Bottom			
6. Top			
7. Over			
8. Under			
9. High			
10. Low			
11. In front			
12. Behind			
13. Beside			
14. Above			
15. Below			
16. Between			
17. First			
18. Last			
19. Middle			

PLAY DOUGH MANIPULATION

Name _____

	Attempts	Emerging Needs Work	Skill Present	Developmentally Not Appropriate	Notes
1. Manipulates dough					
2. Pounds dough					
3. Squeezes dough					
4. Pulls apart dough, pinches					
5. Makes flat round cakes					
6. Cuts with cookie cutter					
7. Makes rolled ropes/snakes					
8. Makes balls					
9. Rolls with a rolling pin					
10. Makes crude objects not always recognizable					
11. Makes refined objects, recognizable by others					
12. Makes name/numerals with dough					

BEAD STRINGING

Name _____

	Attempts	Emerging Needs Work	Skill Present	Developmentally Not Appropriate	Notes
1. Picks up string in one hand, and bead in opposite hand					
2. Places 1" to 2" beads on stiff string					
3. Places string through bead					
4. Places 1/2" beads on stiff string					
5. Pulls string through bead					
6. Places 1/4" beads on stiff string					
7. Pulls string through bead					
8. Strings objects (e.g., macaroni, straws, cereal with needle and thread or yarn)					

Evaluation—Fine Motor

CUTTING

Name _____

	Attempts	Emerging Needs Work	Skill Present	Developmentally Not Appropriate	Notes
1. Places scissors on fingers and holds correctly					
2. Opens and closes scissors					
3. Snips or makes small cuts in paper					
4. Holds paper for cutting					
5. Cuts 1/2″ strips					
6. Cuts 1″ strips					
7. Cuts 3″ × 5″ card in half (shorter distance)					
8. Cuts 3″ × 5″ card in half (longer distance)					
9. Cuts 3″ × 5″ card on 1/4″ bold line					
10. Cuts 1/2 sheet of construction paper on bold line: a. vertical b. diagonal c. curved d. zig-zag e. multiple curve					
11. Cuts out shapes on bold line					
12. Cuts out simple objects on bold line					
13. Cuts simple objects with contrasting background					
14. Cuts out line drawings					
15. Cuts out magazine pictures					
16. Cuts materials other than paper					

PREWRITING

Name: _____

	Imitate after watching adult	Copy from prepared sample	Notes
1. ○			
2. │			
3. —			
4. H			
5.			
6. /			
7. ∨			
8. +			
9. □			
10. △			
11. ▭			
12. First name			
13. Full name			

BLOCK BUILDING

Name _____

	Attempts	Emerging Needs Work	Skill Present	Developmentally Not Appropriate	Notes
1. Builds a tower with 2″–3″ blocks (2,4,6,8,10)					
2. Builds a tower with 1″ cubes (1,2,3,4,5,6,7,8,9,10)					
3. Copies 3-block bridge (1″ cubes)					
4. Copies stair steps (1″ cubes)					
5. Builds 6-cube pyramid					
6. Places 1″ cubes on pattern cards					
7. Copies pattern with 1″ cubes					
8. Places 1″ cubes on colored pattern cards					
9. Copies multicolored patterns with 1″ colored cubes and pattern cards					

Evaluation—Perception

PUZZLES

Name _____

	Attempts	Emerging Needs Work	Skill Present	Developmentally Not Appropriate	Notes
1. Removes pieces					
2. Organizes pieces (turns right-side up)					
3. Completes single piece (form board) puzzles through trial and error					
4. Completes single piece puzzles utilizing shape					
5. Completes inset puzzles through trial/error (4,6,8,10,12,14,16,18)					
6. Completes inset puzzles utilizing color, shape, position (4,6,8,10,12,14,16,18)					
7. Completes interlocking puzzles through trial/error (4,6,8,10,12,14,16,18)					
8. Completes interlocking puzzles utilizing color, shape, and position (4,6,8,10,12,14,16,18)					

PEGS AND PEGBOARDS

Name _____

	Attempts	Emerging Needs Work	Skill Present	Developmentally Not Appropriate	Notes
1. Removes large plastic pegs from rubber mat pegboard.					
2. Places large plastic pegs into rubber mat pegboard.					
3. Removes 2″ sticks from wooden pegboard.					
4. Places 2″ sticks into wooden pegboard.					
5. Removes 1″ plastic pegs from plastic pegboards.					
6. Places 1″ plastic pegs into plastic pegboards.					
7. Places 10 pegs into board following 2-color pattern.					
8. Places 10 pegs into board following 3-color pattern.					
9. Continues pattern on board alternating 2 colors.					
10. Continues pattern on board alternating 3 colors.					

OBJECT AND BODY MOVEMENT

Name _____

	Attempts	Emerging Needs Work	Skill Present	Developmentally Not Appropriate	Notes
1. Copying unilateral movements					
2. Copying bilateral movements					
3. Moving to music					
4. Jumping over objects					
5. Jumping consecutively					
6. Eye tracking objects					
7. Catching a ball					
8. Throwing a ball					
9. Bouncing a ball					
10. Running					
11. Hopping					
12. Skipping					
13. Galloping					
14. Standing on one foot					
15. Walking a line					
16. Walking a balance beam					
17. Walking backward					
18. Stair climbing					
19. Side-to-side rolling					
20. Forward rolls					
21. Backward rolls					
22. Scooter boards					

QUANTITATIVE CONCEPTS

Name _____

	Receptive	Expressive	Notes
1. Big			
2. Little			
3. Tall			
4. Short			
5. Long			
6. Short			
7. Few			
8. Many			
9. Empty			
10. Full			
11. More			
12. Less			
13. Small			
14. Medium			
15. Large			

NUMBERS, NUMERALS, COUNTING

Name _____

	Counts rote to	One-to-one correspon- dence	Numeral recog- nition	Match quantity with symbol	Notes
zero					
1					
2					
3					
4					
5					
6					
7					
8					
9					
10					

SUN	MON	TUE	WED	THU	FRI	SAT